Get the eBook FREE!
(PDF, ePub, Kindle, and liveBook all included)

We believe that once you buy a book from us, you should be able to read it in any format we have available. To get electronic versions of this book at no additional cost to you, purchase and then register this book at the Manning website.

Go to https://www.manning.com/freebook and follow the instructions to complete your pBook registration.

That's it!
Thanks from Manning!

Interview Speak
WHAT YOUR INTERVIEWER REALLY WANTS TO KNOW

BARBARA LIMMER
LAURA BROWNE

MANNING
SHELTER ISLAND

For online information and ordering of this and other Manning books, please visit www.manning.com. The publisher offers discounts on this book when ordered in quantity.

For more information, please contact

    Special Sales Department
    Manning Publications Co.
    20 Baldwin Road
    PO Box 761
    Shelter Island, NY 11964
    Email: orders@manning.com

© 2025 Manning Publications Co. All rights reserved.

No part of this publication may be reproduced, stored in a retrieval system, or transmitted, in any form or by means electronic, mechanical, photocopying, or otherwise, without prior written permission of the publisher.

Many of the designations used by manufacturers and sellers to distinguish their products are claimed as trademarks. Where those designations appear in the book, and Manning Publications was aware of a trademark claim, the designations have been printed in initial caps or all caps.

♾ Recognizing the importance of preserving what has been written, it is Manning's policy to have the books we publish printed on acid-free paper, and we exert our best efforts to that end. Recognizing also our responsibility to conserve the resources of our planet, Manning books are printed on paper that is at least 15 percent recycled and processed without the use of elemental chlorine.

The author and publisher have made every effort to ensure that the information in this book was correct at press time. The author and publisher do not assume and hereby disclaim any liability to any party for any loss, damage, or disruption caused by errors or omissions, whether such errors or omissions result from negligence, accident, or any other cause, or from any usage of the information herein.

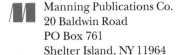

Manning Publications Co.	Development editor:	Marina Michaels
20 Baldwin Road	Technical editor:	Paula Nordhoff
PO Box 761	Review editor:	Kishor Rit
Shelter Island, NY 11964	Production editor:	Kathy Rossland
	Copy editor:	Kari Lucke
	Proofreader:	Olga Milanko
	Typesetter:	Tamara Švelić Sabljić
	Cover designer:	Marija Tudor

ISBN 9781633436220
Printed in the United States of America

brief contents

PART 1 PREPARATION 1

  1 ▪ Welcome to Interview Speak 3

PART 2 TRANSLATIONS 23

  2 ▪ Common questions and special situations 25
  3 ▪ Interpersonal skills questions 48
  4 ▪ Perseverance skills, failures, and negative situations questions 64
  5 ▪ Leadership, hiring, and motivating skills questions 77
  6 ▪ Problem-solving, time management, negotiation, and change questions 90
  7 ▪ Questions by job function 110

PART 3 DON'T MAKE THESE MISTAKES 121

  8 ▪ Not doing your homework, not being real, or leaving without . . . 123
  9 ▪ Not hearing the question, the whole question, and the heart of the question 133
  10 ▪ Giving answers that sound good to you (but aren't) 139

iii

BRIEF CONTENTS

PART 4 INTERVIEW STAGES AND INTERVIEWERS 147

11 ▪ Interview stages and translations before, during, and after 149

12 ▪ How to deal with bad interviewers (and really good ones) 161

PART 5 WRAP-UP 181

13 ▪ Next steps 183

appendix A ▪ Interview questions by chapter 192
appendix B ▪ Questions to think about 203
appendix C ▪ Interview preparation checklist 211
appendix D ▪ Post-interview evaluation 213

contents

preface   xiii
acknowledgments   xv
about this book   xvi
about the authors   xviii

PART 1 PREPARATION 1

1 Welcome to Interview Speak   3

What's so hard about interview questions?   4

How to use this book   6

What this book is and is not   7

Prepare yourself for interviews   7

Get to know the company   7

Get to know the job   9

Get to know the interviewer   12

Know yourself   13

What could get in your way   14

Different kinds of questions and how to answer them   15

Breadth vs. depth questions 15 ▪ Behavioral or competency-based questions 16 ▪ Hypothetical questions 16 ▪ General questions 16 ▪ Answer frameworks 16

v

vi CONTENTS

Tips and traps to avoid 17

Weakening words and phrases 17 ▪ Filler words 17 ▪ Generic answers 17 ▪ "I" vs. "we" 18 ▪ The "negative sandwich" 18 "Or" questions 19 ▪ Rising inflection/uptalking 19 ▪ Answer length and timing 19

Think about 20

Key takeaways 20

PART 2 TRANSLATIONS 23

2 Common questions and special situations 25

Most commonly asked questions 26

Tell me about yourself 26 ▪ Why are you looking for a new job OR why did you leave your last job? 29 ▪ What are you looking for next? 30 ▪ What do you not want to do? 31 ▪ What kind of salary are you looking for? 31 ▪ Why are you interested in this job? 32 ▪ What do you know about our company? 33 What are your career goals? 33 ▪ What are your strengths? 33 What are your weaknesses? 34 ▪ What did you enjoy most about your last job? 38 ▪ What did you not like about your last job? 38 Why should we hire you? 39 ▪ What questions do you have? 40

Special situations 42

What have you done since you left your last company? 42 Why have you changed employers so frequently over the last several years? 43 ▪ Because you were with your last employer for so long, do you think you may have a hard time adjusting to a new company's way of working? 43 ▪ What makes you think you know our industry and will be able to become productive right away? 44 ▪ This job is a lower level than your current (or last) job; why would you be interested in taking a step down in your career? 44

Think about 46

Key takeaways 46

3 Interpersonal skills questions 48

Approachability, credibility, and humility 48

Give an example of an initiative you led that required you to interact with various levels within the company 48 Tell me about a time when humility played a role in your being successful 49 ▪ Describe a situation where you had to build credibility 51

CONTENTS

Influencing and gaining support 52

Give me an example of a time when you convinced leadership in your organization to make a significant change 52 • Describe a situation where you had to delicately let a key stakeholder know that their expectations were unrealistic 53 • Tell me about a situation in which you built needed support for a goal or project from people who didn't report to you and over whom you had no direct authority 55

Diversity, equity, and inclusion 55

How has your background and experience prepared you to be effective in an environment that values diversity and is committed to inclusion? 56 • In what ways do you think diversity is important to someone in this role? 58 • What kinds of experiences have you had with people whose backgrounds are different from your own? 59 • What programs or initiatives have you been part of that focused on working with diverse populations, and what was your role in those efforts? 59

Conflict management 60

Describe a time when you successfully defused a conflict 60 Give me an example of a time when you found yourself in the middle of conflict; what did you do or say to get to a resolution? 60

Think about 62

Key takeaways 63

4 · Perseverance skills, failures, and negative situations questions 64

Failures and negative situations 64

Tell me about one of your failures 65 • What was the most useful criticism you ever received? 66 • Describe for me a decision you regretted after having made it 68 • Give an example where you failed to persuade someone to do something you felt would be good for the organization 69

Overcoming obstacles and difficult situations 69

Tell me about a time when you were most persuasive in overcoming resistance to your ideas or point of view 69 • Give an example of a situation when you had to think on your feet to get yourself out of a difficult situation 72

Perseverance and drive 73

Tell me about a situation that shows your perseverance, persistence, and ability to remain positive when faced with adversity 73

What can you tell me about yourself that best illustrates your personal drive and motivation? 74 ▪ *Describe a situation that required you to make sacrifices or put in extra effort to achieve the goal. How did your drive and perseverance contribute to your success? 75*

Think about   76

Key takeaways   76

5   *Leadership, hiring, and motivating skills questions*   77

Leadership and management   77

What is your leadership style? 77 ▪ *Discuss a situation in which you were able to create a high level of trust, morale, and team spirit 80* ▪ *Tell me about an occasion when you pulled the team together and improved morale during challenging circumstances 82* ▪ *Describe a difficult experience you've had while leading a group with different opinions and personalities. What issues arose, and how did you resolve them? 83*

Hiring and motivating staff   83

What kinds of things have you done to both attract new talent and guard against poor hires? 84 ▪ *What do you do to create an environment that inspires and motivates your team? 86*

Think about   88

Key takeaways   89

6   *Problem-solving, time management, negotiation, and change questions*   90

Analysis, problem-solving, and decision-making   90

Describe a complex problem you solved 91 ▪ *Tell me about a time when you missed an obvious solution to a problem 93* ▪ *What was the most difficult decision you ever had to make on the job? 93 Describe for me your decision-making process 96*

Time and project management   97

Tell me about a time when you were juggling multiple projects with overlapping deadlines, tight time frames, and conflicting priorities 97 ▪ *Recall for me a major project you initiated and worked on through to completion. How did you proactively manage changes in project priorities, scope, and expectations? 98*

Negotiation   100

Tell me about a difficult negotiation in which you were involved. What challenges arose during the negotiation, and how did you work through them? 100 ▪ *Describe a situation that demonstrates your ability to negotiate skillfully when costs were critical 102*

Change management 103

Give an example of your ability to implement change and influence people to accept that change 103 ▪ *Describe something you instituted or changed that required collaborative planning with other departments and resulted in improved customer relationships 105* ▪ *Tell me about a time when you had to deal with frequent changes or unexpected events on the job 107*

Think about 107

Key takeaways 108

7 *Questions by job function 110*

Senior leadership 110

Be sure to sell 111 ▪ *Sample questions 111* ▪ *Think about 111*

Operations 111

Be sure to sell 112 ▪ *Sample questions 112* ▪ *Think about 112*

Sales 112

Be sure to sell 112 ▪ *Sample questions 113* ▪ *Think about 114*

Marketing 115

Be sure to sell 115 ▪ *Sample questions 115* ▪ *Think about 117*

Finance 117

Be sure to sell 117 ▪ *Sample questions 117* ▪ *Think about 118*

Information technology 118

Be sure to sell 118 ▪ *Sample questions 118* ▪ *Think about 119*

Human resources 119

Be sure to sell 119 ▪ *Sample questions 120* ▪ *Think about 120*

Key takeaways 120

PART 3 DON'T MAKE THESE MISTAKES 121

8 *Not doing your homework, not being real, or leaving without . . . 123*

Not doing your homework 123

Assuming being an interviewer will make you a good interviewee 124 ▪ *Not investing time in preparation or thinking that you can wing it 124 ▪ Not practicing your answers to difficult or delicate questions 125 ▪ Not planning good questions (or enough questions) to ask the interviewer 125 ▪ Not testing out your tech in advance (for video interviews) 126 ▪ Not mapping out your directions, parking options, and commute time (for on-site interviews) 127 ▪ Not arriving early 127 ▪ Dressing inappropriately or wearing cologne or loud jewelry 127*

Not being real 128

Not being yourself in your answers 128 ▪ Trying to pass off a memorized answer as authentic 129 ▪ Trying to pass off a BS answer as authentic 130 ▪ Ignoring the importance of rapport-building 130

Leaving without . . . 130

Finding out the next steps and time frames 131 ▪ Getting the names and contact information of all interviewers 131 Closing the sale 131

Think about 131

Key takeaways 132

9 Not hearing the question, the whole question, and the heart of the question 133

Not letting the interviewer finish their question before planning your answer 133

Not taking a brief pause to allow yourself to truly understand the question prior to starting your answer 134

Rambling as you try to come up with an answer 135

Not explicitly tying your answer to the heart of the question 136

Think about 138

Key takeaways 138

10 Giving answers that sound good to you (but aren't) 139

Answers that are too long 139

Answers that are too short 140

Using acronyms, talking in Tech Speak or Industry Speak that may be unknown to your interviewers 140

Focusing your answer mostly on what you did rather than how you did it and why it mattered 140

CONTENTS

Not giving answers that relate to the job, company, and industry   140

Leaving out the results in stories   141

Overusing "we" and underusing "I"   143

Failing to balance confidence with humility   143

Bringing things up that you shouldn't: lack of experience, negatives, compensation, time off or other benefits   143

Not answering the "why should we hire you?" question from the employer's perspective   143

Giving a general answer instead of a past example   145

Think about   146

Key takeaways   146

PART 4   INTERVIEW STAGES AND INTERVIEWERS 147

11   Interview stages and translations before, during, and after   149

Interview stages and mindsets   150

First screening 150 • HR/Talent acquisition 151 • External recruiters, headhunters, and staffing agencies 151 • Hiring manager 152 • Direct reports 152 • Peers 153 Boss's boss 153 • Internal clients 153 • External clients 154 Panel interviews 154 • Presentations 155

Translating other things interviewers say before, during, and after the interview   156

Before the interview 156 • During the interview 157 After the interview 159

Think about   160

Key takeaways   160

12   How to deal with bad interviewers (and really good ones)   161

The poker-faced interviewer   161

The lackadaisical or disinterested interviewer   162

The talkative interviewer   162

The interviewer who asks very few questions   162

The interviewer who tests you   162

CONTENTS

Multiple interviewers 163

The inexperienced interviewer 164

The highly experienced interviewer 164

Interview example 164

*Interview preparation 166 ▪ Initial phone interview 170
Interview review summary 179*

Think about 180

Key takeaways 180

PART 5 WRAP-UP 181

13 Next steps 183

What Clueless Clark learned 184

*Chapter 1: Welcome to Interview Speak 184 ▪ Chapter 2:
Common questions and special situations 184 ▪ Chapter 3:
Interpersonal skills questions 185 ▪ Chapter 4: Perseverance
skills, failures, and negative situations questions 185
Chapter 5: Leadership, hiring, and motivating skills
questions 186 ▪ Chapter 6: Problem-solving, time management,
negotiation, and change questions 186 ▪ Chapter 7: Questions
by job function 186 ▪ Chapter 8: Not doing your homework, not
being real, or leaving without . . . 186 ▪ Chapter 9: Not hearing
the question, the whole question, and the heart of the question 187
Chapter 10: Giving answers that sound good to you (but
aren't) 187 ▪ Chapter 11: Interview stages and translations
before, during, and after 187 ▪ Chapter 12: How to deal with
bad interviewers (and really good ones) 188 ▪ Chapter 13: Next
steps 188*

What's next for you 189

What could hold you back 189 ▪ How to move forward 190

appendix A *Interview questions by chapter 192*

appendix B *Questions to think about 203*

appendix C *Interview preparation checklist 211*

appendix D *Post-interview evaluation 213*

index 215

preface

Thank you for purchasing *Interview Speak*. We hope this information will help you start or strengthen your search for a new job.

The idea for this book came about after many years of Barbara conducting mock interviews to help job candidates improve their interview skills. In these sessions, it was common for her to tell candidates when they missed the mark because the answer they gave to a particular question was actually answering a different question. When she told them what she was really looking for in her question, the candidate would have a "light bulb moment," saying that if they had known that was really what the question was asking, they would have answered it differently. Then, when they had an opportunity to redo their answer, it would be spot on. This is why we came to realize that a book on translating Interview Speak was needed.

Using our experiences from both sides of the interviewing desk, we take the most common and difficult interview questions, provide their translations, and then describe how to answer each one. We present examples of how to answer and suggestions about what your answers should and shouldn't include. We do not provide canned or scripted answers; instead, we offer insights on how candidates should think through and develop their own best answers.

In some cases, you'll see sentence diagrams that analyze interview questions, meaning we call out and specifically define the words in an interview question to increase your understanding. For example, we take a question such as, "What did you not like about your last job?" and review what the interviewer means in each part of that question, showing you how you can use that information to create a more complete answer. This analysis can help your preparation for interviews.

xiii

You'll read examples of different job interview candidates and their good answers to a variety of questions. Each applicant's answer is critiqued to show what they did well and how each answer can be dramatically improved. The book also includes examples of ineffective answers and how to avoid them, as well as insider stories about real situations from our experience to give you insights about hiring that can help you better understand the process.

Thank you for reading the book and for taking us with you on your journey to a new job.

acknowledgments

We are grateful to our friends, colleagues, and clients who contributed stories of their real interview situations for this book. To protect their privacy, we have changed their names and other identifying characteristics.

We want to thank the team at Manning Publications, especially Mike Stephens; Marina Michaels, our amazing development editor; and Paula Nordhoff, our superb technical editor. Paula is a career consultant working with executives on a global scale to manage and upscale their careers.

To all the reviewers: Alex Ware, Alireza Aghamohammadi, Amy Lavelle, Andy Miles, Anita Trupiano, Anuj More, Archana Rao, Bang Nteme Jean-Baptiste, Bruno Couriol, Cesar Aguirre, Dave Corun, Dottie Hunter, Douglas Puenner, Earl Bingham, Eli Richmond Hini, Gaurav Toshniwal, Harinath Kuntamukkala, Harsha Patil, Hilde Van Gysel, Ian O'Connor, Jagadish Kamisetti, Jaganadh Gopinadhan, Jason Simon, Javid Asgarov, Jon Feraro, Julie Tyree, Kalai Chelvi Erudia Nathan, Ken Alger, Marcos Paulo Rocha, Mary Anne Thygesen, Nadir Doctor, Nathan Brouwer, Ninoslav Cerkez, Pavel Bazin, Philippe Vialatte, Piotr Jastrzębski, Pradeep Bhattiprolu, Pradeep Kumar Saraswathi, Radhakrishna MV, Ron Lease, Sameer Wadhwa, Satish Prahalad Gururajan, Scott Morrison, Serenity Smile, Shantanu Kumar, Shruti Singh, Sofija Jaglicic, Stacie Shannon, and Vinit Dhatrak, your suggestions helped make this a better book.

This book would not have been possible without the support of our wonderful friends. A special shoutout to our beloved Career Moms Club, without whom Laura and Barbara would never have met—thank you so much!

Finally, thank you to Chuck, Robbie, and Julianne, who believed in us since the time this book was just an idea and a dream. We will forever be grateful!

about this book

Most people walk away from interviews feeling they did well and are then shocked when they don't get invited back for the next round or get the job offer. That is because their answers all sounded great to them. They don't know that each interview question has a real question behind it—that is, what the interviewer is really looking for. The goal of this book is to help you develop your own best authentic answers so you can have successful interviews and get the job you want.

You'll learn the difference between good interview answers and great ones, and see how you can improve your own answers by reading the sample interview responses throughout the book. Each answer is critiqued to show what the candidates did well and how each answer can be dramatically improved.

The book also includes examples of ineffective answers and how to avoid them. You also get the transcript of a full initial interview so you can see how it flows and how to adjust if an interviewer interrupts. We include insider stories about real situations to give you insights into the hiring process.

Who should read this book

This book is written primarily for readers applying for business positions spanning from entry level up through manager and executive roles and everything in between. The information can also be useful for people applying for nonbusiness roles and for those applying to both technical and nontechnical positions.

Whether you have limited experience with interviews or have been interviewing for many years (as either an interviewee or interviewer), this book can help you.

How this book is organized: A road map

This book contains 13 chapters organized into 5 parts and also includes 4 appendices. The first part focuses on preparing for an interview. Part 2 provides specific interview questions and translations and discusses how best to answer. Part 3 talks about common mistakes and how to avoid them. Part 4 is about interview stages and how to succeed with both good and bad interviewers. Part 5 concludes the book by discussing the next steps.

Here's how you can get the most out of this book:

- Read chapters 1 to 4. These are for everyone.
- Read chapter 5 if the job includes supervising others or the need to motivate a team.
- Read chapter 6. If your job does not include any negotiation, that section is optional; however, we still recommend you review it because most jobs include some form of negotiation, even if informal.
- Chapter 7 includes information for jobs in senior leadership, operations, sales, marketing, finance, IT, and human resources. You can choose to only read the section that pertains to the type of job for which you are applying.
- Read chapters 8 to 13, because they contain critical information about common mistakes candidates often make without even realizing they are making them.
- Review appendices A to D. These include a list of interview questions by chapter, the questions to think about contained throughout the book, an interview preparation checklist, and a self-evaluation form you can use after each interview.

Are you ready to learn what interviewers are really asking so you can get your next job? If so, let's get started.

liveBook discussion forum

Purchase of *Interview Speak* includes free access to liveBook, Manning's online reading platform. Using liveBook's exclusive discussion features, you can attach comments to the book globally or to specific sections or paragraphs. It's a snap to make notes for yourself, ask and answer technical questions, and receive help from the authors and other users. To access the forum, go to https://livebook.manning.com/book/interview-speak/discussion.

Manning's commitment to our readers is to provide a venue where a meaningful dialogue among individual readers and between readers and the authors can take place. It is not a commitment to any specific amount of participation on the part of the authors, whose contribution to the forum remains voluntary (and unpaid). We suggest you try asking the authors some challenging questions lest their interest stray! The forum and the archives of previous discussions will be accessible from the publisher's website as long as the book is in print.

about the authors

BARBARA LIMMER is a professional career coach and consultant who has personally coached thousands of professionals and executives from around the world. She brings extensive experience working on all sides of the hiring process, including career management, human resources, and executive search. She previously worked with MBA students and alumni as a Career Management Director at Thunderbird School of Global Management and in a variety of human resources roles focused on recruiting, training, and employee relations for companies including Bank of America and MetLife. She also worked as a headhunter in New York City while attending graduate school. In all her positions, she continually conducted either real or mock job interviews, providing real-time, detailed, and in-depth feedback on what could be improved in candidates' answers.

LAURA BROWNE has extensive experience in leadership and management development. She was a Senior Director of Human Resources for a global tech company where she taught managers how to be better interviewers. She is a speaker, trainer, and coach who helps global leaders and individuals be more successful. At Career Coffee Break (www.careercoffeebreak.com), she shows clients how to get promoted and make more money at work by negotiating raises and higher starting salaries.

Laura is the author of three business books and two fiction books including *Help! My Company Swiped Left!*, *Increase Your Income: 7 Rules for Women Who Want to Make More Money at Work*, and *A Salary Cinderella Story (Or How to Make Money Without a Fairy Godmother)*. Laura has written for *Forbes* and has been quoted as a business expert in major publications including *Cosmopolitan*, *Family Circle* magazine, and *USA Weekend*.

Part 1

Preparation

Welcome to Interview Speak. In this part, we discuss what's so hard about interview questions, how to use this book, and what this book is and is not. We go over how you can prepare for interviews, what to research and think about in advance, and what could hold you back.

We also talk about different kinds of interview questions and how to answer them and provide frameworks to help you structure your answers.

Lastly, we cover tips and traps to avoid that could undermine your effectiveness in the interview.

Welcome to Interview Speak

Have you ever left a job interview thinking you absolutely nailed it and were then surprised when you didn't get the job? You wonder, what happened? You were so sure that the job was yours.

Here's what might have happened. You thought you said all the right things, but it wasn't what the interviewer was looking for. The interviewer smiled at you and couldn't wait to get done with the interview.

We've seen this happen way too often. So many people think they have great answers, but they actually don't. One big reason for this is that people don't understand what the interviewer is really saying and really asking for. If you understood that, your answers would be much better.

We wrote this book to show you what the interviewer is really asking and why. Think of this as a way to translate "Interview Speak." By understanding Interview Speak, you can be better prepared to answer an interviewer's questions and give them exactly the information they need.

We've learned this from many years of interviews and corporate work. Barbara spent many years as an internal recruiter where she sourced and interviewed candidates, referred some to hiring managers, and then debriefed with both candidates and hiring managers. Interestingly, about 99% of all candidates thought they did well in their interviews, but in talking with hiring managers, most did not.

In one position, Barbara's office was right next door to the VP of Human Resources (HR), so she'd catch candidates after their interviews to see how they felt they did. Again, nearly all of them said they did well. Barbara would then go into the VP's office to get her take, and in over half the cases, she got a thumbs down. It turns out this VP's modus operandi was to be very engaging, smiling, and actively listening during her interviews, so practically everyone walked away loving her and thinking they really hit it off well, even when their answers were off the mark.

Laura has spent many years in corporate HR, so she knows what goes on behind the scenes at companies. She trained hiring managers in what to say during interviews. She explained to them why it's important to ask certain questions. She helped them understand what to listen for in the answers and how to spot red flags that could indicate a person might not be right for the role. She also heard managers share their thoughts about memorable applicants—both good and bad.

When Laura left the corporate world, she used that experience to write two books about how to negotiate higher salaries at new jobs and current jobs (one nonfiction book and one fiction book). She now coaches and trains people through online courses on how to ask for and get more money at work.

This book is for you if you want to learn how to improve your interview skills, even if you think you've done well at past interviews, so you can get the job you want. We'll share what we've learned to help you know what to say and what to avoid saying. In these chapters, we'll journey together, uncovering the true questions behind interview questions and how to respond with effective answers that will impress your potential employer.

You might be thinking that interviewing is common sense and that you just need to prepare and give some good positive answers.

Unfortunately, that's just not true. Even though answering basic interview questions may appear obvious, there are many nuances that most people are not aware of. And, even if some of the things we cover seem like common sense, they are definitely not common practice. You'd be surprised how often, in the context of a job interview, people say things that make no sense!

What's so hard about interview questions?

Why are interview questions so hard? They're just questions, yes, but they are questions that you have to answer in a stressful situation, and you don't have much time to think. You need to be prepared and ready so you can use the few minutes you have to impress the interviewer enough to get to the next stage in the hiring process.

One of the unique perspectives that Barbara brings is she wasn't just an interviewer for a variety of positions, industries, levels, and hiring managers. She also spent many years conducting mock interviews to help job candidates improve their interview skills. In these sessions, Barbara would create interview questions based on job descriptions and then conduct role-plays where she asked questions, listened to answers, and then gave real-time, detailed feedback to the interviewees. Throughout those years, it was common for her to tell candidates when they missed the mark because the answer they gave to a particular question was, in fact, answering a different question.

For example, when she asked the popular "Tell me about yourself" question, she'd often get long, rambling answers about the candidate's life story, including where they grew up, what they did after college, all the jobs they've had since then, etc. By the time they got to the relevant parts (skills and experience that qualify them for the job), Barbara was no longer listening (she had completed a mental grocery list of things to pick up on her way home, all while smiling and nodding along).

She would then explain what she was looking for in her question, and the candidate would have a light bulb moment—saying that if they had known that was really what Barbara was looking for, they would have answered the question differently. When they had an opportunity to redo their answer, it would be spot on. This is why we came to realize that a book on translating Interview Speak was needed.

Every job interview question has a question behind the question—that is, what the interviewer is really looking for when they ask it. For the questions we cover, you'll get a translation that explains what that question means and what the interviewer is looking for. You'll then get some examples of how to answer or suggestions about what your answers should and shouldn't include.

For example, the previous question, "Tell me about yourself," seems straightforward, and some people think it's simple to answer, but it can be easy to mess up if you don't realize what's behind it. Yes, the interviewer wants to know about you, and they also want to get an idea of how you answer an open question like this. Are you prepared? Do you get to the point? This question is especially important because it's normally asked at the beginning and sets the tone for the rest of the meeting.

Another issue we've seen is with people who have been on the other side of the desk as interviewers. They can be quite confident in their skills as interviewees. They have their own opinions on which questions they would ask and why and which questions they would never ask. We tell everyone that there is a whole world out there of possible interviewers, and you need to be prepared to deal with people who have different styles and approaches. This book will help you translate a variety of common interview questions so that you can answer them well and achieve the ultimate goal: a job offer.

It's time to start our interview journey to see how your answers can move you in the right direction. Are you ready for better and easier interviews? Let's go.

Insider story: Why it's hard to tell how you're doing in an interview

Some interviewers will make it obvious during the interview if you're doing well (or not), but many show only a poker face. Many people think that they're good at reading body language in social and business settings, so they assume that would be the case during job interviews. However, I (Barbara) have worked with many hiring managers who have good interpersonal skills, smile, and are engaging during their regular work activities and meetings, but when interviewing candidates, they are serious, don't smile, and just nod after each answer to their questions. It's almost as if they were taught that it's a bad thing to show any emotion or indicate what they're thinking when they're interviewing people. One time, I was telling an executive client that many interviewers put on a poker face as interviewers, and he said, "Oh, yeah, I do that." He

(continued)

wasn't sure why he did it, but he knew that he did. Therefore, don't assume that you'll know how you're doing!

There's also the story we mentioned earlier in this chapter about the HR VP who makes a point to be extremely engaging when she interviews others. She knows that if she makes them feel quite comfortable, she'll get to see the "real" person. In that case, people almost always walked away from being interviewed by her feeling that they did extremely well, even when they did not.

It should be noted that there are times when a candidate walks away from an interview feeling like they didn't do well, but these situations are much rarer than people thinking they did well. These situations often include people who lack confidence in general, or occur if a hiring manager is putting candidates through some sort of test to see how they react under pressure. We know of one recent candidate who, after feeling like she didn't do well with a hiring manager who confronted her about her desired salary, ended up getting the job offer.

How to use this book

Use this book to help you learn a new language: the language of interviewers. The questions you get asked may seem straightforward, but beneath many of them are subtleties that give you opportunities to showcase who you are and the value you bring—that is, if you know how to answer them.

When you travel to a foreign land and don't know the language, you need some way to translate what people are saying so you can understand them. That's why we're here. We want to help you understand what recruiters are really saying. Consider this a guidebook on your journey to a new job.

The key to success lies in your ability to understand what's behind the questions so your answers address what the interviewer wants to know, not just what they explicitly say. To help you, we'll break down some of the questions and clearly explain the different parts.

You'll get examples that show how an interviewee provides a good answer to a question. You'll then see what makes that answer good as well as how it could be improved.

We're also going to have some fun by introducing you to "Clueless Clark." He'll show you what a poor interviewer might do and say. Clueless Clark thinks he's great at interviewing and doesn't feel the need to prepare very much. He thinks it's much better to wing it because the right answers seem so obvious to him, and he wants to feel natural in the interview. He leaves every interview convinced that he's got the job and is quite surprised when he doesn't get the offer. From his examples, you'll see what to do to avoid being a Clueless Clark. Some of his answers may seem a little exaggerated, but he's an amalgam of real people that we and other interviewers have experienced. We include him to highlight potential mistakes that people make and what to do instead.

What this book is and is not

It's important to remember that there are no perfect answers. Every interviewer is different, so no matter how much you prepare, it's still a guessing game. You might wonder why you should bother preparing then, if there are no guaranteed responses that will always work. Let's look at the options: if you take the time to be fully prepared, the interview will most likely be less stressful for you, and even if you aren't asked all the questions you've prepared answers for, you'll most likely still have a good interview. In addition, you're prepared for questions that may be asked in the next round of interviews. Or you could decide not to prepare, think you did a good job, and get surprised when you are rejected.

Obviously, we believe that the right preparation makes all the difference. To help you prepare, we provide both translations and advice on how to answer questions, but we don't give you scripts of what to say. You must personalize your answers and customize them to fit your background, experience, personality, and the job for which you're interviewing. Memorizing a script will not build rapport, and it simply won't work (unless you're seeking a job as an actor).

This book is not an encyclopedia of all possible interview questions. Instead, we give you common interview questions that everyone should be prepared for, as well as lists of many other typical questions.

Prepare yourself for interviews

Congratulations: you've received a message asking you to schedule an interview! Now what? Let's look at some areas to start working on. You're going to want to get to know the company and find out information about the interviewer(s). You'll also need to analyze your background, compare it to the employer's needs, and anticipate any potential objections they may have and how to overcome them.

It's helpful to think about the interview as a sales process. You're the product, and the employer is the consumer. To get the job offer, you need to understand their needs so that you can match your features and benefits to those needs.

Get to know the company

To get to know the company, start by reviewing the "About our company" part of the job description because employers often reveal important characteristics about candidates who will fit their culture.

Here is an excerpt from one employer's job posting that gives insight into the kind of candidate it seeks:

> *Company X is recognized as a premier provider of _____ located in _____. We are known for providing our customers with exceptional service and outstanding experiences. The person in this role will ensure that the operational goals of the organization are being met through proactive, visible leadership while also paying attention to the fine details. These important attributes along with a necessary intuitive collaboration style will contribute to the overall success of the company. The successful candidate*

will be an integral part of a select team recognized for its superior service, quality work environment, and focus on continuous improvement for both its customers and staff.

To prepare to interview for this job, candidates should "translate" this description and have examples ready that demonstrate the following:

- Providing exceptional service and outstanding experiences to customers
- Using a proactive and visible leadership style that is also detail oriented
- Engaging in an intuitive collaboration style
- Contributing to a quality work environment
- Executing continuous improvement practices

It's also important to thoroughly review the company's website and its LinkedIn page. Other resources include YouTube and other social media sites. Pay attention to how it describes its leadership and culture. As you go through the information, consider how you could use it in your answers or your questions in this interview or future interviews.

For example, if the company lists its values, you can highlight how you showed these values in the examples you give. Or you might find out that the company offers a volunteer day for employees and highlights some nonprofit organizations that it supports. You can mention your support of these or other similar organizations.

You want the interviewers to see that you spent time on your research to show that you are a serious candidate who is interested in working for *this* company, not just someone who is applying for any job and accepting any interviews. (Even if you are applying for a lot of jobs, you want the recruiters to feel that you are focused on this job.)

You'll also want to review any recent press releases about the company. What events, product news, or other stories is it focusing on? These could be areas to mention or ask about. Part of your research into a company can be looking into what others say about it. If it's been in the news for positive reasons, you can comment about that.

You can also look at sites that show employee reviews, such as Glassdoor.com. Don't be overly concerned with negative reviews, as the people who are most likely to post these are disgruntled employees. In addition, it's helpful to focus on the most recent reviews. A company that got bad reviews last year could have made changes leading to more positive reviews. This is for your research only; it is not an area that should be brought up in initial interviews.

Insider story: Companies known for certain types of interviews

When I (Barbara) was working as an internal recruiter for a major bank, I met a technical recruiter for a major aerospace company at a networking event, and he thought I'd be a good addition to a new team they were creating for positions that were challenging to fill. He referred me to the director, who then scheduled me to interview with three people onsite. I talked to people about this company's interview process and was told by everyone that they did behavioral interviews (i.e., "Tell me about a time when you did X"). As an interviewer, I was familiar with that style of interview and prepared accordingly. However, during the actual interviews, I wasn't asked any

> behavioral interview questions. In fact, they didn't ask me many questions but rather spent the bulk of our time explaining why this new team was being created, what they were going to do, the types of people they wanted to hire for the team, etc. The "interviews" were more like casual conversations.
>
> I ended up getting the job, at a significantly higher salary, but the lesson here is that companies don't interview—people do, so just because a company is known for a certain style, don't be surprised if your actual interviewers don't follow that style.

Get to know the job

Go through the job description in detail and think through each bullet point. Be ready to describe your experience in each item listed and to give examples. While you can supplement your preparation by using AI to analyze a job description and generate lists of possible interview questions, we feel there is much more value in studying and analyzing the job description yourself as your primary method of preparation. The easy way is not the best way to prepare for a job interview.

As an example of how to anticipate possible interview questions, we've selected a job posting that we all can relate to—not because we've been in a similar role but rather because we know what it's like to be on the receiving end of a telemarketing call. Recruiters often develop their interview questions based on the content of job descriptions, and you can use the very same approach to anticipate possible questions and prepare how to answer them.

In the next section, we show an example of a job description for an outbound customer service representative and how to deconstruct it.

Example: Outbound customer service representative

At XYZ Corp, we value and seek exceptional thinkers with the heart and humility to match. Join us on a mission to improve lives and make a lasting difference.

As part of the member engagement team, you will contact members of various plans by phone to offer, explain, and schedule a free in-home or virtual evaluation. You will work diligently to meet department productivity, quality, and customer service goals.

This role will report to a member engagement manager.

Responsibilities:

- Make an average of 50 outbound calls per hour placed by an automatic dialer system to offer, explain, and schedule a free in-home or virtual evaluation.
- Follow 20+ approved scripts, ensure members understand and are comfortable with the terms, and respond to rebuttals persuasively and with professional courtesy.
- Present a positive, professional, and high-energy approach to clients and team members.

- Meet daily goals set by the department (i.e., 300–400 outbound dials per day, 24 appointments set per day, shift and attendance policy adherence, quality targets) in an office or remote environment.
- Adjust, reschedule, and cancel appointments as requested.
- Monitor performance results including appointments, calls, and productivity using designated reporting systems.
- Report complaints and escalations immediately to member engagement managers.
- Participate in peer side-by-side coaching as needed.
- Follow security and privacy guidelines when handling protected information accessed during normal work activities.

Qualifications:

- A high school diploma or equivalent is preferred.
- 1+ year call center experience OR 2+ years general work experience required.
- Previous outbound call center or high-volume experience working in a metrics-driven environment, with an auto dialer, and/or using scripts is preferred.
- A desire to work in an efficient, results-oriented outbound call center environment.
- Persuasive with the ability to handle rebuttals while treating all members with professional courtesy.
- Good communication skills, friendly and conversational.
- Ability to adhere to a fixed daily schedule, including start, breaks, lunch, and end times.
- Strong computer skills and the ability to use multiple systems at the same time while making calls.

Here is how you can deconstruct this description to identify possible interview questions.

In the job description	Key words and phrases	Possible interview questions
At XYZ Corp, we value and seek exceptional thinkers with the heart and humility to match. Join us on a mission to improve lives and make a lasting difference.	Exceptional thinkers Humility Improve lives	Describe an example of you being what could be considered an exceptional thinker. Give an example of your being humble. Why are you interested in improving lives?

Get to know the job

(continued)

In the job description	Key words and phrases	Possible interview questions
As part of the member engagement team, you will contact members of various plans by phone to offer, explain, and schedule a free in-home or virtual evaluation. You will work diligently to meet department productivity, quality, and customer service goals.	Explain and schedule a free in-home or virtual evaluation Work diligently Department productivity, quality, and customer service goals	Describe your experience in explaining services and scheduling appointments with potential customers. Give a personal example of working diligently to meet productivity, quality, and/or customer service goals.
Make an average of 50 outbound calls per hour placed by an automatic dialer system to offer, explain, and schedule a free in-home or virtual evaluation.	50 outbound calls per hour placed by an automatic dialer system	Describe your experience using an automatic dialer system to make outbound calls, including your typical volume per hour.
Follow 20+ approved scripts, ensure members understand and are comfortable with the terms, and respond to rebuttals persuasively and with professional courtesy.	Follow 20+ approved scripts Respond to rebuttals persuasively and with professional courtesy	What experience have you had following scripts to explain available products or services? Give an example of your responding to a rebuttal using both persuasion and courtesy.
Present a positive, professional, and high-energy approach to clients and team members.	Positive, professional, and high-energy approach	In what ways have you displayed a positive, professional, and high-energy approach in your previous positions? Give a personal example of displaying a positive, professional, and high-energy approach when interacting with a customer or potential customer.
Meet daily goals set by the department (i.e., 300—400 outbound dials per day, 24 appointments set per day, shift and attendance policy adherence, quality targets) in an office or remote environment.	Meet daily goals	What were your goals in your last position? To what extent did you meet them?
Monitor performance results including appointments, calls, and productivity using designated reporting systems.	Monitor performance results Using designated reporting systems	How was your performance in your last position monitored? What kinds of systems have you used to report your performance?
Report complaints and escalations immediately to member engagement managers.	Report complaints and escalations immediately	How did you handle complaints and escalations in your last position?

(continued)

In the job description	Key words and phrases	Possible interview questions
Participate in peer side-by-side coaching as needed.	Peer side-by-side coaching	What experience have you had in coaching peers in your previous positions?
Follow security and privacy guidelines when handling protected information accessed during normal work activities.	Follow security and privacy guidelines	What kinds of security and privacy guidelines have you had to follow in your past positions?
1+ year call center experience OR 2+ years general work experience required. Previous outbound call center or high-volume experience working in a metrics-driven environment, with an auto dialer, and/or using scripts is preferred.	1+ year call center experience OR 2+ years general work experience required Previous outbound call center or high-volume experience preferred	Describe your general work experience. What experience have you had working in either an inbound or outbound call center? What experience have you had working in a high-volume, metrics-driven environment?
A desire to work in an efficient, results-oriented outbound call center environment.	Efficient, results-oriented outbound call center environment	In what ways would you describe yourself as efficient and results-oriented? Give an example.
Persuasive with the ability to handle rebuttals while treating all members with professional courtesy.	Persuasive Ability to handle rebuttals while treating all members with professional courtesy	Give a personal example of responding to a rebuttal using both persuasion and courtesy.
Good communication skills, friendly and conversational.	Good communication skills Friendly and conversational	Give a personal example of being friendly and conversational when interacting with a customer or potential customer.
Ability to adhere to a fixed daily schedule, including start, breaks, lunch, and end times.	Ability to adhere to a fixed daily schedule	What kind of schedule did you have in your previous positions?
Strong computer skills and the ability to use multiple systems at the same time while making calls.	Ability to use multiple systems at the same time	Describe your computer skills. Give a personal example of using multiple computer systems at the same time.

Get to know the interviewer

You need to get to know the interviewer. It is critically important to be yourself and build rapport, likability, and a human connection with the interviewer. If you do, the interviewer will be more likely and willing to consider you, even if you don't match 100% of the job qualifications. On the other hand, if you do match 100% but come across as either arrogant or robotic, with canned and rehearsed answers, the interviewer will find a reason not to hire you. The reason they give will usually be something like "You just weren't a fit."

Laura remembers hearing hiring managers talking about candidates who didn't have all the required qualifications, but the manager really liked them. They said that they could teach someone the needed skills. What mattered to them most was whether they wanted to work with the person or not.

The initial people you meet with may not be working with you directly if you get hired, but if they are internal interviewers, they want to make sure that you'll fit in with their colleagues. Do your homework on the interviewers and look at their LinkedIn profiles to review their backgrounds and how they describe themselves. It's okay for them to see that you viewed this; it shows that you're someone who does their homework (and no, it's not viewed as creepy). Look for anything you have in common that you can use to build rapport during the interview. For example, did you go to the same school, live in the same state, or work for the same company in the past? These are all things that you can comment on.

If you go to their site for the interview, look around their office and comment on something you have in common or that you are impressed by, or compliment the photos on their desk. Granted, some interviewers may have a poker face and make it difficult to build rapport, but do everything you can to really connect on a human level and not just as a job candidate.

It can be helpful to look at the interviews from the interviewer's point of view. The interviewer is not your enemy in this process. They are looking for the best fit for this position so they can support their company and make their boss and the hiring manager happy. They don't want to have to conduct interview after interview where they don't find the right person. It makes their jobs much simpler when they can find the right person fast. Your job is to help them clearly see that you're the best candidate so they can help you get hired and wrap up this position quickly and easily.

Know yourself

Part of preparation is knowing yourself. This is the time to go through your resume and review it from the perspective of this job. Go through each line and prepare to tell the story of what you did, the results you obtained, and how this example pertains to this position and organization.

After your detailed review of the job description that we discussed earlier in this chapter, identify your most relevant and compelling stories to share in the interview based on the areas of experience and competencies listed there. For each story, you want to clearly state the actions that you took and the results. Stories should be brief (no more than 2 minutes in duration) and impactful. You may want to practice talking through your stories out loud or tell them to someone else to see how much time they take and gain their feedback. Remove unimportant details such as people's names or locations and focus on the key message that you want to give the interviewer.

You may wish to put together a prep chart such as one shown here, where the competencies (like problem-solving and decision-making) are included in the job description and the stories are from your experience that relate directly to those competencies.

Interview prep chart

Competency	Story including actions and results

You'll want to identify your top three to five selling points for why you are a great fit for the position. Be sure to include your unique combination of skills, knowledge, and experience. The interviewer needs to hear why you are the best choice.

You'll also want to clearly state what may be obvious to you, and don't make assumptions that the interviewer understands everything that you're saying (hint: avoid your previous company's acronyms unless they are widely known). For example, it might be clear to you that your experience in a certain area connects with what the job needs; however, the interviewer might not realize that unless you say it. This is especially true in initial screening interviews, where the interviewer probably only knows the basics about the position. Always make it easy for the interviewer to see your value and why you're the right person for the job.

What could get in your way

During the preparation stage, consider what could possibly get in your way. It's important to identify any potential objections the interviewer may have. For example, you might have experience in a different industry or may have worked in a company much larger or smaller than this company. Or maybe you don't have a specific degree or certification that they've specified they would like to have. Consider what they might be concerned about and develop your answers. This process can feel uncomfortable, but it's an important part in helping you feel confident that you can address any question.

Your answers should include a brief mention of the potential problem and a focus on how you will overcome it. It can be helpful to use past examples. It's important to answer the question asked; do not offer any additional information.

Remember, even if they've asked for a specific degree or something you don't have, they are interested enough to invite you in for an interview. Obviously, there is something about your application that interested them, so don't get caught up in what you don't have and instead focus on what you do bring to the job.

There are several reasons that candidates may not be selected for a job, and we've divided them into three categories: reasons that have nothing to do with you, things about you that you can't control, and things about you that you can control.

Reasons that have nothing to do with you include things like open positions being put on hold (which may be due to reorganizations, reductions in force, or cost control initiatives), or the hiring manager may have decided to hire someone from within the company, someone they used to work with, or someone referred to them by someone they trust.

Things about you that you can't control include reasons such as wanting to hire someone from their same industry, but you come from a different industry, you lack experience in their exact same job function, or you haven't worked on the same system they use or with their same types of customers. Hiring managers often feel that hiring someone who basically did the same job for a direct competitor (or a company in their same industry) will make the new person's learning curve flat, therefore giving the new hire a more direct path to success. We don't agree with that philosophy, but we must acknowledge that some hiring managers feel that way.

Things about you that you can control are your preparation and performance in the interview. The fact that you're reading this book shows that you're someone who wants to learn how to improve in both of these areas, so congratulations on taking the first step toward improvement! By following the steps outlined in this and subsequent chapters, you're well on your way to successful interviews leading to the goal of getting a job offer.

Now it's time to start working on your answers to the interviewer's questions.

Different kinds of questions and how to answer them

To help you understand the types of interview questions you could be asked, let's look at the different types of questions: breadth versus depth, behavioral, hypothetical, and general questions. We cover these types at a high level in this chapter; in later chapters, we discuss specific questions and how to translate them. In this chapter, we also cover frameworks that help to structure your answers. Use one of these frameworks to organize your thoughts when preparing and answering questions.

Breadth vs. depth questions

Interview questions either cover breadth or depth. You could be asked questions about the breadth of your experience ("What experience have you had in X?") or the depth of experience you've had in a particular scenario ("Give a personal example of having to face X situation"). These depth questions are also known as behavioral interviews or competency-based interviews (more on that in the next section).

It's important to listen very carefully to the topic of the question and how it is being asked. If the interviewer uses words like "Describe your experience in . . ." or "What experience have you had in . . . ," then you'll know it's a breadth question. If they use words like "Give an example of" or "Describe a situation . . . ," then it's a depth question.

When asked a breadth question, mention several examples you've experienced, preferably at different organizations or in different positions. Do not "go deep" into any one situation but rather stay on the surface when describing the experiences you've had in that area and the results you've achieved. In response to a depth question, mention only one circumstance but describe how you handled that situation in more detail, including your results.

If you're not sure if it's a breadth or depth question, it's okay to ask. For example, you could ask, "Would you prefer to hear about the kinds of experiences I have in this area, or would you rather hear the details of one specific example?" The interviewer's question might make it clear, but if you're not sure, it's best to clarify.

Behavioral or competency-based questions

Behavioral or competency-based questions directly ask for examples, typically by using phrases such as "Tell me about a time when . . . ," "Give an example of . . . ," or "Describe for me . . . ." You need to be ready with examples that directly pertain to the position and have impactful results.

Hypothetical questions

Hypothetical questions ask how you would handle a certain scenario instead of how you have handled it in the past. The questions include verbiage such as "How would you handle X situation?" If you've had experience in that kind of situation, it is best to describe your actual experience and results instead of how you would hypothetically handle it. If you have not had that exact experience, then talk about something similar from your background.

General questions

General questions ask how you typically handle a certain scenario instead of how you would handle it in the future or have handled it in the past. These questions are asked in the form "How *do* you handle X situation?" instead of "How *would* you handle X situation?"

Whenever possible, you should answer hypothetical and general questions by giving an actual example with real results, which will have a much more impact than answering with general statements about the kinds of things you typically do or hypothetical scenarios about what you would do. The best way to begin is with a sentence like "I think the best way to answer that is to tell you about the time in my last position when I . . . ," which allows you to provide a specific example with impact in a natural way.

Answer frameworks

How do you talk about an actual example in your answer? You need to have a structure, or it will be too easy to ramble. There are a few recommended structures that you can use; we call these *answer frameworks*. Using one of these frameworks makes it easier to prepare your examples and get your message across. There are several frameworks for how to articulate your stories or examples: here are three that we recommend:

- Problem Action Result (PAR)
- Situation Task Action Result (STAR)
- Situation Obstacle Action Result (SOAR)

Some employers may tell you their preferred framework (STAR is the most used); if they do not, then choose the one that you're most comfortable with. Typically, entry-level or less experienced candidates use PAR, and SOAR is more applicable to senior-level candidates. One issue that is common in interviewees, even at the executive level, is to water down the description of their actions, perhaps because they don't want their answers to be too long or because what they are describing came easily to them. This has the unfortunate consequence of diluting the impact of their answers. You need to show a good balance of both complexity and brevity by articulating the challenge behind your actions. What made this situation difficult or challenging, or what obstacles did you have to overcome to accomplish your results?

Tips and traps to avoid

In our years of doing interviews, we've noticed a variety of things that people do that either weaken their message and should be avoided, or help them get their message across more clearly and effectively. Also, employers commonly ask certain kinds of questions that could be perceived as traps, so we want you to know how to answer them.

Weakening words and phrases

Be careful of using weakening words or phrases. Some people do this without realizing it, including things like "I try to," "I think," or "I'm pretty good at." Practice eliminating these words in your stories. Think about what Yoda from *Star Wars* said: "Do or do not. There is no try."

Overall, you should demonstrate a balance of confidence with humility. Too much confidence will make you appear arrogant, but too much humility will not lead to job offers. Be proud of what you've accomplished (which is not bragging) while still being likable.

Filler words

While everyone uses some filler words when talking, in an interview this could be seen as a sign of nerves and therefore should be minimized. These are words such as "um," "uh," and "ah," and people tend to include these when they are trying to think while speaking. It is much better to pause than to use too many filler words in your answers. If you need help minimizing these, we suggest attending a few Toastmasters meetings or practicing recording yourself.

Generic answers

You should provide customized answers for each interview question. Select examples that pertain directly to the role for which you're interviewing and are from your recent past (within the last five years or so, depending on your level). If too many of your answers are from a totally different kind of job or from too long ago, the interviewer is likely to conclude that you lack the needed experience.

"I" vs. "we"

We've all heard the expression "There's no 'I' in Team." When people talk about things they personally did, they often use the word "we" when what they really mean is "I." Be intentional in when to use "I" and when to use "We." Use "I" when describing things you personally have done. Use "we" when describing what you've done, either as a leader or part of a team. When describing something your team accomplished as a result of your leadership, use both. For example, "I led the team, and we accomplished X."

If every pronoun you use is "we," the interviewer will not have a clear idea of what they would be getting when they hire you. Also, if every pronoun you use is "I," they may conclude that you're not a team player who is good at collaborating with others. Lastly, avoid starting your sentences with "you" (as in "You need to do X") because that can be perceived as lecturing.

The "negative sandwich"

Use a "negative sandwich" in your answers to negative questions. It has become quite common for interviewers to ask about negative scenarios, including the reason why you're looking to leave your current position (or why you left your last one), and they may ask about your weaknesses, a time you failed, a mistake you made, a decision you've regretted, etc. These aren't necessarily traps and can provide a good opportunity to build rapport and likability by being real (both confident and humble).

The best way to answer these questions is by using a "negative sandwich"—start with a positive, describe the negative, and end on a positive. For example:

- *Positive*—"I'm really proud of my ability to manage a variety of details."
- *Negative*—"One time, however, two people in the department were out sick, so I was not only juggling my own projects but also filling in for my colleagues, and unfortunately, I missed one of the deadlines. As soon as I recognized this, I went to my manager and explained what had happened. I took the extra time to get caught up and made sure the other deadlines were met."
- *Positive*—"I learned an important lesson; now what I do is create a spreadsheet with specific dates for all aspects of my projects and check that spreadsheet every night before I leave and every morning when I get to work. I'm pleased to report that I haven't missed any deadlines since then."

If your answer to the "failure" question is that you've never failed or made a mistake, you will likely lose credibility and come across as being dishonest (nobody is perfect!). Don't miss the opportunity to build likability and rapport by being candid about something that didn't work out as well as you had hoped. Get to what you learned and do differently now, and that way you are selling yourself as someone who learns from their mistakes and from difficult circumstances.

"Or" questions

Be prepared to answer "or" questions. You might be asked to choose one thing or another. Examples include "Are you more of a leader or a manager?" "Do you prefer to be a manager or an individual contributor?" "Would you like to work on X or Y?" (e.g., a project, job, department, division, location, or product.) It really doesn't matter. It might as well be "Are you more like an apple or an orange?"

Resist the urge to choose one because whichever you don't choose can be used against you (e.g., if you say you're more of a manager than an individual contributor, but they only have an individual contributor role open).

The way to answer this type of question is to divide and conquer: "It depends on the situation; in X kind of circumstance, I am more like an apple (and then explain), and in Y kind of circumstance, I am more like an orange (and explain). In my experience, I've learned to adapt my approach to the specific scenario and people involved."

Rising inflection/uptalking

Some people have a tendency to end a declarative sentence with a rising pitch, making their sentence sound like a question. This is called uptalk, upspeak, or high rising inflection. Talking in this manner makes you sound less certain or less confident, which can affect your credibility in an interview. For example, it would sound different if you said, "I'm proud of the work I did with my team?" instead of "I'm proud of the work I did with my team."

To minimize this tendency, record yourself speaking. Notice the times you use uptalk, so you become aware of this tendency and will be more conscious of this during interviews. Practice speaking and ending your sentences using a consistent and even pitch or a downward pitch and then record yourself again to hear the difference.

Answer length and timing

Plan and prepare for the length of your answers. If your answers are too long, the interviewer might lose interest and no longer be listening by the time you get to the important part of your answer. Sometimes people are so concerned with giving answers that are too long that they make the opposite mistake, and their answers are too short and lacking enough substance to truly answer the question. Allow enough time to address the important key points of the message.

A good rule of thumb is that your answer to the opening "Tell me about yourself" question should be no more than 1 minute in length, and the same is true for nonstory questions (i.e., strengths, interest in position, why you're in the job market, etc. Examples and stories should be no more than 2 minutes in duration.

Next applicant, please

Think about

The following are some things to think about before moving to the next chapter:

- How have you prepared for interviews in the past? What will you do differently now?
- Which of the types of interview questions described have you been asked in previous interviews?
- Which of the traps mentioned have you fallen into? What will you do differently in your next interview?

Key takeaways

- Every interview question has a question behind the question. By translating Interview Speak, you can understand what the interviewer is really asking so you can give them the information they need.
- Think of the interview as a sales process: you're the product and the employer is the consumer. You have to understand what they need so you can match your features and benefits to those needs. To do that, you'll need to get to know the company, the interviewer, and the job. You can deconstruct the job description to help you develop possible interview questions and think through your answers.

- A critical part of preparation is understanding yourself and why you're a great fit for the position.
- There are different kinds of questions that require different approaches. Using answer frameworks can make it easier for you to clearly get your message across.
- Learning a variety of tips and tricks is important so your answers will make an impression. For example, one way to address negative questions is to use the "negative sandwich," which will help you address issues and show that you are someone who learns from mistakes and difficult situations.

Part 2

Translations

In this part, we translate questions that you could be asked in your interviews. For each question, we'll state a typical version of the question and then provide a "translation" to help you understand what the question really means (i.e., the "question behind the question"). We'll explain why the interviewer is asking it and what they're looking for in answers. We'll highlight some things to say and some things you should avoid because they could be interpreted negatively by the interviewer.

We include chapters on the most commonly asked questions and special situation questions such as those directed to unemployed or career-changing candidates.

Also, in this part we provide translations of interview questions that are designed to gather information about how you behave in different situations. These are also known as behavioral competencies. Each chapter covers a question about a different set of competencies. As you review these questions, consider to what extent they pertain to the kind of job you're applying for. This will help you determine how prepared you should be for those questions. For example, if your job involves interacting with others, you'll want to make sure you spend time on chapter 3.

Everyone should be prepared to answer questions about negative situations, overcoming obstacles, and difficult situations (chapter 4), since they can be asked of all interviewees (and are quite common).

Some questions include example answers from candidates, as well as critiques on what they did well and what could be improved. We also include examples from Clueless Clark, and we talk about what he did wrong and what he should have said. These examples are taken from combining answers from real situations and candidates. The questions that include these sample answers are common and are relevant to a wide variety of candidates.

In most job interviews, you'll be asked some questions that are specific to your job function. These can be either breadth questions ("What experience have you had in X?") or depth questions ("Give an example of a time when you did X"). In these cases, the interviewer is interested in hearing about what you did *and* how you did it. This book will not address all possible job functions or job types within those functions. We have included the most common business functional areas: senior leadership, operations, sales, marketing, finance, information technology, and human resources.

For these function-specific questions, instead of providing direct translations, we include important areas that need to be included in your answers, examples, and a list of typical questions. These sample questions will help you recognize the questions you're asked during the interview so you can address the most appropriate issues.

Common questions and special situations

Initial interviews almost always include at least some version of the common questions we describe in this chapter because the interviewer is trying to get to know you and determine whether you meet their basic qualifications before moving you to the next round of interviews. These questions are used in all kinds of industries, companies, and jobs at all levels of an organization. While we can't guarantee that you won't be surprised in your interviews by an unusual question you hadn't anticipated (our favorite is "If you were a superhero, what would your special power be?"), the questions in the first part of the chapter are so common that you need to be prepared for them.

In this chapter and in subsequent Q&A chapters, we provide translations of each question so you'll know what the interviewer is looking for and instructions on how to answer them. The How to Answer sections provide ideas and suggestions for how to plan your answer. It's important to take these suggestions and use them to create answers of your own. Interviewers don't want to hear canned responses; they want to learn about the real you and feel that they're getting to know you.

"Tell me about yourself" is the most common first question asked and not only serves as an icebreaker but also allows you to introduce yourself in a way that highlights your specific qualifications for the job. Questions like "What are your career goals?", "What kind of job are you looking for next?", and "Why are you interested in this job?" serve as initial screening questions; if the interviewer feels that they can't

26   **CHAPTER 2** *Common questions and special situations*

accommodate your interests and goals, no matter how qualified you are, it's unlikely you'll be invited to further interviews.

Answering questions like "Why are you looking for a new job?", "Why did you leave your last job?", "What are your salary requirements?", and "What are your strengths and weaknesses?" can be tricky. If you're not careful in how you word your answers, you can provide the interviewer with red flags about you, inadvertently shooting yourself in the foot.

In addition to translating these and subsequent interview questions for you, we want to help you develop your answers so that you give the interviewers the key things they are listening for. They will then see that you're a match and will want to move you to the next step in the interview process.

We'll also look at specific situations that may or may not affect you. For example, if you're unemployed, have worked for a long time at the same company, or are applying for a lower-level position, you'll want to be prepared to answer questions about those particular topics.

Throughout the Q&A chapters, you'll meet four people looking for jobs: Jen (sales), Lucas (customer service), Ari (engineer), and Davina (manager). They'll give good answers to interview questions, and then we'll show how each answer can be turned into a great answer.

Before you read our suggestions, you may want to pause and take some time to consider what you would do to make the responses better. Then read our feedback and use that information to adjust your interview answers.

You'll also meet another job applicant, Clueless Clark. Clueless Clark is in marketing, and he believes that he's great at marketing himself. Although Clark hasn't personally been a hiring manager, he has served on several panel interviews for his company, and based on that limited experience, he thinks he knows what interviewers will ask and what he should say. We'll follow Clueless Clark as he stumbles through interviews and show you what he should do differently to help you avoid making similar mistakes.

Most commonly asked questions

Candidates should be prepared to answer all of the following questions since they are likely to be asked at some time during the interview process.

Tell me about yourself

"Tell me about yourself" is the most common opening question. Interviewers ask this as an icebreaker and because they want to give you the chance to introduce yourself in a way that makes them want to learn more about you. They may also be looking for possible red flags on how you will be perceived based on how you communicate.

It is *not* an invitation for you to ramble, share your life story, or give a verbal resume. Rather, it is an opportunity for you to build rapport and immediately focus their attention on the specific aspects of your background that pertain to the position.

Next applicant, please

TRANSLATION

Before I start asking you my real questions, I'd like to get to know you a bit and also give you an opportunity to share things that you'd like me to know about you.

HOW TO ANSWER

Keep your answer to 30 to 60 seconds maximum:

- Thank them for taking the time to speak with you.
- If you haven't yet, say something brief to build rapport, such as where you're from, or mention any mutual connections you have, something you noticed from their LinkedIn profile, or anything that connects you to their company and/or role.
- Name a few of your skills that relate to the position: "Some of my top skills are . . ."
- Describe one or two accomplishments you're especially proud of that directly relate to the position: "One of the things I'm most proud of is . . ."
- Say why you're so interested in this company and this specific position. For example, you can reference specific aspects such as their expansion into a new geography and say something like "I've been involved in multiple expansion plans generating up to X million dollars in new revenue, and I look forward to learning more about your plans."

Example: Ari, engineer

The interviewer begins by asking, "Tell me about yourself."

Ari's answer

I'm a technical professional with a strong background in engineering. I've worked in many roles where I've been responsible for customer projects.

My journey began with a degree in mechanical engineering. Over the years, I've honed my skills, enabling me to tackle complex challenges effectively.

I'm particularly proud of a project I was responsible for at my current company, where we designed a new system for a long-term customer. The customer wanted us to do this for them even though it was in an area that wasn't our specialty.

My team took the time to review all the potential problems and came up with a solid design plan within the parameters they had requested. The project stayed in scope and was done on time. This experience showcased both my problem-solving and planning abilities.

What excites me about the opportunity at this company is the chance to work with cutting-edge technology for a firm known for quality. I believe my analytical and technical skills can contribute effectively to the company's goals.

What Ari did well

The timing of this answer is excellent—about a minute in length. Ari gave a good introduction to his background and his profession and included a project he's proud of that relates to the position for which he's interviewing. He did not get stuck in the details of the project and instead gave a very high-level overview, including that the project ended on time and within scope. He also mentions his soft skill strengths of problem-solving and planning, and he closed with why he's excited to be there, why he's interested in this job, and how he can benefit the company.

What would make this even better

In his opening, he says, "Over the years, I've honed my skills, enabling me to tackle complex challenges effectively." This would be more impactful if he named some specific skills that he excels at, which can be a combination of both job-related and soft skills. In interviews, he is selling not only his past experience but also the skills he brings to the table now.

In the description of the customer project, he says, "We designed a new system." He should be clearer on what his role was; did he lead this team or was he a member of the team? Was it purely an engineering team or was it a cross-functional team? Also, he could add in a brief tidbit showing the scope of the project, like how long it took and/or what the budget was.

Ari mentions that this project was not in an area that was their specialty; how did he (or they) overcome that challenge? He may have missed an opportunity to sell the fact that he learned new skills, knowledge, and abilities.

While Ari came close to including a result (on time and within scope), he did not include what the overall benefit was to the customer and his company. Why did it matter that this project was completed? Did it improve any metrics like reduced costs, improved efficiency, or increased revenues? Did it allow his company to sell this type of work to other customers, thereby expanding their business offerings? Even though Ari is a tech person, he will stand out from others if he shows understanding of the overall business benefit his technical work provides.

Why are you looking for a new job OR why did you leave your last job?

Interviewers ask this question not only because they want to know why you're looking for a job but also because they are wondering if your reason is something they should be concerned about. We call this the "exit" question; your answer should be brief and should roll off the tongue with no hesitation. The interviewer is looking for honesty and transparency in your answer.

TRANSLATION

Why are you in the job market, are there any red flags in your past such as performance or personality issues, and are you going to badmouth your last employer or manager?

HOW TO ANSWER

Use the "negative sandwich" model:

- Start with a positive about your current or last job, such as really enjoying the job/people/company or feeling pride in what you accomplished there.
- Then go into the negative by giving the business reason for leaving or looking to leave, such as cost-cutting measures, reorganization, or merger or acquisition, or perhaps, based on the structure or organization chart, there is no room for further career growth.
- End on a positive by saying what you're looking for next, showing excitement and enthusiasm about your next career chapter. You can even say what specifically excites you about this job and company, showing that you've done your research.

Example: Ari, engineer

The interviewer then asks, "Why are you looking for a new job?"

Ari's answer

I believe that a change in my career aligns with my long-term goals and aspirations. Specifically, the first reason is my continued interest in growth and career advancement. While my current role has provided me with valuable experience, I'm looking to join a team that will expose me to new and different technologies that will help me to keep my knowledge current and enable me to work on cutting-edge solutions. My current company does not have opportunities for growth.

Also, I'm looking to work in an innovative environment. Your company is known for its commitment to new technology and for driving industry standards.

CHAPTER 2 Common questions and special situations

(continued)

Lastly, through my research, I've been impressed by your company's values and how they align with my own. The emphasis on sustainability and contributing positively to society resonates with me on both a personal and professional level.

What Ari did well

This answer is short and to the point, and it also shows that he's done some homework on the company. He does a good job of answering the implied second part of this question: ". . . and why are you interested in our company?" He states the lack of growth potential in a straightforward, matter-of-fact way with zero blame or negative implications.

What would make this even better

Ari's first sentence is basically "filler" because it tells the interviewer nothing that is unique about him. "I believe that a change in my career aligns with my long-term goals and aspirations" could have been said by any candidate for any job, so it should not be included in his answer. Ari then discusses his own interests and goals rather than directly answering the question. This is where the "negative sandwich" approach should be used.

A better answer

After modifying his answer based on the previous feedback, Ari's even better answer is now this:

"I'm really proud of the work I've done at my current company and have really enjoyed working with the people there. However, I feel that the opportunities for growth and learning new technologies are limited, and I love how innovative your company is and the cutting-edge solutions you offer to your customers. I've also been impressed by your company's values; the emphasis on sustainability and contributing positively to society resonates with me on both a personal and professional level."

What are you looking for next?

Interviewers want to know what you're looking for in your next position so they can determine if this job can accommodate your interests and goals. They want to make sure that you'll be happy in the job and that you will stay in the position for a while. If your answer makes it sound like this job is simply a stepping stone for another job that you actually want, it would be a red flag and might make them not want to hire you.

TRANSLATION

I'm wondering how closely my open position matches the kind of job you now seek.

HOW TO ANSWER

Say that you're looking for a position that includes a, b, and c (name some of the work activities that are listed right in their job description) and would allow you to use your skills in x, y, and z (name some of your top skills that are specifically needed in this job). You do not have to mention a specific job title unless the titles are quite common across organizations in your field.

What do you not want to do?

Interviewers want to know the things you don't want to do in your next position for a similar reason to why they ask what you're looking for next—so they can determine if this job will align with your interests and goals.

TRANSLATION

What kind of job would you not enjoy, so that I can determine to what extent this job would be a match for you? (If the job we have open is like what you describe, then even if you qualify, you likely won't last long.)

HOW TO ANSWER

After going through the job posting or job description in detail, identify either a role or specific work activities that you would not expect to be included in this job. Ideally, describe something in a totally different function or industry. For example, if you're interviewing for a position in finance, you could say that you enjoy recording and tracking sales information but do not want to engage in selling directly to customers.

What kind of salary are you looking for?

Interviewers want to know your desired salary range to see whether they can match your compensation requirements.

TRANSLATION

I don't want to waste my time continuing to interview you or risk my credibility with my boss, colleagues, and/or direct reports by introducing you to others if I can't afford to hire you, so let's get this out of the way now. I also don't want to waste time if your salary expectation is too low. That will make me wonder if your skills and experience are at the level that we need.

HOW TO ANSWER

Here are instructions on how to best answer this question:

- If possible, avoid giving a number because you don't want to be too high or too low. Just like Goldilocks and the three bears, you want the answer to be just right. If their salary range wasn't included in the job posting, then try to get the range out of them by admitting that you don't know anything about their salary structure or budget and then ask, "What is the salary range?" Your attitude should be one of intelligent curiosity rather than avoidance, noncompliance, or any kind of game-playing. You may be surprised how often interviewers will tell you if you simply ask. When you hear the range, confirm that the range works for you.
- Also, do not say you're looking for a salary "commensurate with your experience." First, the word "commensurate" is never used in real conversations—only salary discussions—so avoid it. Second, this is the epitome of a "BS" answer that has been around for decades and will likely lead to their next question, which is "Oh really, what number would you consider to be commensurate with your experience?" Don't put yourself into that trap!

- If they push you for your salary expectations a second time, have a range ready that you've determined is appropriate for the position based on your research. Always give a range rather than a number because it shows flexibility and share the range with a caveat: "Much would depend on the entire package but based on what I've seen out there for similar positions, it seems that somewhere in the X-Y neighborhood would be fair." Do not avoid answering this question if they ask it a second time, because you will risk irritating them, which is never a good idea when you're trying to build rapport!
- If you already have their range, just say that you understand their range is X-Y and that sounds reasonable.
- The goal here is to get past this part of the interview as comfortably as possible by letting them know that you're in the correct salary range. In many cases, even if a range is stated, there's still a possibility for some flexibility if they've decided you're the right candidate.

> ### Insider story: The money question
>
> The most common answer to the question "What kind of salary are you looking for?" is something like "Salary isn't the most important thing to me; I care more about the company and culture." One time when I (Barbara) heard this answer one too many times, I said to the candidate, "Oh, good, so you won't mind then if we pay you minimum wage for this project manager job? Since, after all, salary isn't important?" After a surprised look and some silence, he finally gave me a range. I didn't hold this against him, because I knew he was just following what many of the books say to do. Because he really did have good qualifications and answered the other questions well, I ended up referring him and he was hired. When I saw him a month or so later, I could tell he was a bit embarrassed, but I made a joke about it and told him he got the prize for being the 50th person to give me that answer that month.

Why are you interested in this job?

Interviewers want to know why you're interested in this job to learn your motivation and level of interest in their open position. This is especially true if the candidate is unemployed, because interviewers want to know why the candidate wants this specific job and not just any job.

TRANSLATION

Even if you qualify, I need to know that this is a job that you want, are passionate about, and will find challenging. I don't want to hire someone who can do this in their sleep, will become bored, and will require me to replace them in a short time frame because they found a better job.

HOW TO ANSWER

Identify a few work activities that are part of this job and describe how you not only have succeeded in those things previously but also that you really enjoy doing them.

You need to sell that this job represents the sweet spot—that is, the intersection of both what you're very good at and what you're passionate about.

> **Insider story: What not to say**
>
> I (Barbara) remember one candidate who was extremely confident in his qualifications for the job. It was a lateral move for him, and he had recently been laid off after his company had been acquired. When I asked him why he was interested in this job, he gave a bit of a smirk and said, "Why not?" That was not the answer I wanted to hear, and he missed the opportunity to further sell himself for the job. Needless to say, that pretty much ended his candidacy at that point!

What do you know about our company?

Interviewers want to find out what you know about their company to learn whether you've done your homework, and, if so, to what extent. They want to know if you are a serious candidate who is willing to take the time to research and get to know their company or if you are someone who just applies to lots of different jobs.

TRANSLATION

Are you the kind of person who prepares for important meetings? Have you done your homework, or did you just glance at the About Us part of our website?

HOW TO ANSWER

Here's your chance to not only show that you've done more homework than your competition but also to state why you're so interested in working there. Show excitement and enthusiasm about their company and its products or services.

What are your career goals?

Interviewers want to know your career goals to determine whether they can accommodate them. If your goal is to be promoted within two years and that conflicts with their typical time frame, giving that answer may negatively affect your chances of getting hired.

TRANSLATION

Even if you qualify for this job, will our company be able to help you achieve your goals? If not, you might leave in the near future, and I will have to replace you.

HOW TO ANSWER

Say that you don't have specific titles and time frames in mind—only that you want to continue developing skills in a, b, c, and d (name some of the skills that are relevant and needed in this job) and that you'd like the opportunity to advance to whatever other positions might become available at this company at the appropriate time when you have the necessary experience.

What are your strengths?

Interviewers ask about your strengths so they can learn what you consider your top skills and selling points. It may also be combined with the next question as "What are your strengths and weaknesses?" Our example answer from Lucas in the next section uses the combined question.

TRANSLATION

What skills do you feel are your strongest, and to what extent will they be utilized in this job?

HOW TO ANSWER

Name some skills that relate to the position that you've developed or come naturally to you and that you're especially proud of. After each strength, give a brief example of how you've used that skill. These can be both hard skills (functional job skills) and soft skills (behavioral skills that aren't job-specific, such as problem-solving, collaboration, influencing, and decision-making).

What are your weaknesses?

Interviewers ask about your weaknesses to get a sense of your self-knowledge and to find out how honest and realistic your answer will be. Do *not* give any of the typical BS answers, such as being a perfectionist, working too hard, getting frustrated by others who don't work as hard as you, or being bad at work–life balance. We've all heard them before, so if you use one, you're saying that you are more of a BS artist than a transparent and honest human. The goal here is to build rapport, which cannot be done by making something up.

Next applicant, please

TRANSLATION

Are you going to be real, honest, and candid with me, or will you give me a typical BS answer by disguising a strength as a supposed weakness? Are you someone who has both the confidence and humility to admit you're not perfect? Will we be able to work around your weaknesses in this job, or will they end up causing problems?

HOW TO ANSWER

If they ask for one weakness, give one, and if they ask for the plural "weaknesses," give two. Some people ask for three strengths and three weaknesses, so you must be ready. You have two options here:

- Go back in time. Pick one or more things that earlier in your career you weren't very good at, didn't come naturally to you, or you really had to work on and then describe what you've done to improve.
- Take a strength and identify under what circumstances that strength could actually be a weakness. Then say that you've come to recognize those situations and describe what you do to compensate for that tendency.

In either case, use the negative sandwich model, starting with a positive, then stating the negative, and ending on a positive. For example:

- *Go back in time*—"I'm really proud of my ability to do X. But that wasn't always the case. Earlier in my career, I really struggled when faced with X" or "I had a mentor who gave me feedback on X, and I did these things to work on it."
- *Start with a strength*—"I'm really proud of my ability to do X. But, under this particular circumstance, that strength is actually a weakness, and here's why. So what I do in those situations is this . . ."

What you are selling here is self-knowledge and the idea that you're aware of your shortcomings and have worked to improve them. Don't miss the opportunity to build rapport and a human connection with your interviewer by admitting that you're not perfect (nobody is). Just don't choose anything that is central to the job (like an accountant who isn't good with numbers)!

We acknowledge that there are psychological barriers to admitting weaknesses, and many of us are afraid to admit that we've made mistakes or were wrong about something. The emphasis in this interview question, though, is not about the weakness; what's important is what you learned from this experience and what makes you a better candidate now that you've gone through it.

HOW NOT TO ANSWER THIS QUESTION

Many interview guides and websites tell you how to answer this question, but beware! Interviewers read these books, so they will recognize them if you try to pass these answers off as your own. We've all heard these answers hundreds of times:

- "I give everything I do 100% of my effort, and I get really frustrated when other people don't work as hard as I do." Our response: "Sorry, buddy, but being frustrated by other people's weaknesses isn't really a weakness of yours!"

36   **CHAPTER 2**   *Common questions and special situations*

- "I'm a perfectionist." Our response: "Yeah, that's what many others say to this question, so now we know that you're just trying to disguise a strength as a weakness (which is what the other interview guides tell you to do). We'd rather hire someone who has the confidence and humility to admit they're not perfect and are working to improve their real weaknesses than a BS artist."
- "Work–life balance is my weakness." Our response: "Great, so assuming you are working on overcoming your weaknesses means that you *used to* work long hours, but now that we are considering hiring you, you'll be leaving early every day to preserve your work–life balance. Thank you, but we'll keep looking!"

Insider story: What the other books tell you to say

After hearing the same answer to this question over and over from so many candidates, one day I (Barbara) decided to have some fun. I asked this question, and the guy said, "I give every project 110%, and I get really frustrated when other people don't work as hard as I do."

I then said, "Yeah, I've read those same books on interviewing that tell people to give that answer. Come on, give me your real answer!" He was taken aback and remained quiet as he tried to come up with something. He ended up saying he was a perfectionist, which, of course, I've heard about as many times as his first answer, but at that point I no longer had enough energy to call him on it, so I just said, "Thank you" and moved on to the next question, ending the interview shortly afterward. It's no surprise that he was not referred to the hiring manager.

Lucas is a customer service representative who was asked the combined version of this question.

Example: Lucas, customer service

The interviewer asks, "What are your strengths and weaknesses?"

Lucas's answer

I believe my calm and empathetic approach with the customers is a significant strength. I'm very good at paying attention and really listening to customer concerns and addressing them with patience and understanding. This helps me to build rapport and give great support even during difficult situations.

I really take pride in giving customers the best experience possible. I believe happy customers are the key to a company's success, and when they share their experiences with others, it helps our company.

I work very well in a team atmosphere and look for ways to support my teammates. On my current team, we're often asked to cover for each other, and I'm often the first person who's asked because they know that I try to be very flexible. I'm looking to join a great team, and I've heard that your company is known for that.

As for a weakness, I realize that my quiet nature can sometimes be seen as a weakness. While I'm great in one-on-one interactions, I'm working on improving my assertiveness in larger group settings.

To work on this, I've been looking for opportunities to speak up in team discussions. I have also taken classes on confident communication, and I'm considering joining Toastmasters. I believe this will help me continue to provide excellent customer service and enhance my group communication skills.

What Lucas did well

Lucas described several strengths, including his ability to be calm, empathetic, patient, and flexible; listen well; build rapport; be part of a team; and act on self-improvement. He also did a great job following our instructions to take what some might consider a strength (his quiet nature) and admitting that his style can sometimes be seen as a weakness. He went on to say what he's doing to improve. He also demonstrated his focus on the customer, which is of critical importance in this role.

What would make this even better

While Lucas does mention several strengths, his answer would have more impact if he gave an example of when these strengths resolved a problem with a customer, including what he said to demonstrate empathy, patience, and rapport-building. Then he should include results with metrics. If his strengths helped save a multimillion-dollar customer account, his answer would really be powerful! Lastly, he mentions that he is the first to be asked by his teammates for back-up because he *tries to* be flexible. "Tries" is a weakening word, so instead, he should just say that he *is* flexible.

On his weakness answer, he should use the negative sandwich approach by starting with his strength, then describing the negative, and ending with a positive. He could say something like

"As I mentioned, I have a calm and quiet nature, which can be really helpful when working through customer problems." (This would be the first slice of bread in the sandwich.)

He then should go into why this is sometimes a problem (and say why):

"However, sometimes this demeanor can be seen as a weakness, because I don't speak up much during team meetings." (This is the meat in the sandwich.)

The second slice of bread is ending on a positive, which Lucas does, but he could add even more impact by saying what he's actually doing rather than simply "looking for opportunities." Has he spoken up and taken a more active role as a result of the classes he's taken? What else has he learned and applied from those classes? He could also show that he's taken more action regarding Toastmasters, including finding a meeting that he will be attending on a specific date within the next week or two. It's very general to say that he's "considering joining," which many people might say, but how many actually did join?.

What did you enjoy most about your last job?

Interviewers ask what you enjoyed most about your last job to help them determine whether you'd enjoy this new job.

TRANSLATION

What work activities do you enjoy most, so that I can determine to what extent they will be a part of this job? (If they are only a minor part, then even if you qualify, you likely won't stay long.)

HOW TO ANSWER

After going through the job posting or job description with a fine-toothed comb, identify the major parts of the job that you've been both successful at and enjoy doing. Then describe these same things as the activities and responsibilities that you have enjoyed the most and have been extremely successful at. Remember, you're selling this intersection of both strengths and passions.

What did you not like about your last job?

Interviewers ask what you didn't like about your last job so they can ascertain whether you would not enjoy this new job

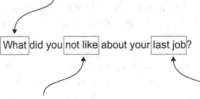

"What" refers to work activities such as completing paperwork, analyzing numbers, compiling spreadsheets, writing documents, interacting with customers, and collaborating with colleagues.

"Not like" doesn't necessarily mean that you hated it; it could just mean that this part of the job wasn't your favorite aspect of the work.

"Last job" refers to any of the jobs you held in the present or recent past and may include something about your manager, colleagues, or the company in general.

TRANSLATION

What are the work activities that you do not enjoy, so that I can determine to what extent those things will be a part of this job? (If you will have to do those things here, then even if you qualify, you likely won't last long.)

HOW TO ANSWER

After going through the job posting or job description in detail, identify a work activity that you would expect to either not be included in this job or be a very small part of it. Then say that there wasn't anything that you flat out didn't like about your last job, but there was one thing that you liked less than everything else, and go on to describe it briefly. Many jobs involve things like administrative work, reports, or other "paperwork," so those are examples of safe answers (as long as the job you're interviewing for isn't focused on those things!). State that you understand why this activity was needed in the job, so you gave 100% to that effort.

Why should we hire you?

Interviewers ask why they should hire you to get additional information to help them determine if you'd be a good fit for the job. This is your chance to sell yourself and your skills, knowledge, and experience.

TRANSLATION

Please summarize for me the top qualifications you have for this job and what makes you unique among all the other candidates I'm interviewing.

HOW TO ANSWER

Describe the top three to five areas of skills/knowledge/experience that make you an ideal fit. Then talk about the unique combination you bring. For example: "I not only have A and B but also C and D." By ending that way, you're implying that it would be difficult to find that unique combination in another candidate and in only one person.

Example: Clueless Clark, marketing

The interviewer asks, "Why should we hire you?"

Clueless Clark's answer

I think I'm going to be a great asset to the next company that I work for. I'm an awesome marketer—probably the best marketer you'll ever find. My previous boss loved how I promoted the company and pushed the boundaries.

Okay, my current boss, not as much, which is why I'm looking for the right company who will appreciate my skills.

It looks like your company would be great to work for. I'll be all in and will make sure that your marketing really reaches your customers.

And don't worry, I'm great at jumping right in and getting things done. I won't need a lot of ramp-up time. Just give me some basic info and I'll be off and running.

What Clueless Clark got wrong

Clueless Clark may think that he needs to appear very confident to get hired, but here he comes across as arrogant. He describes himself as "a great asset" and "the best marketer you'll ever find." He needs to show much more of a balance of being confident but with some humility to be likeable. People who aren't liked don't get hired. He can show humility by not using superlatives when describing himself and by offering more specifics when talking about the work he's completed both individually and as part of a team.

CHAPTER 2 Common questions and special situations

(continued)

Clark says that he promoted the company and pushed the boundaries but gives no specifics on what he did or the results he achieved. He also hints that his current boss doesn't appreciate his skills, and experienced interviewers will either probe that comment for more information or just assume there were personality issues there, which could be Clark's fault given the way he comes across.

What Clueless Clark should have done

In addition to showing less bravado, Clueless Clark should have provided specifics about his experience that qualifies him for this job, including quantified results, which are especially important in marketing roles. He also should say something about the unique combination of skills, knowledge, and abilities that he will bring to this position.

Clark could use some work on his communication skills. It would help if he could better understand how other people hear what he has to say. We recommend one of Laura's books on communication: *Why Can't You Communicate Like Me? How Smart Women Get Results at Work*. Even though the title mentions women, everyone can benefit from it. In this book, readers take an assessment, learn how they prefer to communicate, and discover what small changes they can make to communicate more effectively with others.

What questions do you have?

Interviewers want to know what questions you have so they can gauge your actual interest level based on what you ask. This is also your chance to impress them with the research you've done on their company. You should always be prepared to ask a few questions that show your interest.

TRANSLATION

What are you interested in learning more about? Do you care more about our benefits and time-off policy, or are you so interested in this job, our team, and our company that you have several questions about them?

HOW NOT TO ANSWER

The questions you ask your interviewers should not be any kind of "What's in it for me?" questions, like those about pay, hours, benefits, or paid time off. During the interview, your entire focus should be on what you offer to them and how you can help them accomplish their goals, not what they will offer you. It does not become about you until after you have the job offer, because that is when the power shifts, and you become the one with the power to decide whether to accept their offer.

Some interview guides say that job interviews are a two-way street; that is, you are interviewing them as much as they are interviewing you. We disagree, because the interviewer and interviewee are not equal during the selection process. Interviewers have the power in so many ways, including what questions they ask, how they interpret your answers, whether you qualify for the position, and whether you'd be a good fit for their organization.

What is important to realize is that if you come across as someone who is "shopping" them to decide if they match your needs, that alone might prevent you from getting the offer. They want to hire someone who is sure about their interest in both the job and company, not someone who is trying to decide whether they'd want to work there. (We realize this may not be the case if there is a scarcity of talent in your field or specialization, but for most of us, this applies.)

HOW TO ANSWER

Pretend it's your first day on the job and you're meeting with your boss. What are their top projects and priorities? What would they want you to get started on right away? What does success in this position look like?

You have an opportunity to impress the interviewer with the questions you ask and to demonstrate your research on the company and knowledge of your field. You also have an opportunity to demonstrate what it will be like to work with you by diving in immediately to address the interviewer's priorities. The following are some ideas of questions you may wish to ask, depending on their relevance to the position for which you're interviewing:

- What will be my top priorities in this position?
- What would you want me to get started on right away?
- What does success in this position look like?
- What is the most important area that you will view when judging my success?
- What are the major challenges the department or team is facing?
- Are there any immediate problems that need to be addressed?
- What are the successes that the team is proud of?
- What are the team's weaknesses?
- Tell me about the customers I'd be interacting with and what their expectations of me would be.
- Which other departments are the most important to collaborate with to be successful in this position?

If you're being interviewed by someone from human resources, talent acquisition, or recruiting, your questions should be more about the company, since they may lack knowledge of the specific daily activities of the position or department. Here are some questions to consider asking those interviewers:

- Can you tell me more about the team I would be working with?
- How would you describe the company culture?
- What are the common characteristics of people who are successful at this company?
- What do you enjoy most about working here?
- Would you tell me more about your career at this company?

Special situations

Now that you've seen some of the most common questions, let's consider some special situations to see whether you might need to be prepared to answer these questions.

Interviewers often focus on the length of time at previous companies. If a candidate has left their company after a short period of time, they want to know why. They are looking to determine whether that's a pattern and if you are likely to leave this job soon as well. On the other hand, if someone has stayed a long time at their most recent employer, they want to learn whether the person is so set in their ways that they will find it hard to adjust to a job at a new company.

Another specific situation that can be difficult to address is if the applicant is unemployed. Questions on that topic can be uncomfortable to deal with, so it's very important that applicants prepare their answers in advance and can confidently discuss their reasons for leaving.

Applying for a lower-level position can also be a difficult situation. Applicants need to be prepared to clearly explain why they are a good match for this job because interviewers want to be sure that they won't get bored and quickly leave.

When interviewers deal with these special situations, they need confirmation that these will not be problems for you and that you really are a good match for their open position.

What have you done since you left your last company?

If you're currently unemployed, you need to be prepared to talk about what you've been doing since you left your last job. Employers ask this question because they might be concerned that your skills have gotten stale during the time you were unemployed. They also may think that you're desperate and will take any job and then not perform well or last very long. They also may worry that you enjoyed not working so much that it will be difficult for you to become productive in this new job.

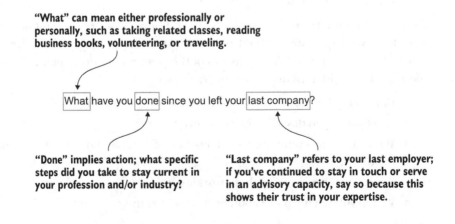

TRANSLATION

What can you say to convince me that your skills haven't gone stale and that you still have the energy to work hard from day 1 here?

HOW TO ANSWER

You can say that you've been doing volunteer work or consulting, but only if you have real projects to speak of (regardless of whether you were paid). Also, talk about what you've done to stay current in your field, including reading books, taking classes, watching webinars, and staying in touch with colleagues. The longer you've been unemployed, the more important it is to say what you've been doing to be productive, especially to keep your skills current.

If you needed to take a break for medical or personal reasons, it's okay to be honest; just say that you took a break to travel, take care of an ill or elderly family member, or spend time with friends/family. If you personally had a medical situation, decide whether you're okay with revealing that and, if so, mention it in a general way without going into details. Clearly state that those medical problems have now been addressed, and you are ready and excited to get back to work.

Why have you changed employers so frequently over the last several years?

If you were at your last job or company for less than two years, you'll need to show that you're not a job-hopper. If they hire candidates who leave after a short period of time, it will reflect badly on them as managers, so they need to believe that you won't do that.

TRANSLATION

What can you say to convince me that you're interested in committing to a company for the long term and succeeding in this job and that you won't leave in the next year or two, causing me to have to go through this whole hiring process again?

HOW TO ANSWER

Give a very brief overview of why you changed your last two to three jobs, especially if you were laid off or left due to no fault of your own (see how to answer the "exit" question earlier in this chapter). Then explain that you are looking for long-term employment, are excited about growing your career with their company, and why you're a great fit to enter their company in this particular position. Remember to state not only that you fit their qualifications but that you love doing the exact kind of activities included in this position. You're selling not only your experience and skills but also your passion for the work.

Because you were with your last employer for so long, do you think you may have a hard time adjusting to a new company's way of working?

If you've worked for the same job or company for a long time, you'll need to show that you'll be able to adapt to a new company quickly.

TRANSLATION

What can you say to convince me that you're flexible and adaptable enough to switch to our job and the company's environment, processes, and systems?

How to answer

Talk about how things were constantly evolving and changing at your last company and, if you changed jobs and departments at your last company, how each time you made a change you learned the ropes very quickly. Share some of the early successes you've had after starting in one of the new departments or positions. Show that you thrive on change, and it excites you!

What makes you think you know our industry and will be able to become productive right away?

If you're interviewing with a company in a different industry than the companies you've worked for previously, you'll need to show that you'll be able to get up to speed and be productive right away.

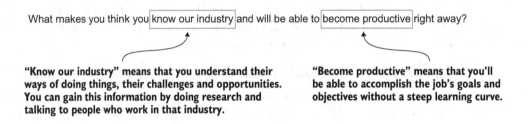

Translation

What can you say to convince me that you won't have a steep learning curve and that we won't have to wait for you to have an impact?

How to answer

Your answer should contain two parts:

- Show that you've done your homework, talked to people in their industry, and understand that there are similarities in the challenges faced by both industries.
- Give brief examples of how you've overcome similar challenges in your previous roles.

The end result is that you'll come across as someone who can "speak their language" and who knows much more about their industry than they initially thought. It's as if they only speak Portuguese, and they initially dismissed you as someone who only speaks Spanish. Your job is to show them how similar Spanish is to Portuguese and that you can understand them in conversation.

This job is a lower level than your current (or last) job; why would you be interested in taking a step down in your career?

If you're interviewing for a lower-level position, the employer will likely view you as overqualified and, therefore, not hire you unless you convince them otherwise.

TRANSLATION

What can you say to convince me that you won't be bored in this job and leave, causing me to have to go through this whole hiring process again?

HOW TO ANSWER

To avoid their thinking of you as a "flight risk" or someone who will continually be asking for higher-level work, you must sell not only the reason why you're looking for a lower-level position but also that you're excited about this role specifically. You're not just "willing" to do this job—it is a perfect fit for you at this point in your career. The best way to convey that is to identify the specific work activities in the position that you love to do and show that those very things get you up in the morning. Say that those work activities represent the intersection of what you've been extremely successful at and what you enjoy doing the most. Also, say that the things you had in your job which are not a part of this job are things you are specifically looking to no longer do, either because you didn't enjoy them or because they don't speak to your strengths.

Example: Lucas, customer service

Lucas is currently a customer service lead applying for a customer service representative position.

The interviewer asks Lucas, "I want to be clear that this is a customer service representative position. This is a lower level than your current job; why would you be interested in taking a step down in your career?"

Lucas's answer

I've been at the XYZ company for five years and have worked my way up from my first position in customer service to my current lead position. What I've found during that time is that my favorite parts of the job are when I can directly help the customers. While I enjoy being the team lead and supporting the other customer service representatives, that's not the part of the job I like the most.

I'm excited about this position because it would allow me to get back to what I'm passionate about—really helping customers. My understanding of the role is that I would be responsible for supporting customers on particular projects, and it would mean working with the same customers over time and helping them with their problems. That's what I really enjoy—working directly with customers and helping them to have the best experience possible.

I believe that I would bring the experience from my position as a lead that I can apply to this role. In addition, I'm always looking for new ways to build my communication and problem-solving skills, which this role would help me to do.

I'm looking for a long-term career at a growing company like yours. I believe that starting in this position will give me a solid foundation working on something I enjoy, in a company that has values I believe in, so I can make a difference for people every day.

(continued)

What Lucas did well

One of the things that Lucas did well is that he didn't give the answer most people give when in this situation, which is that they're willing to do this job and that they're fine with the title and pay. But interviewers don't want to hire those who are willing; they want to hire people who are excited to do the job.

Lucas did a beautiful job explaining the work activity that he loved the most, which is the main part of this job. He conveyed excitement and passion for this role specifically and did not frame it as just a stepping stone to further advancement. He also said that he's looking for a long-term career at a company just like this one.

What would make this even better

Lucas's answer would have more impact if he added in a specific example or two of his successes in customer service, with quantified results. Also, he mentions that he would bring the experience from his position as a lead that he can apply to this role, but he doesn't describe how that experience as lead will make him a better rep. For example, he could talk about understanding the call escalation process, how he successfully handled those, and how that experience will make him better at resolving customer issues without having to escalate them to his supervisor.

Think about

Applicants need to be prepared to answer all common questions since these are used by many interviewers. The following are some things to think about before moving to the next chapter:

- How would you answer the question "Tell me about yourself?"
- How would you describe the reason you exited (or are looking to exit) your last (or current) job?
- What three things would you list as your weaknesses, and how would you use the negative sandwich to describe each of them?
- How would you answer the "Why should we hire you?" question?
- If any of the special situations apply to you, such as being unemployed, having multiple short-term jobs, being with one employer for a long time, or wanting to change industries, how would you address them?

What other similar interview questions on these topics might you be asked? For additional examples, see appendix A.

Key takeaways

- To get to know applicants, most interviewers ask some common questions. They include questions like "Tell me about yourself."; "Why are you in the job market?", and "Why are you interested in this job?"

- The goal of the interviewers is to get to know you and see whether you meet their basic qualifications so they can decide whether to move you to the next round of interviews. They are also listening for any potential red flags that may come up.

- It's important for you to be prepared to answer these common questions. For each question, we provide a translation of the meaning behind the question as well as suggestions for what to include and not to include in your answers.

- One of the most difficult common questions is about your strengths and weaknesses. This is an area where a lot of people make a mistake by trying to disguise a strength as a weakness. For example, someone may say that they are a perfectionist. The problem is that interviewers have heard this answer plenty of times before and see it as BS. Instead, they want an honest answer.

- Your answers should address what the interviewers are really asking while also being true for you. They do not want to hear typical BS answers and will view them negatively.

- Interviewers are looking for confirmation that you are a good fit for the job and are likely to stay for a while. They don't want to have to fill the position again in a few months.

- Some typical situations that interviewers watch for include applicants who have changed jobs frequently, stayed a long time at one job or company, worked in a different industry, are unemployed, or have applied for an obviously lower-level position. If any of the special situations apply to you, it's important for you to understand the interviewer's concerns and clearly address them. If not, it may be difficult to advance to the next round of interviews.

Interpersonal skills questions

Interviewers want to know if you will be a good fit for the company as well as for the job. They may ask questions to determine how you connect with other people and whether you're seen as approachable and easy to work with. While they won't directly ask if you are difficult to work with, they may ask questions about your ability to manage conflict.

They may also ask about how you build credibility and trust with different individuals and groups. This is especially important for jobs where success involves interactions with people at different levels and in different areas. Many roles require some sort of influence. Candidates will want to show they will be able to convince people to listen to new ideas or make important changes.

Another topic that is important to some companies is diversity, equity, and inclusion. Candidates should be prepared to address their experiences and views.

Approachability, credibility, and humility

Interviewers want to know if candidates have a good balance of confidence and humility, will be approachable by people at all levels inside the company, and will display the authority needed to be viewed as credible by others.

Give an example of an initiative you led that required you to interact with various levels within the company

Interviewers want an example of how you build credibility with people at different levels of the organization, including senior leaders. They also want to know whether you would be approachable by people at lower levels and how you avoid being intimidating because of your position. Questions like this are frequently asked in a more complex way, such as "Give an example of an initiative you led that required you to interact with various levels within the company. How did you build credibility with those at the top and avoid being intimidating to people at lower levels?" If you're asked this longer question, be sure to cover all components (how you dealt with whom you interacted, how you built credibility, and how you avoided being intimidating) in your answer.

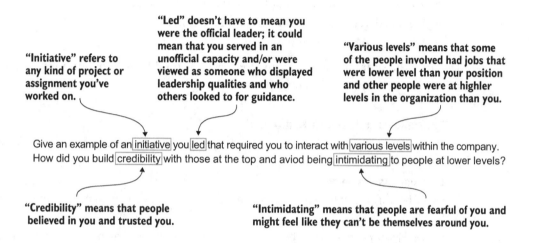

Translation

We need someone who can quickly establish themselves as credible with senior management and who will also be approachable and respected by the entry-level staff. Give an example of a time when you demonstrated that ability.

How to answer

Start with an example that shows how you established new relationships and built trust, specifically with senior management. What did you do to build trust? Describe what you said, how you interacted with the executives, and how you overcame any doubts that others may have had about you.

Then describe what you did with and said to lower-level staff to build trust, show respect, encourage interaction, and welcome your involvement in their project or tasks.

Tell me about a time when humility played a role in your being successful

Interviewers want an example of a time you showed humility at work because they want employees who have emotional intelligence, particularly for roles that are customer facing or require working with a variety of personality types. Perhaps previous people in the role had large egos and were unsuccessful.

CHAPTER 3 *Interpersonal skills questions*

TRANSLATION

We need someone in this role who is confident but also humble and who can play well with others. Convince me that you are that kind of person.

HOW TO ANSWER

Give an example of when you displayed confidence and humility, which could require you to admit things like

- Someone else had a better idea than you.
- You were wrong about something.
- You were new at a particular task and had a learning curve.
- You needed to ask for help, direction, or guidance.
- You know that you're not perfect.

Describe the situation, who was involved, what you said and did, and provide an end result that demonstrates a successful outcome.

Example: Clueless Clark, marketing

The interviewer asks, "Tell me about a time when humility played a role in your being successful."

Clueless Clark's answer

I can be very humble. As a matter of fact, people have complimented me on my humility.

I normally let people know about my great ideas, but there are times I choose not to. For example, when other people take the lead on projects, even if I think I have better ways to do it, I let them run it. Sure, I'll offer a suggestion or two, because I really know my stuff, but I don't make a big deal out of it. I'm humble enough to let the other person do what they think needs to be done.

Of course, I let my boss know about my ideas so he knows that I have the capacity to do these things, and even though he agrees with me, he says it's a learning experience for the other person, so it's important to let them try things out.

So yes, I can be humble and let other people learn.

What Clueless Clark got wrong

Clueless Clark made a very common mistake: instead of providing a specific example that demonstrates his humility, he only spoke in generalities by saying what he normally does. Also, he shows a lack of humility by talking about how he has been complimented on his humility, referring to his great ideas, and saying he really knows his stuff. He also risks giving the impression that he is prone to tooting his own horn by making sure his boss knows about his ideas. (That may not be the case, but in job interviews, we must recognize that it's the interviewer's perception that matters.)

Clueless Clark should have provided a specific example, such as a time when he had a good idea but recognized that it was important for someone else to take the lead on a project so they could learn and grow professionally. He could talk about what obstacles they faced, the coaching he provided to this person, what he said to the project leader to encourage and be helpful to them, what questions he asked to prompt them to realize something without directly telling them, how the project progressed, and what the overall results were.

Describe a situation where you had to build credibility

This is an opportunity to show how you built credibility.

TRANSLATION

In this role, you'll need to establish yourself as someone who is credible, trustworthy, and knows their stuff—perhaps with someone who doubts your qualifications. Give an example of a time when you had to do this in a short period of time.

HOW TO ANSWER

Describe a situation where you were new and still establishing your relationships with the team, customer, colleague, or department. What did you do to build trust? Describe what you said, how you interacted, and how you overcame any initial hesitation that others had about you. Then give the overall result of what you or the team accomplished because of your positive relationships.

Example: Davina, manager

The interviewer asks, "Tell me about a time when you had to build credibility."

Davina's answer

I remember a time about seven years ago at my previous company when I was brought in to take over a group that had experienced a lot of problems and turnover. Since I was new to the company, I had to build relationships with the team as well as with the other departments that we supported.

First, with my team, I scheduled one-on-one meetings with each person to understand what their concerns were. One of the themes that came out was that people said priorities changed weekly and sometimes daily. I committed to putting together a two-week schedule for the team with clear priorities so everyone knew what to work on.

To do this, I had to build credibility with three other departments that gave us work to do. I met with their leaders and helped them to see that the current system of just sending over lots of emails with problems was not working, and it would be better for them to change to a daily summary. The department heads sent them directly to me so I could review them and determine how to get it all done.

In addition, I believe it's important to lead by example, so I took on one of the most difficult team tasks so my employees would know I was in the trenches with them.

What Davina did well

Davina chose a highly relevant example because she will be in a similar situation when and if she gets hired at this company. She shows an understanding of the

(continued)

importance of building relationships with both her team members and the leaders of other departments, and she does that by having initial one-on-one meetings. She demonstrated her ability to draw out people's main concern and then acted on it. She provided a good amount of information about her style and showed not just her credibility but also her humility in personally taking on one of the most difficult tasks.

What would make this even better

While this example is relevant, it's from seven years ago, so a more recent example would be better. Her answer would also have more impact if she included what questions she asked when meeting with her team members, including more specifics on what she said to help them feel comfortable opening up to her and sharing their concerns.

The same is true for her meetings with the other department leaders. What did she say to get them to understand that the current system wasn't working without alienating them or putting them on the defensive? How did she present her idea of moving to a daily summary so the new system would be accepted as a benefit rather than a burden?

Lastly, her example did not include any results. What happened after she implemented the two-week schedule for her team and the daily summary of problems with the other departments? She missed an opportunity to show the improvements that came as a result of her implementation of new ideas.

Influencing and gaining support

Interviewers want to know candidates have the communication skills necessary to clearly explain benefits to others and get them to support goals and initiatives.

Give me an example of a time when you convinced leadership in your organization to make a significant change

For jobs that require you to implement change to improve the organization or customer experience, you need to be prepared to influence management, gain their buy-in, and, in some cases, gain their approval.

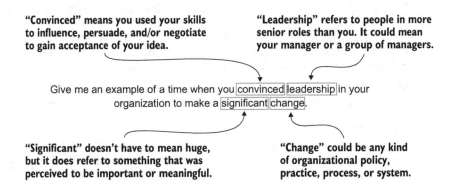

TRANSLATION

We're looking to hire a change agent, but our leadership team sometimes is resistant to change. Show me you'll be able to convince them of needed changes.

HOW TO ANSWER

Describe a situation when you had an idea that you knew would result in a major improvement to the team, department, organization, or customer. Explain what the objections were and who had them, and then describe what you did or said to overcome them. Usually this involves knowing your audience (company leadership), what their priorities are, their decision-making style, what the benefit of the change will be, and what kind of data you can show as evidence of this benefit. Then describe your involvement in the implementation of the idea and the results.

Describe a situation where you had to delicately let a key stakeholder know that their expectations were unrealistic

The question is about your ability to handle difficult situations with stakeholders, which could be people either inside or outside the company. This skill is important because it's usually inappropriate to just tell the stakeholders directly that they have unrealistic expectations. Instead, they need to be educated on why their request may not be feasible given the company's time, budget, system, or staff limitations and offered options that would be doable given those limitations.

TRANSLATION

Our internal and external stakeholders often have unrealistic expectations of how long things will take or how much money or other resources projects will require, but we can never simply say, "That's not possible" or "That won't work." Convince me that you'll be able to convey to them that their expectations are unrealistic in a way they will understand and accept.

HOW TO ANSWER

Give an example where your internal or external customer, someone in management, or an investor wanted you or your team to get something done in a manner, cost, or time frame that wasn't feasible. Give specifics of what you said, including factual evidence rather than subjective opinions, and how you explained this to them. Then state what you offered as alternatives or compromises and how you worked through this to ultimately deliver what they wanted.

> #### Example: Lucas, customer service
>
> The interviewer asks, "Describe for me a situation where you had to delicately let a key stakeholder know that their expectations were unrealistic."
>
> #### Lucas's answer
>
> At my previous company, we had a situation where one of our big customers requested a highly customized product with a short time frame. In addition, the customer

(continued)

bypassed our sales team and just tried to order it through customer service, which was not the approved process for a product like that. We were able to accept basic reorders but not a new order for something customized.

I started by thanking the customer for the order and went on to explain that due to the nature of the order, he would need to talk with the sales department. The customer then got annoyed because I was working a Saturday shift and he didn't want to wait until Monday to discuss it with someone in sales. He pushed me to just take the order.

I listened to his concerns and respectfully replied that our main goal was to make sure the final product met expectations and to do that it was important that he works with the sales team. I offered to contact sales and ask them to call him back on Monday.

The customer pushed and asked if I could call the sales manager at home so we could start working on it right away. I was not going to do that, so I assured the customer the best answer was to talk to sales on Monday, and I assured him I would get it to the sales manager as soon as possible and ask him to give it high priority.

When I followed up with the sales manager on Monday afternoon, he let me know he appreciated how I handled it.

What Lucas did well

Lucas did a good job of talking through how he handled this delicate situation with the customer, including first thanking him for the order, listening, and then explaining why this situation required a different process. He did what he could to be respectful and also follow his company's proper procedure. Offering to contact sales himself rather than make the customer do that was a nice gesture. His answer also demonstrated his willingness to work on a Saturday.

What would make this even better

This answer would have more impact if Lucas provided the context for this customer's request, including how long customized products typically take (if he knew this) and the short time frame the customer requested. He could also include how unusual this kind of situation might have been for his company, whether that kind of customization had been done before for other customers, or if the requested customized features were things his company had ever done before.

The results Lucas included in his answer were solely about the sales manager appreciating how he had handled the situation with that customer, but he did not say anything about what happened. Did the customer ultimately get his customized product, and how long did it take? What kind of revenue did that purchase bring to the company? Did the company retain this customer as a result, and what kind of annual revenue did that customer represent? Did the customer end up referring any other business to the company after being pleased with these interactions?

The point of this question is to see how a candidate influences and educates stakeholders who may not realize their expectations are unrealistic. While this story shows Lucas's communication skills with a demanding customer (a core competency needed in this job), it would have been better to use an example where he was ultimately able to gain buy-in and understanding from the customer as a result of his explanation and one where he could include more definitive results.

Diversity, equity, and inclusion 55

Tell me about a situation in which you built needed support for a goal or project from people who didn't report to you and over whom you had no direct authority

Interviewers want to know how you successfully gain support from people who don't report to you. This is important for anyone who interacts with other departments, either as an individual contributor or a manager.

TRANSLATION

To accomplish the goals in this position, you'll have to gain buy-in from people in other departments or at higher levels; we need someone who can influence those folks so they'll support our projects.

HOW TO ANSWER

Give an example where you served in a leadership role, even if unofficially, and interacted with stakeholders in other departments or at higher levels. State what their priorities and agendas were and what you did or said to find out their top priorities. Then explain how you described the benefits they would receive because of your project. Perhaps the result was that ultimately they supported you and your team, and were big fans of your work because it made their jobs easier.

Diversity, equity, and inclusion

You may wonder: do I really need to be prepared for questions about diversity, equity, and inclusion (DEI) if I'm not in human resources? Even though not all companies focus on these areas, it's still important to be prepared. (Of course, if you are applying for a role in human resources, you already know you should be ready for questions on this topic.) For many companies, DEI is an important value. Other related terms include equality, belonging, and access.

There are many ways to define DEI, but for the purpose of this book, we define it generally as follows:

- Diversity refers to the range of human differences including race, gender identity, age, religion, sexual orientation, and physical abilities. It can also refer to personality, communication, and social differences.
- Equity means having fair practices that ensure access, resources, and opportunities are provided for everyone.
- Inclusion means involvement and empowerment whereby people feel valued, respected, and supported.

Overall, these terms refer to a workplace that seeks to promote fair treatment and full participation of all people, particularly groups who have historically been underrepresented or subject to discrimination.

Interviewers want to ensure employees support these values and practices. You can learn more about the importance of DEI to a company by looking for information on the company's mission, values, or goals, which are typically listed on its website.

Companies that ask this question want to make sure you will fit into their culture of appreciating people's differences. Interviewers want to know whether you value people for who they are, even if they are different from you, and that you will support other employees.

Interviewers will want to hear about your experience in these areas and how you display actions that align with the company's views and practices. If the role is directly related to DEI areas (for example, a role in human resources), applicants will be expected to give clear examples of how they've supported DEI in the past.

For any role, it's important to acknowledge and support differences. Candidates can clearly state how they have worked with people who have different backgrounds and experiences. This can be a tricky area, because interviewers may ask you to share your personal views so they can understand how you would fit into the team and company culture.

When you are asked about DEI, do not say what many people say in interviews: that you don't see race or gender and you see everyone as the same. Most interviewers will want to roll their eyes at that point. The fact is we do all see that people are different from us; it's what we do with that knowledge that is important. Instead, say you recognize people are different and you make it a point to get to know people as individuals. You want to show that you believe, when different people work together, it can lead to much better outcomes and success.

This topic has become controversial for some companies and industries, so make sure you clearly understand what the company says on its website and in any current messages on media so you will be able to match its messaging.

How has your background and experience prepared you to be effective in an environment that values diversity and is committed to inclusion?

Interviewers who ask this question are emphasizing that diversity, equity, and inclusion are important values for the company. They want to know that you have experience supporting people who are different from you and that you can give examples of how you have shown that commitment.

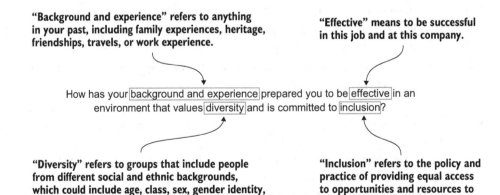

Diversity, equity, and inclusion 57

TRANSLATION

Convince me you value diversity and will be inclusive in performing and succeeding at our company.

HOW TO ANSWER

Share something from your personal or professional life that shows your passion for diversity and inclusion. Then provide an example from your professional experience that shows either how you played a key role in improving diversity at your previous organization or team or how you were inclusive while collaborating with others. Describe the context, the challenge, what specifically you did or said, and the result that benefited the organization.

Example: Davina, manager

The interviewer asks, "How has your background and experience prepared you to be effective in an environment that values diversity and is committed to inclusion?"

Davina's answer

My company does value diversity, and I really appreciate our emphasis on being inclusive.

I think my experience has really helped me in this area. Throughout my career, I've had the privilege of working in diverse teams and groups, and that has given me a deep appreciation for the benefits of diversity. For example, early in my career, I worked for a great boss, Marco, and he was known for bringing in diverse talent even though the rest of the company was not known for that.

He taught me the importance of bringing in people with different backgrounds and from different groups. He told me that the key to his team's success was that we all had different ideas and were willing to listen to each other. It's true: his team meetings were very different from any other meeting I had ever been to at that point. In other teams, when someone came up with an idea, the rest of the team often went along with it because they came from the same backgrounds or thought the same way. In this team, people listened to the ideas and then questioned them in a respectful way and added to them. The ideas were much better because of all the different ways of looking at it.

That experience taught me the importance of working with people who are different and the importance of appreciating their differences. So I make it a practice to look for people who have diverse backgrounds, experience, or ideas.

Mentoring is something that is important to me because I feel we need to give back and build tomorrow's leaders. I make it a practice to mentor people from various backgrounds.

You had asked me earlier about hiring. It's also very important to me to look for diverse candidates. At my current company, my recruiting team is great at that and has built connections with many different groups so it can attract different candidates.

(continued)

That was not always true at previous companies. I remember one time when I was hiring for a position and all the candidates looked and sounded the same. I had to push back on the recruiters, and we were able to bring in more diverse candidates. I was really proud that we were able to do that and not just go for the usual candidates. I did end up hiring a diverse candidate, and he was very successful in the position.

What Davina did well

Starting her answer with a brief general statement and then immediately providing an example that demonstrates how and why she values diversity and her commitment to inclusion was effective. Many candidates state a lot of generalities, philosophies, and beliefs when answering this question, but Davina gave an example of a manager she admired and whose practices she adopted, including the things he did and how those actions benefited the team and company. This real-world example that includes specifics is very impactful.

What would make this even better

Davina included some results at the end of her Marco story, but they were general in nature: "The ideas were much better because of all the different ways of looking at it." She could have given examples of improved business results that came from some of those ideas.

Davina then goes on to talk about mentoring but adds nothing of substance about what she has done or why it mattered. She also discusses hiring and gives all credit to her recruiting team (and it's not clear what her involvement was with that team). The brief example she shares of pushing the recruiters at one of her previous companies to improve the diversity of candidates and ultimately hiring one lacks impactful results, because "he was very successful in the position" is far too general to have any meaning.

In what ways do you think diversity is important to someone in this role?

Interviewers want to know that your values match what is important to the company and that you will fit in with their company culture.

TRANSLATION

Convince me you value diversity and will be inclusive in performing this job.

HOW TO ANSWER

Give a specific example of a time when you worked with someone who was different from you and what you did to learn more about them so you and others could understand them better. Your answer should show that you are open to learning from people who are different from you and that you value people for the individual strengths they bring. The overall message you want to convey is that you have successfully worked with diverse groups in the past and you are committed to supporting individuals who are different from you.

Diversity, equity, and inclusion

What kinds of experiences have you had with people whose backgrounds are different from your own?

Interviewers are looking for specific examples of how you have exhibited actions which show that you work well with people who are different from you.

TRANSLATION

Convince me you value diversity and have learned the importance of working with a variety of different people and backgrounds, and describe how being inclusive will bring value to our company, customers, department, and team.

HOW TO ANSWER

Share examples of when you worked with people who were different from you and you learned something useful from their differences. Or give examples of when you helped other people see the value of someone else's differences and their contributions.

When you think about people with different backgrounds, it can be helpful to go beyond the typical examples of gender or race. Think about examples when you worked with someone who was from a different generation, a different part of the world, or had different physical abilities. Let the interviewer know that you appreciate many types of differences. Show that you were curious, didn't make assumptions, and instead listened respectfully to that person's experiences and tried to understand even though the experiences were very different from yours.

Reinforce that you want to make sure everyone feels they belong. You also want to show you believe everyone is a unique individual and should be appreciated for their uniqueness and the special things they bring to the job and company.

What programs or initiatives have you been part of that focused on working with diverse populations, and what was your role in those efforts?

Interviewers want to hear about other ways you have supported diversity, including training programs and special projects.

TRANSLATION

Convince me you value diversity and inclusion by providing examples of when you played a significant role in programs that involved diverse populations.

HOW TO ANSWER

If you're applying for a human resources job, be ready to share initiatives or training programs that you started or were an important part of. Be specific about how the programs began and the results that were achieved.

For roles outside of human resources, describe any training or other programs you were involved in and clearly explain your role. If there were small-group meetings, did you help facilitate the discussions or make sure that someone who was not speaking up was heard?

If your company did not have any DEI initiatives, you can talk about what you've read about the subject and how important it is to you that everyone feels included, valued, and appreciated.

Conflict management

Candidates must convince interviewers that they will be able to deal positively with conflicts as they arise and preserve relationships following a conflict. This is especially true in high-pressure jobs and those that require working with external groups such as vendors and customers.

Describe a time when you successfully defused a conflict

Interviewers want to know that you can defuse conflict.

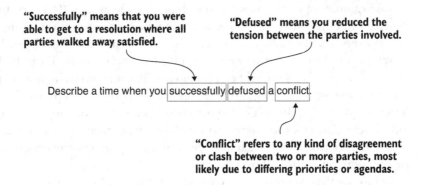

TRANSLATION

Conflicts may arise from time to time, so we need someone who can defuse them rather than escalate them. Give an example of when you did just that. (See the next section for how to answer this question.)

Give me an example of a time when you found yourself in the middle of conflict; what did you do or say to get to a resolution?

Interviewers want a specific example of what you said and did to resolve a conflict so they can better understand how you communicate during difficult situations.

TRANSLATION

There may be conflicts that arise from time to time, so we need someone who can resolve them rather than exacerbate them. Give an example of when you did just that.

HOW TO ANSWER BOTH

Describe a time, preferably from your professional life (but it can be from your personal life), that required you to mediate or collaborate with two people or groups that were having a conflict. This could be about any kind of disagreement between two where you took the lead on resolving the problem. Your answer should show how you used your ability to ask questions to get at the root of the conflict, your listening skills, and your ability to influence others to reach a compromise. Avoid talking about any

Conflict management   **61**

personality differences and instead focus on the differing priorities of the two people or groups.

Provide the context, what made it challenging, what questions you asked, what the responses were, and what you said to defuse the emotions involved and reach a resolution where both parties felt heard and satisfied with the outcome, even if they both had to make compromises.

Example: Jen, sales

The interviewer asks, "Give me an example of a time when you found yourself in the middle of a conflict; what did you do or say to get to a resolution?"

Jen's answer

We don't have many conflicts at work because we work really well together as a team; however, I do remember a time when two of my colleagues had a problem and I was able to help out with it.

There was a problem with a new territory with two other sales reps. There were some overlapping areas that they both felt they should be responsible for.

I'm not going to get into the details, but both of them, Jack and Liz, had some good points. Unfortunately, things got a little nasty because of an email one of them sent. The message probably could have been worded in a better way.

I was concerned because their focus on this was affecting how we worked with some of the other departments, and things were taking longer to get done.

I decided to meet with them individually to find out what was really bothering them. I focused on really listening to them, so they felt heard. I made sure in the meetings not to take sides. Instead, I helped them to see some facts and offered some different perspectives.

After the meetings, I suggested that we all go out to lunch and chat about it. I feel like having some good food can help make things easier. And in this case, it did. By the time the coffee came, we had developed two options to consider. We brought it to our manager, Ruth, and she discussed it further. She implemented one of the proposals.

That meant that Jack and Liz could get back to doing their jobs, it made things easier for the other departments that we work with, and we could all continue to focus on hitting our numbers for the quarter. And I not only hit my numbers; I beat them by over 25% that quarter.

What Jen did well

Jen gave a good description of the situation without providing too many details on what led to the conflict. She also clearly explained how and why she got involved. Her answer included great results—not only resolving the conflict but also improving the collaboration between departments. It's especially good that she found a way to include her own sales achievement.

> **(continued)**
>
> **What would make this even better**
>
> While Jen provided some good contextual information to set up her story, she left out some key details on what she specifically said to the two people involved (she didn't need to include their names).
>
> She says she focused on listening but doesn't say what questions she asked them to get to what was really bothering them. She also said she made sure not to take sides, but what specifically did she say to sound neutral? What facts did she point out, and what did she say to show a different perspective?
>
> Leaving out these key details makes it sound too simple, which then undersells her ability to work with people to resolve differences.

Think about

The following are some things to think about before moving to the next chapter:

- Which scenario would you select to describe when humility contributed to your success? In what way was it important to be humble in that situation?
- When you had to build credibility, what kinds of things did you do or say that allowed others to have confidence in your abilities?
- Which project would you describe if asked about interacting with different levels of staff within your organization?
- Which projects or ideas required you to gain higher-level approval? What did you say or do to get that approval?
- Have you ever had to tell someone that their expectations of you or your team were unrealistic? If so, what did you say to help them understand?
- Which example would you select to describe a situation where you had to gain support from people who didn't report to you? What did you do or say to gain their support?
- What are your personal beliefs on diversity, and why do you think this topic is widely discussed these days? How do you think this topic relates to the kind of role you are targeting?
- Which of your experiences interacting and collaborating with people whose backgrounds differ from yours would you talk about in interviews if asked?
- How comfortable are you in sharing aspects of your personal background that may have shaped your views on diversity?
- Which example would you select to describe a conflict in which you played a key part in its resolution? What did you do or say to reduce the tension between the parties?
- There is a difference between being a mediator between people who have a conflict and being in the middle yourself as someone who has a conflict with another

person. Which examples do you have of having a conflict with others on a project, deadline, or priority?

- What kinds of tools or methods do you typically use to calm people down during heated discussions?
- What other similar interview questions on these topics might you be asked? For additional examples, see appendix A.

Key takeaways

- Interviewers need to know that candidates will be able to get along with others and fit into the company culture. They want people who can build credibility and trust at different levels of the organization. They will ask questions to determine whether applicants are seen as approachable and willing to admit they're not perfect.
- Candidates should be prepared to give examples of situations when they used their influencing skills to get buy-in from others and gain support for changes.
- DEI is an important area for many companies. Interviewers want to learn about an applicant's beliefs and experiences. This information will help them determine whether someone will be a good fit for the team and company.
- Applicants should research the company's values and mission statement to learn more about their approach to DEI. This can be a tricky question, so it's important to be prepared with an answer that aligns with those values.
- Effectively dealing with conflict is an important skill needed in many jobs. Interviewers want to know that applicants will be able to handle potential problems and manage them positively.

Perseverance skills, failures, and negative situations questions

Most jobs include dealing with problems and difficult situations occasionally. Interviewers want to know how applicants overcome obstacles and whether they will be able to deal positively with setbacks. Most people will say they can do this, but interviewers want specific examples of how applicants showed drive and perseverance, especially when facing potentially difficult situations.

Talking about failures can be uncomfortable since people typically don't want to dwell on their mistakes. The fact is, we all fail at some point, and interviewers want to know if applicants have enough self-awareness to admit that. They also want to know what the applicant learned and what changes were made based on that experience.

Choosing a good example is very important here. Even though interviewers may use the word "failure," it doesn't mean applicants are expected to share the most awful and humiliating thing that's ever happened to them. Instead, they are looking for something that had some importance and could have been handled another way.

Interviewers also don't want to hear examples that are too simple or aren't really failures or challenges. They don't want to hear someone forgot to send an email until the next day or ordered the wrong sandwich at lunch.

Failures and negative situations

Interviewers want to know how candidates handled real problems and uncomfortable situations in the past, and gain a sense of how they would deal with those kinds of issues in this job.

Failures and negative situations

Tell me about one of your failures

This question is about more than explaining a failure. As we said earlier, this is an opportunity for you to build likeability and rapport by being transparent about something that didn't work out as well as you had hoped.

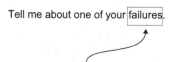

A "failure" doesn't have to be major (and doesn't have to be an actual failure). It can simply be something that didn't work out as well as you had hoped.

Remember to use the "negative sandwich" model by starting with something positive; then briefly describe the negative, and end on a positive.

TRANSLATION

Are you someone who has both the confidence and the humility to admit that not everything in your professional life has worked out perfectly? Are you the kind of person who learns from failures? In what ways are you a better candidate now that you've learned some important lessons?

HOW TO ANSWER

Describe a project from a past job that didn't work out as well as you had hoped. This could be from any time in your career. Give the context for the project, what you did, what the result was, and why that result wasn't as stellar as you thought it would be. Then state what you learned from this and, most importantly, what you do differently now. Remember, you are selling yourself as someone who learns from their mistakes or from difficult circumstances; demonstrate how you have shown resilience and how you will be a tremendous asset now that you've gone through this experience.

> ### Example: Jen, sales
> The interviewer asks, "Tell me about one of your failures."
>
> ### Jen's answer
> Early in my career at the XYZ company, I was asked to work on designing some new sales materials for customers by my boss. I was happy to take it on because I want to do whatever I can to support our customers. The problem was that I'd never worked on anything like that before. I really should have spoken up and let my boss know that.

(continued)

I threw myself into it and did the best I could, but I had trouble getting into our system since I was new. I asked for some help, but when my access was delayed, I didn't push. And I didn't let them know the deadline.

In addition, the person who was supposed to partner with me went on vacation without giving me instructions. Instead of letting my boss know, I waited, hoping that it would turn out okay in the end.

All of this together meant that when my boss asked for the materials, I had to let him know that they weren't finished yet and that actually, I had just started on the project.

He reassigned the project to someone else who had more experience designing these kinds of materials, and they finished a week later.

One thing I learned was that it's important to ask questions and let people know what you don't know. I also learned the importance of keeping my boss and other stakeholders up to date, especially when something might not meet a deadline.

I used the information I learned during that time to make sure I never missed another deadline. Now when I work on projects, I make sure other people know the milestones and deadlines. And I keep people apprised of the progress to ensure no one is surprised.

What Jen did well

It's clear that Jen is giving a real example and is displaying candor, honesty, and humility in admitting that she's not perfect. This story demonstrates some of Jen's many good qualities, such as her willingness to take on new things even when new, her positive attitude, and her desire to help her boss and her customers.

She clearly described the situation, provided enough but not too much detail, and gave the actual result: that she didn't have it ready for her boss when he asked, and he then assigned it to someone else who was able to get it done.

Jen also articulated what she learned from this situation, including the importance of being honest with others when she doesn't know something or lacks experience and keeping her boss and stakeholders informed on project progress (or the lack thereof).

What would make this even better

Jen's answer would have more impact if, rather than talking in general about what she does differently now, she gave a specific example of a project that she handled next, including the tools she used to track milestones and timelines and the communication methods she used to keep stakeholders informed of any setbacks. Because this would be an example rather than a generality, she could then talk about the positive result of achieving the project deadline.

What was the most useful criticism you ever received?

Interviewers want to learn about feedback you've received in the past and how you used it to improve. The criticism you describe here is less important than how you applied that feedback going forward.

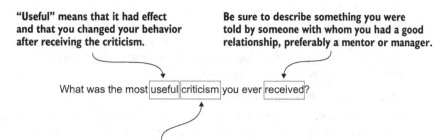

Translation

Are you someone who can take criticism, learn from it, and change your behavior?

How to answer

Choose something that you were given feedback on from a prior boss, mentor, or colleague and describe it in a neutral way (without emotion). Talk specifically about what you were told and how you reacted (without getting defensive). Then describe how you took that criticism to heart and worked on it until you improved. Share what you do differently now as a result of getting this feedback.

It's important to show you did not get defensive when receiving this feedback. In our experience, the more open someone is to feedback, the better they become as professionals; people who aren't open to feedback never improve. Interview candidates who get defensive display a trait that could make them difficult to work with, which will likely be a red flag.

> ### Example: Clueless Clark, marketing
> The interviewer asks, "What was the most useful criticism you ever received?"
>
> **Clueless Clark's answer**
> Let me start off by saying that I don't get a lot of criticism. I do the best job possible, and I always go above and beyond on my projects.
>
> But if I were to pick one time when I got some criticism, I would say it was when a previous boss said I was too much of a perfectionist. I was working with a team, and I wanted to make sure that my high standards were their high standards, as otherwise it would reflect badly on the team and company.
>
> I explained that to my boss, and he agreed that we needed to keep high standards.
>
> What I learned from that is that perfectionism is not always understood, but it's important to talk to people so they realize how important it is.
>
> **What Clueless Clark got wrong**
> Clueless Clark is using the classic example of a weakness answer that isn't really a weakness (see our description of what not to say when asked for a weakness in

68 CHAPTER 4 *Perseverance skills, failures, and negative situations questions*

(continued)

chapter 2). Most interviewers will be able to see through this answer and will conclude that Clark is not only being disingenuous but is also pretending that he's perfect when we know that's not the case.

What Clueless Clark should have done

If Clueless Clark wanted to use this perfectionist answer and come across as honest, candid, and humble, then he'd provide more information on the situation that prompted his boss to give that criticism, what specifically was said, how Clark responded, and what he has done since then to improve.

He should not have described something so commonly used as perfectionism but rather something specific that he was criticized for—for example, a project that he spent either too much or not enough time on—and then what he does now to ensure that doesn't happen.

Describe for me a decision you regretted after having made it

Interviewers want to learn about a problem you had with a decision after having made it and what you did as a result. What matters here is not necessarily the actual decision but rather how you managed that situation afterward. They want to know what you did (if anything) to rectify the situation, what you learned from this situation, and why you are a better candidate now that you've gone through that process.

Next applicant, please

TRANSLATION

I'd like to learn more about how you make decisions, and if faced with regret about one such decision, are you someone who takes action to rectify that situation quickly?

HOW TO ANSWER

Choose a decision you made that did not have a catastrophic ramification (e.g., nothing that cost your organization a great deal of money, caused an important customer to leave, or opened the company to legal action). State the circumstances of why you made the decision you did and then why you later regretted it. Then talk about what you did to correct the situation, including the people affected, and describe the (hopefully) positive result.

Give an example where you failed to persuade someone to do something you felt would be good for the organization

Interviewers often want to learn about your communication and influencing skills. Using persuasion is a key component in many jobs, and this is the negative form of the question.

TRANSLATION

I'd like to learn about your ability to influence other people and how you react when you don't get your way.

HOW TO ANSWER

Select a situation where you had an idea and tried to convince your boss or someone else who you had no authority over to make a change, but because they had information you weren't privy to, they didn't agree to make that change. Talk through your example in a matter-of-fact way, describing what your idea was, who you presented it to, what you said, and what they said in response.

Be sure to note that you reacted in an understanding way and did not get defensive. Then say that you later learned more information about the situation and that it wasn't that your idea was bad but rather it just wasn't the right time, the organization didn't have the resources necessary to implement your idea, or something similar.

Overcoming obstacles and difficult situations

Recruiters want to know how candidates successfully managed past issues to see how they will be able to successfully resolve problems at this job.

Tell me about a time when you were most persuasive in overcoming resistance to your ideas or point of view

Overcoming resistance to ideas is a commonly needed skill in many jobs, including those that require interactions with people in other departments and/or vendors, suppliers, and customers outside the company.

CHAPTER 4 *Perseverance skills, failures, and negative situations questions*

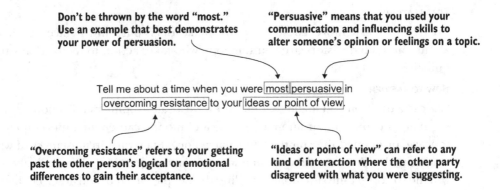

TRANSLATION

We're looking for someone to bring new ideas, but there will likely be resistance to any new ideas you have. Convince me that you'll be able to overcome people's natural resistance to change.

HOW TO ANSWER

Describe a time when you had a new idea for how something could be improved and presented it to your boss or colleagues but they said it wouldn't work. Then talk about what you said or did to increase their understanding of why it would benefit everyone involved to make that change. Mention that you used the "what's in it for them" approach and that, ultimately, they agreed. Discuss your involvement in the idea's implementation and the overall positive result.

> ### Example: Jen, sales
>
> The interviewer asks, "Tell me about a time when you were most persuasive in overcoming resistance to your ideas or point of view."
>
> #### Jen's answer
>
> In my current company, our team was facing strong resistance to implementing a new sales strategy that I strongly believed would significantly boost our results because it would incorporate a new customer segment. The resistance mainly came from the more traditional members of our team who were skeptical of change. They said that we were targeting the correct types of customers and there was no reason to change. However, I could see that the market was changing, and more customer types were looking for the kinds of products and services we offer.
>
> To deal with this resistance, I decided to get some information by meeting with a select group of current customers as well as staff in other departments that I had relationships with. I asked them questions to understand their perspectives. Then I used a combination of data I had obtained from our CRM system and real-world examples to illustrate the potential benefits of the new strategy. I highlighted how it would make their jobs easier after a brief initial rollout period.

Overcoming obstacles and difficult situations

I then took this information back to the team and held a brainstorming session to deal with potential issues and adjust the approach.

We didn't get 100% buy-in at that meeting, but I could see a shift in attitudes as people could clearly see the value of the new strategy. It wasn't about me pushing my idea; it was about creating a shared vision everyone could rally around.

The result of that meeting was the development of a pilot program that I led with five other team members. The first quarter results after that pilot showed that time from initial contact with a potential customer to a signed contract was reduced by more than 20%.

Once we presented the pilot results to the team and leaders, more people wanted to use the new strategy, and we designed training to help everyone get up to speed more quickly. At the annual meeting, my boss mentioned that shift as one of our major wins for the year, and I was really pleased with the way it all turned out.

What Jen did well

This is a good success story that allows Jen to demonstrate multiple competencies in addition to her persuasion skills and ability to overcome resistance: collaborating with others, strategic thinking, project management, and presentation skills. Resistance to change is a very common thing, so this story will be relatable and relevant to the interviewer. She showed the scope of the pilot project by stating that she led a team of five people, and she also remembered to include quantified results.

What would make this even better

This story is already about 2 minutes in length, so to add any specifics, she would need to remove content that is less relevant to the question and the position for which she's interviewing. The story would have more impact if she "put us in the room" as she describes taking the information she gained from customers and staff back to her team. What were the team's objections, and how did she address them?

She mentions that she didn't get 100% buy-in, and it's never a good idea to include a negative unless you're specifically asked for one. Instead, she could say that she achieved buy-in from 95% of the people (or whatever the percentage was).

Her results were about reducing the time from initial contact to signed contract by more than 20%, but she doesn't include any improvement in sales, revenue, margin, or customer growth as a result of adopting this new sales strategy.

She says that "we" presented the pilot results; what was her role in that presentation? More people wanted to use the new strategy; how many more?

The training piece should be removed from the story, because including specifics on exactly what she said to persuade and overcome resistance is more relevant and important than talking about training. However, if she is asked a question about training, she should say more about what kind of training, who designed it, who delivered it, and what the specific result of the training was.

She should leave in the part about her boss mentioning in the annual meeting that this was one of their major wins for the year, which would make a perfect ending to the story after naming the specific sales, revenue, margin, and/or customer growth metrics that were improved.

CHAPTER 4 Perseverance skills, failures, and negative situations questions

Give an example of a situation when you had to think on your feet to get yourself out of a difficult situation

If you're interviewing for a position that will require you to interact with management, customers, or vendors, you'll need to be prepared to think on your feet, because you may be asked questions or presented with a problem that you hadn't anticipated.

TRANSLATION

We need someone who can react quickly and is able to handle unexpected situations with customers, colleagues, or senior leaders. Tell me about a time when you were successful in dealing with that kind of situation.

HOW TO ANSWER

Think of a time when you had to react quickly to solve a problem or answer questions that you hadn't expected. Describe the situation and include the pain point—that is, what made it difficult or delicate. Then describe what you did or said to rectify the situation and how it worked out favorably.

Example: Lucas, customer service

The interviewer asks, "Give an example of a situation when you had to think on your feet to get yourself out of a difficult situation."

Lucas's answer

Early on at my current company, I encountered a particularly challenging situation where a customer was very upset due to a shipping error that was out of our control. The customer had a tight deadline for receiving their order, which had been delayed.

To diffuse the situation and find a solution, I empathized with the customer's frustration and assured them that I would do everything I could to help. I asked my boss for help as well as the team lead, and then I contacted the delivery company to see what could be done to expedite the delivery. I informed the customer and my boss of all the steps we were taking to resolve the issue.

My understanding and quick response to the problem not only calmed the customer down but also left a positive impression. By directly contacting the carrier and working with them, we were able to expedite the delivery. In addition, I was able to offer the customer a discount on their next purchase as a goodwill gesture to compensate for the inconvenience they had experienced, even though it was not our responsibility.

The customer appreciated our dedication to resolving the problem promptly and our willingness to go the extra mile. In the end, we not only retained a customer but turned a potentially negative experience into an opportunity to strengthen our relationship with them.

What Lucas did well

Once again, Lucas selected a good example to share in this interview, because it is a common occurrence in his customer service role. He included a lot of great things in his answer, like how he showed empathy for the customer, assuring them that he'd do everything he could to help, and how he worked with his boss, the team lead, and even the delivery company to resolve the situation. He also kept both the customer and his boss informed about the steps he took. Offering a goodwill gesture to the customer in the form of a future discount likely made them happy, and through Lucas's actions, the company retained the customer, so there was a successful outcome.

What would make this even better

In short, he should have included more specifics. Lucas says that he empathized with the customer, showed understanding, and calmed them down—but by saying what? It is easy for anyone to say that they empathized with a customer and got them to calm down, but for this to be believed, Lucas needs to include what he said to the customer. (We call this "putting the interviewer in the room," which means allowing the interviewer to feel as if they were there listening to Lucas during the customer interactions.)

In terms of the results part of this story, Lucas says that he was able to expedite the delivery, but we don't know how long the initial delay was, how quickly he was able to get the shipment to the customer, or whether the customer received it prior to their tight deadline. He also says that he offered a discount, but he doesn't say how much, either in terms of a percentage or dollar amount. While we did learn that the customer was retained, including the overall value or total volume that the customer purchased annually would give this answer a great deal more impact. He mentions that this scenario strengthened the company's relationship with that customer but provides no metric for that claim. Did the customer increase their annual volume after this scenario? If yes, then Lucas should say so; if not, then he should leave that last part out.

Perseverance and drive

Interviewers want to know that candidates won't give up when faced with challenges.

Tell me about a situation that shows your perseverance, persistence, and ability to remain positive when faced with adversity

Many roles require people to persevere and remain positive during difficult circumstances.

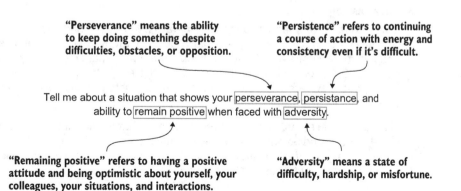

74 CHAPTER 4 *Perseverance skills, failures, and negative situations questions*

TRANSLATION

In this job we need someone who is highly driven, a self-starter, and can persevere in what can sometimes be difficult situations. Convince me you can handle that and be successful in that kind of environment. (See the next section for how to answer this question.)

What can you tell me about yourself that best illustrates your personal drive and motivation?

If the job you're interviewing for requires drive and self-motivation, which are much-needed skills in sales and customer-facing roles, you may be asked a question like this.

TRANSLATION

We need someone in this job who is highly driven and self-motivated, so tell me a story that shows me you fit that description.

HOW TO ANSWER BOTH

This is a great opportunity to build rapport and allow the interviewer to get to know you by sharing something about the personal side of your life. If you played a sport in high school, have run a marathon, or done anything involving facing adversity head-on, staying motivated, and coming out the other side as a better person, talk about that. Or you can talk about working through the COVID pandemic and staying positive and motivated to succeed despite the difficult circumstances. Describe what you did and still do to manage your emotions and retain a positive outlook on life, whether it be working out, doing yoga, talking to friends, or something else.

You can also give an example from your work if you were in a sales role, had to build a clientele and achieve a quota, or were one who survived a layoff but then had a much larger workload, for instance. The key here is to talk through the situation; what you did to motivate yourself, overcome obstacles, and succeed; and why you're a better candidate now as a result.

Example: Jen, sales

The interviewer asks, "What can you tell me about yourself that best illustrates your personal drive and motivation?"

Jen's answer

My personal drive and motivation have always been the driving force behind my successful career in sales. Ever since I was a kid, I've always had an insatiable curiosity and relentless desire to achieve my goals. I remember that I had some of the highest sales for Girl Scout cookies in my district for the six years that I sold them. And it's not because my parents bought them all! I sold to lots of neighbors and had a table outside the local grocery store.

In my first job in sales, I was so eager to learn and prove myself that I practically lived in the office. I studied our products inside and out and consistently met and exceeded quarterly targets after my first few months. I believe in setting high standards for myself and constantly pushing my boundaries.

But my real passion is helping customers. I have a Brian Tracy quote on my vision board that says, "Approach each customer with the idea of helping him or her to solve a problem or achieve a goal, not of selling a product or service." My calling is to help each of our customers get what they need. When I help the customers, that helps the company and me.

What Jen did well

Jen did a great job painting a picture of who she is and what matters to her, allowing the interviewer to build a connection and get to know her, which is always important. She could have gone on and made her answer quite long, but instead she kept her answer to about a minute in length, which is appropriate (and she could have even taken a bit more time as described next). She maintained a good balance of discussing both her sales success and her personal traits, including explicitly stating her passion. We also like that she included some humor by saying that her parents didn't buy her cookies!

What would make this even better

Jen spent most of her time discussing her very early successes. While mentioning her start in Girl Scouts is a nice personal touch, she should then provide a more recent example of an important sales success and include metrics.

By how much did she exceed quota? Did she win any sales awards or contests? How many new customers did she bring in last year, and what amount of revenue did they bring in? How specifically did she help the company drive revenue, improve performance, increase profit, and save time or money? Including a story about a recent and relevant sales success would really capture the interviewer's attention and speak directly to her ability to do the same for this employer.

Describe a situation that required you to make sacrifices or put in extra effort to achieve the goal. How did your drive and perseverance contribute to your success?

In today's business environment, it's often necessary to make sacrifices to achieve company, department, customer, or individual objectives. This question is asked so the interviewer can evaluate your work ethic and dedication, and it also gives you the opportunity to showcase your ability to stay motivated during challenging times.

TRANSLATION

We need someone in this job who is not only willing but also happy to put in extra effort to achieve success, so describe an example that shows me you have what it takes to get this difficult job done.

HOW TO ANSWER

Describe a time in the recent past when you had to go above and beyond the normal call of duty to complete a project on time or satisfy a customer's request. Provide the context, what was at stake, what you did that was outside the norm, what amount of time was needed, especially if your work was outside of regular work hours, what you

CHAPTER 4 *Perseverance skills, failures, and negative situations questions*

said to those involved, and what the result was. Be sure to explicitly say that, without your perseverance and drive to succeed, that result would not have been achieved.

Think about

The following are some things to think about before moving to the next chapter:

- Which example would you select if asked to demonstrate perseverance and persistence?
- When was the last time you had to persuade someone to accept your idea or point of view? What factors contributed to their resistance? What did you say or do to gain their acceptance?
- What example would you give if asked about a time you had to think on your feet?
- What were the obstacles you had to overcome to be successful in your last job?
- What kinds of things do you typically do to remain calm during stressful situations?
- What situation would you describe if asked about one of your failures? What did you learn after this experience, and what do you do differently now?
- What constructive criticism have you received that you would describe if asked about this in an interview? In what ways did you take it to heart and change your behavior as a result?
- Can you think of a decision you made that, if given the chance, you would change? What did you learn from that experience, and what do you do differently now?
- Which example would you share about failing to persuade? What did you say at that time, and how would you word it differently if given a similar situation now?
- What other similar interview questions on these topics might you be asked? For additional examples, see appendix A.

Key takeaways

- Employees often need to deal with problems and unexpected situations. Interviewers want to know whether these issues will stop the applicants from being successful or whether they will be able to persuade others to accept their ideas and suggested remedies to problems.
- Candidates need to be ready with good examples that show how they were able to manage their work when faced with difficulties.
- Interviewers also want to know if applicants have the drive and self-motivation needed to succeed, thrive, and move forward even in difficult situations.
- Interviewers ask about failures and mistakes to gain a better understanding of how candidates handle them. Most importantly, they want to know what the person learned and what specific changes were made based on that knowledge.
- It's important to choose examples that are neither too horrible nor too simplistic and are relevant to the employer.

Leadership, hiring, and motivating skills questions

Interviewers want to know what kind of manager or leader the candidate would be in the organization. Candidates should be prepared to talk about their management or leadership approach and the results they have achieved with their staff. Interviewers are trying to determine if there is a good fit with the current leadership in the company or if there is a potential mismatch.

They likely will ask about how one's style affects direct reports and others in the organization. They can ask these kinds of questions in either a positive way (e.g., how applicants were able to motivate employees), or they can take a negative approach (e.g., how applicants dealt with difficult experiences).

Interviewers also want to know what the candidate has done to successfully hire and motivate staff.

Leadership and management

People who seek managerial roles will be asked questions about what they do to get the best results from people. Senior leaders should also be prepared to talk about how they share their vision with others.

What is your leadership style?

Interviewers want to see if your approach to leading others is a good match for the role and the company.

CHAPTER 5 *Leadership, hiring, and motivating skills questions*

TRANSLATION

I need to know what kind of leader you are so that I can determine whether you'll fit in with our culture and our people.

HOW TO ANSWER

The key here is to not state any one style; rather, say that you modify your approach depending on the situation and people involved. Then give specifics. For example, you might say when leading people who are experienced and performing well, you take a more hands-off approach and when leading people who are new or are not performing well, you monitor their work closely and provide coaching and mentoring. You understand that different people need different things from their managers, and you must show you have the experience and understanding to know what is needed in different circumstances.

Example: Davina, manager

The interviewer asks, "What is your leadership style?"

Davina's answer

My leadership style can best be described in two words: vision and empowerment.

When I was promoted to senior manager two years ago, I took on two additional teams, including one based in Ireland. I brought all the teams together virtually to explain our new mission and vision. We continue to have monthly virtual meetings with the entire team. The vision was added to our PowerPoint template, and we had mouse pads made, which we gave to each employee.

Empowerment to me means setting clear expectations with employees and giving them the support they need to get things done. Let me give you an example. One of my newer employees, Jay, was assigned to be the liaison between our department and another department on a major project. Jay and I met at the beginning of the project to review the deliverables and key stakeholders he had to keep in the loop. Since it was his project, I stayed out of it and let him know that I was available to help him at any time, if he wanted it.

I have biweekly meetings with my direct reports where they give updates and I help them if they need it. Jay gave limited updates on this project but said it was fine. One week I was chatting with the manager of another department, and he mentioned that they were waiting for information from our team. I checked in with Jay, and it turned out that the project wasn't going well, and he had barely been working on it.

Instead of taking over the project, I coached Jay to help him see where some of the issues were. I could easily have solved it myself, but it was his project, and I wanted to empower him to take control of it. It turned out that he had underestimated the time needed for this project and some of his other duties. He identified some potential solutions, and we talked through the benefits of each one; then he chose the ones to start working on.

His work paid off, and he was able to get it back on track. We continued coaching meetings for a few weeks. It was great to see how he was empowered to take control of the project, and at the end, the senior manager of the other team thanked him.

That's just one example. I find it important for all my employees to feel empowered and that they have control. I also want them to know that I'm here to support them to be their best. And I believe that's a big reason why my team continues to meet and exceed all our metrics quarter after quarter.

What Davina did well

It's great that Davina provided a structure for her answer by summarizing her style in only two words. (Interviewers often fear that candidates will ramble on and on in their answers, so providing this structure up front is beneficial.)

Also, rather than only sharing her philosophies (which many candidates do in response to this question), Davina gave real examples that demonstrate her style, including how she coached an employee who was struggling. In the example about Jay, she chose to do the right thing (empowering Jay) rather than what might have been the easier option (taking over his project). Through her coaching, they both achieved the successful result of getting the project back on track.

What would make this even better

In her first example of demonstrating vision, all she said was that she explained her mission and vision to her teams and added them to their PowerPoint template and mouse pads. How those actions benefited the teams and whether the staff embraced this mission and vision is unknown. What else did Davina do to support the vision, aside from making the mission statement more visible? How did Davina embody the mission statement in her everyday work? She also talks about holding monthly meetings, but it is unclear what value came because of those meetings.

It should be noted that meetings aren't important in interview answers; rather, the subjects discussed during the meetings and what results come from the meetings are the key topics to include.

The example about Jay demonstrates Davina's ability to coach a team member to get a project back on track, but it also raises a potential negative: that the project got off track in the first place. Her hands-off style (what she calls empowerment) may have been too hands-off, especially because he was a new employee. Davina said that she "stayed out of it" and let him know that she was available to help him at any time if he wanted it. A better approach would have been to hold regular check-ins, so that she would become aware of the problems prior to being told so by another department. In addition, she could have checked in with the project owner herself proactively.

The only result provided was that the project got back on track; what benefit or value did that project bring to the team, customer, or company? Answering the question "why did it matter?" would have given this answer much more impact.

Lastly, Davina also mentions at the end that her team continues to meet and exceed all their metrics quarter after quarter. Specifically naming these metrics, especially those she exceeded and by how much, would greatly improve this answer.

Discuss a situation in which you were able to create a high level of trust, morale, and team spirit

Interviewers want to understand how you will work with the team.

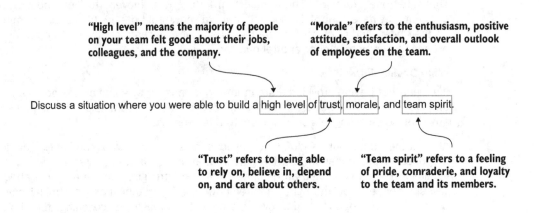

TRANSLATION

We need a leader who can create an environment of trust and team spirit and who can improve morale around here. Give an example that demonstrates you can do that.

HOW TO ANSWER

Provide a situation where either you were new to the team and had to build trust or morale and team spirit were low. What did you do or say to create an environment where people felt good about their jobs and their contributions to the team? Include any concrete outcomes that occurred as a result of this improved morale.

> **Example: Davina, manager**
>
> The interviewer asks, "Discuss a situation in which you were able to create a high level of trust, morale, and team spirit."
>
> **Davina's answer**
>
> Let me go back to the situation that I mentioned, the time when I was promoted and I took on two additional teams. I knew that there would be difficulties because one of the teams had been managed by three different managers in the previous two years. This was the team in Ireland, so there was also a time zone and distance issue.
>
> I immediately went to visit the team and scheduled individual meetings with each person to learn more about them and their interests. It was important for me to build relationships.
>
> Instead of coming in and making changes, I asked them for their feedback on what they wanted changed and what they wanted to stay the same. One of the areas that came up was flexibility with hours. In the past, they had been told that they had to start at 8:00 AM and there was no flexibility. Some of the team members wanted to

start a little later, so I went to bat for them with the leadership team in the US and in Europe and I was able to get them the flexibility they wanted.

I also brought back some of the practices they liked that the last manager had changed, including monthly birthday celebration lunches. It was a small thing, but it meant a lot to them.

I wanted the team to know that I was not just going to meet with them once and leave them, so for the first year, I visited them in person once a quarter. I asked them to choose team-building activities, and they came up with some great ones, including going to see a soccer match and going on a group treasure hunt that was held in a local city.

We also made a change in the timing of all our meetings so that the team in Ireland could easily attend them all. They really appreciated that because in the past, some of the meetings were held in their evenings.

One thing I had been concerned about when I took over the team was that with the manager change, we might lose some key team members. There were two employees in particular I was worried could be looking at other offers. I'm pleased to say that we did not lose anyone at that time, and since then, only one person has left the team, and that was to work for his family business, so he didn't go to a competitor.

What Davina did well

Davina did a lot of things well in this answer. She started her example by not only giving the context (when she was promoted and took on two additional teams) but also stating what made this a challenge (one of the teams had been managed by three different managers in the previous two years, and since this team was in Ireland there were time zone and distance issues).

Rather than just talking about the individual meetings she held, she described the purpose of the meetings (to learn more about the people and their interests and to build relationships). She also described what was accomplished during the meetings (gaining their feedback on what they wanted changed and what they wanted to stay the same). As a result of these meetings, Davina was able to address their concern about flexibility of hours and scheduling of meetings and bring back the birthday celebrations that their last manager had stopped, plus she gained their preferences on team-building activities.

She also gave an important result: zero attrition after she took over and losing only one person in two years, for a reason that likely had nothing to do with her (to work for his family business).

In addition, Davina changed the culture in Ireland, which is no small feat. She likely helped the Irish team feel they were no longer just the offshore team but truly part of the whole team. She also demonstrated listening and collaborated not only on what could change but also on how to make it happen.

What would make this even better

The only thing that would make this answer better is to offer more concrete results as evidence of her creating a high level of trust, morale, and team spirit.

CHAPTER 5 *Leadership, hiring, and motivating skills questions*

> *(continued)*
>
> What was turnover like prior to her taking over this team in Ireland? How many people were on this team, so we know the context for losing only one person in two years (there is a big difference between losing one out of 4 people vs. losing one out of 30 people).
>
> Also, were there any employee surveys done, or 360-degree performance reviews, that showed improved metrics? Were there any quantitative business metrics this team accomplished during the past two years that showed improvement after she took over as manager?
>
> These important results would make her answer even better.

Tell me about an occasion when you pulled the team together and improved morale during challenging circumstances

This is a more negative slant on the previous question about morale.

"Pulled the team together" means that you served in an official or unofficial leadership capacity and worked together in a productive manner.

Tell me about an occasion when you pulled the team together and improved morale during challenging circumstances.

"Morale" refers to the enthusiasm, positive attitude, satisfaction, and overall outlook of employees on the team.

"Challenging circumstances" can mean any kind of situation that was perceived as more difficult than ordinary daily activities. Examples include a project with a tight deadline, an unhappy customer situation, a new system implementation, budget cutbacks, and during or after a reduction in force.

TRANSLATION

Our morale is pretty low, so we need to hire someone who can bring people together and improve the way they feel about their jobs and our company. Give an example that demonstrates you can do that.

HOW TO ANSWER

Talk through a situation where morale was low and there were disagreements or personality conflicts in the team. A "challenging circumstance" could be during or after layoffs, COVID, cost-cutting, implementing a new system, or anything that made the environment stressful. What did you do or say to pull people together, diffuse stress, and ultimately help people feel better about themselves, the team, the company, or the environment in general? Include any specific results that occurred because of this improved morale.

Describe a difficult experience you've had while leading a group with different opinions and personalities. What issues arose, and how did you resolve them?

Applicants should be ready to share how they've dealt with difficult personalities and disagreements within their team.

TRANSLATION

We have some people here who have strong personalities and aren't afraid to speak up when they disagree or have differing opinions. I need to know that (a) you're comfortable in that environment and (b) you can work through and resolve any people issues that might arise as a result of having these personality types on the team.

HOW TO ANSWER

Provide an example where the people involved fit that description: "differing opinions and personalities" (which pretty much exists everywhere!). Describe the disagreements or conflicts that came up and what you did or said to work through them to a positive resolution.

Hiring and motivating staff

Candidates should be able to show what they have done to build and motivate their teams to create successful environments. Interviewers may ask questions about how managers find and interview potential employees. Some companies have specific internal hiring processes that managers must follow. Other companies don't and want to know that the applicant has a process that works. They want to learn how the applicant chooses the best candidates and how they will bring those skills and practices to their new company.

> ### Insider story: Interviewers as interviewees
>
> The majority of clients I (Barbara) have worked with are managers, directors, vice presidents, and C-suite executives, most of whom have spent a great deal of time on the other side of the desk as interviewers. Because of that, they're often quite confident in their skills as interviewees. When we talk about common questions, they have their own opinions on which questions they ask and why and which questions they would never ask. I have to remind them that there is a whole world of possible interviewers out there.
>
> In my years working with job seekers and hearing about their interview experiences, I've concluded that most interviewers aren't very good at interviewing. The people who interview all the time are often quite good (e.g., internal recruiters and external headhunters), but most interviewers do not interview regularly. There are junior talent acquisition people who read from scripts, hiring managers who glance at candidates'

(continued)

resumes just prior to starting the interview, and executives who know which topics they'd like to cover but don't take the time to think through how best to articulate their questions. I tell my clients they should assume they are better interviewers than most of the people they will be interviewed by. I always think about what Forrest Gump said because it applies to job interviewers: "Life is like a box of chocolates; you never know what you're going to get."

What kinds of things have you done to both attract new talent and guard against poor hires?

One of the most important responsibilities of people in management roles is to hire good employees. This question covers both issues of attracting and hiring good people, and interviewers want to make sure you know how to avoid making bad hiring decisions.

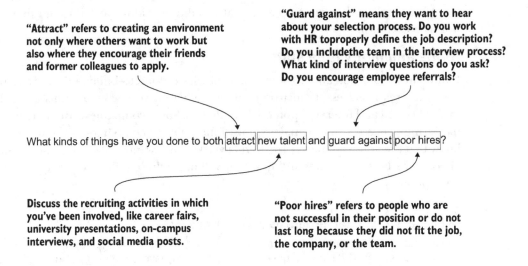

TRANSLATION

The person in this role will be hiring people, and we need to make sure they can do that effectively and not cause problems by bringing in people who don't fit in or can't do their jobs. What do you do to ensure people will want to work for you, and what is your hiring and selection process?

HOW TO ANSWER

The best way to answer this is to give an actual example rather than speak in general about what you typically do. It's okay to begin with some kind of conversion sentence like, "I think the best way to answer that is to tell you about the time in my last position when I needed to hire three people in a short time frame." Give the background, what made the situation challenging, what you did to attract candidates, how many candidates you considered, what your selection and interviewing process was, and how many people at your company were involved in interviews.

Remember to state the result: the time frame in which you hired them and how successful they later were at your organization. If you can mention that later on they were promoted to roles of greater responsibility, that would be the icing on the cake!

Example: Davina, manager

The interviewer asks, "What kinds of things have you done to both attract new talent and guard against poor hires?"

Davina's answer

Having a great team is very important to me. In my current job, I'm pleased to say that I have not had too many openings. But when I've had an opening to fill, one of the first things I do is really look at the job now and how I want the job to look in the future. For example, earlier this year, when putting together a job description for posting, I realized that in the future more time would be spent on global projects instead of projects in the US. I decided that it would make the most sense to adjust the job description to make it more global.

The job description is also very important to me, so I always work with human resources to make sure what I'm looking for is clearly listed. They obviously deal with candidates all the time and have a much better idea of what's working now. To attract great talent, I look at the jobs and see what the future opportunities are that might interest people. I can't expect that people will stay in jobs forever, and I want to help potential applicants see the benefits of the roles.

When I'm interviewing, I use behavioral questions to get information on how candidates have handled specific situations in the past. I talk about our values and ask them for examples of how they have shown those values. In addition, I rely on other people to help me with the interviews. I always have some team members as well as a peer join me in the final interview process to ensure I'm making the best decisions.

I'm pleased to say that in this company and the last company, every one of my hires did well and stayed with the company at least two years. As a matter of fact. I'm still in touch with someone that I hired more than 10 years ago, and she's still at the company. So I think I've had a lot of success attracting and keeping good talent.

What Davina did well

Davina did a good job of talking through her selection process, and she discussed several important components: reevaluating the job description, anticipating trends, working with human resources, using behavioral interview questions, asking candidates for examples of demonstrating the values she feels are important, and including both team members and one of her peers in the interview process.

She also included results in her answer, regarding the retention of all her hires.

> *(continued)*
>
> **What would make this even better**
>
> Instead of talking through the kinds of things she typically (or always) does, she should have converted this answer to give an actual example. When an interviewer asks, "What kinds of things have you done" or "What kinds of things do you do," it's better to pretend that their question is "Give an example that demonstrates the kinds of things you've done," because giving an actual story will have more impact than just saying what you generally do.
>
> Davina could easily do that in this case by talking about a time when she had to replace someone or hire someone new instead of describing what she said in her answer. Then she'd describe things she *actually did* rather than what she typically does.
>
> It was very good that Davina included results, because usually when people say what they typically or always do, there are no results to speak of. What would make her results much more impactful is to provide the context for "every one of her hires." Was that 4, 40, or 400 people? Showing any percentage increase in retention (or decrease in attrition) since she took over as manager would also add impact. Additional information she could share would include any employee survey results or any team or individual recognition within the department or across the organization.

What do you do to create an environment that inspires and motivates your team?

Interviewers want to find out how hiring you can help increase the team's morale.

Next applicant, please

TRANSLATION

We need an inspirational leader in this role who can improve the team's motivation (or if it's already good, someone who won't lower the morale of the team). Provide an example that demonstrates these leadership attributes.

HOW TO ANSWER

Once again, the best way to answer this is to give an example rather than speak in general about what you typically do. Provide a situation where either you were new to the team and had to improve performance, or morale was low due to circumstances outside of your control. What did you do or say to create an environment where people felt good about their jobs, themselves, and their contributions to the team?

Include any concrete outcomes that occurred because of this improved morale and any anecdotes about what people later said as evidence that you inspired and motivated team members.

Example: Clueless Clark, marketing

The interviewer asks, "What do you do to create an environment that inspires and motivates your team?"

Clueless Clark's answer

I motivate my team by getting excited. Our boss is in another location, and the rest of us work together, and I thought it would be a great idea to get together every Monday morning to have a 30-minute rally where I charge them up by reminding them why we're there and what a great week it will be. I usually come up with a motivational quote of the week. Last week it was a quote from Dale Carnegie, "Most of the important things in the world have been accomplished by people who have kept on trying when there seemed to be no hope at all."

After that, if anyone has something they want to share, they do. Often, they don't because they count on me to bring the energy and inspiration to the meeting.

Then we end the meeting by getting together in a circle and putting our hands in the middle and we shout together, "one, two, three, teamwork!" Then we clap and get ready for the day.

We've been doing that for a month, and I know the team appreciates that I take the lead on it because I asked if anyone else wanted to run our Monday rally and they all said that I should do it.

So that's me—I inspire the team.

What Clueless Clark got wrong

Clueless Clark sounds more like a high school football coach than a business leader. He seems to think that holding a weekly rally (as he referred to it) will inspire and motivate his staff. He failed to recognize that people have different motivators, and what inspires one person may not inspire another.

It also sounds like Clark believes that his talking is what motivates his team, rather than his asking questions and listening. It's no surprise that by the time he asks

(continued)

if anyone has something to share, they often don't (and we question whether their silence is really due to their counting on him to "bring the energy and inspiration to the meeting").

What Clueless Clark should have done

Clueless Clark should have discussed his conversations with his team members, both individually and as a group, because not all people feel comfortable talking in front of a group. He should include in his answer what questions he asks his team members to get to know them, learn what kinds of things motivate them, what they feel would inspire them to perform at their highest levels, and what expectations they have of themselves.

He should then talk about how he uses that information to improve the environment and make people feel good about their jobs and working for the company, the department, and him.

If possible, Clark should include any kind of results and metrics that show the high performance, the high retention rates, and low absenteeism and turnover of his team.

Think about

The following are some things to think about before moving to the next chapter:

- How would you describe your leadership style?
- How do you think others would describe you as a leader? Have you ever asked them?
- Do you gravitate toward one style of leadership, or do you adapt your style to the situation and people involved?
- What kinds of things do you do to build trust in you as a leader?
- Have you ever been in a situation where staff had low morale? How did you react?
- What example would you use to describe a time when you built team spirit?
- Which scenario would you describe if asked about leading a team with different personalities and opinions? What did you do as a leader to resolve the issues that arose?
- How would you describe your selection and hiring process? What works well, and what can be improved?
- How would you describe your interview style? Do you follow a process or do you wing it? What kinds of questions do you ask?
- How do you think others would describe what you're like to work for?
- What do you do to identify what motivates the members of your team? Once you have that information, what do you do as a leader to ensure that your team stays motivated to perform at their highest levels?

- What other similar interview questions on these topics might you be asked? For additional examples, see appendix A.

Key takeaways

- Candidates for management positions will usually be asked about their leadership approaches to determine if there is a match with the team and the company culture.
- Applicants should be ready to share examples of how they supported team success and dealt with difficult situations.
- Managers should also be prepared to explain the process they use to hire and motivate staff members.
- Interviewers want to find out if the applicant will be able to support the current team that would report to them in their new role.
- They also want to see how the manager would motivate and grow the team in the future.

Problem-solving, time management, negotiation, and change questions

One of the key skills needed for many jobs is the ability to analyze information. To determine these abilities, interviewers will ask candidates to describe past examples that highlight that skill. They do this by asking about how specific problems were handled and how that led to the desired results. Questions about decisions, both good and bad, are also used to gather this information.

Even though questions may ask about the result, interviewers are really looking to understand the steps in your thinking process. They want to know how you went about it, what you considered, and why it was important.

Most jobs have multiple goals and priorities. Candidates should be ready to share what they do to manage their time effectively to get the necessary results, especially when other departments are involved. Depending on the role, interviewers may also ask questions about negotiation and managing change.

Analysis, problem-solving, and decision-making

Interviewers want to understand the process you use to make decisions. Make sure to describe your example in a way that the interviewer can easily understand, especially if it involved highly technical information or something specific to a previous job. Choose examples that will help them see how you would approach a similar problem in this role. Include enough detail to make the story impactful, but don't get lost in the details. Focus on how you thought through the situation, the obstacles you faced, and why your solution provided the best possible outcome.

Describe a complex problem you solved

Interviewers want a specific example of how you worked through a complex problem to solve it. Your answer needs to show them how you think. Questions like this are frequently asked in a much longer and more complex way, such as "Describe a complex problem you faced. How did you analyze processes, strategically evaluate potential solutions, and ultimately enact change?" If you're asked this longer question, be sure to cover all components (how you analyzed processes, evaluated solutions, and implemented your selected solution) in your answer.

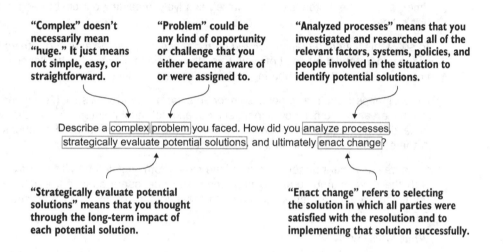

TRANSLATION

This job requires strong analytical and problem-solving skills; give an example that demonstrates your ability to analyze, evaluate, make decisions, and ultimately solve a complicated problem that improves something that impacts the business, team, or customer.

HOW TO ANSWER

Most people say that they have good analytical and problem-solving skills, but here you'll need to demonstrate this strength by showing how you think when faced with a complicated problem. Do not make the mistake many job candidates do by simply stating the problem, describing your actions, and then reporting the result. This will not provide the window into your thought processes that the interviewer is looking for.

Instead, describe the problem, including what made it difficult or complicated, and include any obstacles you faced and needed to overcome. Then describe the analysis you did, even if it was in your own head. Talk about the potential solutions you came up with, how you thought through the pros and cons, which solution you selected and why,

CHAPTER 6 *Problem-solving, time management, negotiation, and change questions*

and then how you implemented that solution. End by describing how your solution benefited the business, team, or customer.

Example: Ari, engineer

The interviewer asks, "Describe a complex problem you faced; how did you analyze processes, strategically evaluate potential solutions, and ultimately enact change?"

Ari's answer

In my previous role, I was tasked with addressing a complex performance issue that was affecting our user experience. The problem was connected to slow response times and frequent crashes, which were negatively impacting our customer satisfaction ratings.

To solve this, I gathered and analyzed performance metrics and engaged with end-users to understand their point of view. This allowed me to pinpoint the bottlenecks and potential root causes contributing to the performance issue.

I then mapped out the various components from start to finish. This helped me identify areas of inefficiency, dependencies, and potential points of failure that were impacting the overall performance. We considered a range of possible solutions and gathered data through performance testing and simulations.

Once we had a clear understanding of the most promising solution, I worked closely with the development team to implement the necessary changes, and we communicated regular progress updates to stakeholders during the implementation process.

What Ari did well

Ari gave a good example of a problem and how he approached it, gave a high-level overview of how he worked with the team to solve it, and didn't get lost in the details of the technical aspects of the problem or its solutions (which is what many technical professionals do in their answers).

What would make this even better

This answer is so high level that we don't get a real sense of what the problem was, how he thought through it, what kind of analysis he did to choose the best solution, and what the overall benefit was once the solution was implemented. It's almost as if he wanted to include as many buzzwords as possible rather than giving us a window into how he thinks and solves problems, which is what this question is truly after.

We're left with the following questions after hearing this answer:

- What was the performance problem, and how was it affecting user experiences?
- What was the actual versus desired response time?
- What was the crash rate?
- What were the actual versus desired customer satisfaction ratings?
- What performance metrics did you analyze, and what did you learn after talking with the end-users?

- What bottlenecks and potential root causes did you identify?
- What areas of inefficiency and potential failure points did you identify that impacted performance?
- Which solutions did you consider, and did you do that alone or as part of a team (the "we" is not clear)?
- How did you or the team decide which solution was the most promising?
- What changes were implemented, and what was the overall benefit? Did response times and satisfaction ratings improve and by how much? Was the crash rate reduced and by how much? Did these changes improve the workflow or productivity of the team? Was this solution considered a new best practice for the organization?
- How long did it take to create and deliver the solution? How were management, sales, and customer support involved?

The length of this answer is about half what it should be; by adding in specifics about the problem, his thought processes, making the "I" and "we" clear in the descriptions of actions taken, and providing specific results, this answer would have considerably more impact.

Tell me about a time when you missed an obvious solution to a problem

Interviewers want to know whether you have enough self-knowledge and confidence to admit that, in overthinking a problem, you missed an obvious and perhaps simple solution.

TRANSLATION

This job requires strong problem-solving skills and attention to detail but also the knowledge and experience to recognize that not all problems are complicated. Give an example that shows you have humility and the ability to learn from a previous problem-solving mistake.

HOW TO ANSWER

Describe a situation from earlier in your career when you were new or lacked experience. Talk through what the problem was and how you came up with several ideas as possible solutions but later learned from your manager or a more experienced colleague that a simple solution existed. This can be something related to a company's systems, processes, or policies that you hadn't yet been trained on or learned. Then describe why this was an important lesson for you and what you did differently from then on. You can even make a joke about the old adage that when you hear hooves, think of horses before zebras!

What was the most difficult decision you ever had to make on the job?

Interviewers want to know what you consider to be a difficult decision and understand how you go about the decision-making process to arrive at the best outcome for your company, team, and/or customer.

Next applicant, please

TRANSLATION

This job requires someone who can make difficult decisions; describe for me a decision you faced that you considered difficult and walk me through how you made your decision.

HOW TO ANSWER

Many candidates who have been in supervisory roles use a scenario that involves either firing someone or implementing a reduction in force and deciding who can stay and who will be laid off. On the surface, this seems like a decision that anyone would find difficult. However, there are dangers in using either of these examples:

- *Firing someone*—As a manager, you are paid to do what is best for the business, and keeping someone on the team who isn't performing well is not good for the business. If you use this as an example, be sure to describe both sides of your brain: the human side that felt bad for this person, because you knew this was beyond their abilities or would have a major impact on their personal life, and the business side, because their lack of performance had a negative impact on the team and you needed to get someone into the role who could do the job well. Present yourself as someone who does not hesitate to make difficult decisions after careful analysis and consideration of multiple factors.

- *Laying someone off*—Unfortunately, sometimes what is best for the business means cutting costs and reducing headcount. If you use this type of scenario as an example, you also need to describe both your human side that felt bad for the person or people involved because they were decent performers, and the business side that recognized and accepted why this was needed. Then talk through the analysis you conducted (even if it was only in your head); the various options you considered; which people you selected and why; how you told the people involved, including the survivors; and the assistance you offered to the affected staff. End by describing how this reduction benefited the business.

If you have not been in a supervisory role or have not had to fire or lay someone off, provide an example of another decision you had to make that you considered difficult at that time. Describe what made it difficult, how you analyzed possible options, how you did a cost/benefit analysis of each (even if this was just in your head), which option you chose and why, and how you implemented that decision. End by describing how your decision benefited the business, team, or customer.

Example: Ari, engineer

The interviewer asks, "What was the most difficult decision you ever had to make on the job?"

Ari's answer

I can recall a particularly challenging decision I had to make while working on a critical project. We were tasked with delivering a project with a tight deadline and budget. As the project lead, I was faced with a decision regarding scope changes and resource allocation.

The project had been progressing well until we encountered unexpected issues that threatened our ability to meet the deadline on budget. After careful consideration, I made the decision to prioritize the core functionalities to make sure those would be delivered.

Here's how I approached the process:

First, I gathered data to understand the impact on our timeline, quality, and budget. I worked closely with the team to estimate the additional time and resources that would be necessary if we stayed with the original project scope.

I then got the stakeholders involved. I presented my analysis and provided information on the tradeoffs of various options. Their input was essential in weighing the pros and cons of these options. We also discussed potential consequences, including the impact on customer satisfaction and the company's reputation.

Once the decision was made, I ensured communication across the team and with stakeholders, including the benefits of prioritizing quality over rushed delivery. I closely monitored the progress and communicated any changes to the stakeholders.

As a result of the decision, we were able to deliver a product within the initial deadline and on budget but with the scope somewhat reduced from the original plan.

96   **CHAPTER 6**   *Problem-solving, time management, negotiation, and change questions*

(continued)

What Ari did well

Once again, Ari provided a very good example of a difficult and quite common decision: whether to adjust the project scope, budget, or timelines as unexpected issues arise. He gave a high-level overview of how he approached the decision and what he did to make the decision. He didn't get stuck in the weeds while describing the technical aspects of the project.

What would make this even better

Just as in the previous answer, the description is so general that we don't get a sense of how he came to make the decision, nor are we clear on how he weighed the options of whether to increase the budget or extend the timeline to deliver the full project scope versus reducing the scope to stay on budget and timeline (which seems to be what he decided to do).

To make this clearer and to showcase his decision-making abilities, Ari should provide more specifics:

- What was the actual project?
- How did he determine and prioritize the core functionalities?
- Did he make the decision before or after his meeting with the key stakeholders? If after, how did stakeholder input influence his decision?
- Did he make this decision alone or together with the group of stakeholders? Was there any negotiation involved?
- What team did he work with to estimate the additional time and resources necessary to stay with the original project scope?
- How did he present the tradeoffs of increasing the budget or timeline to deliver the full scope versus reducing the scope to stay on budget and timeline while preserving the quality of the core functionalities?

Ari also failed to stick the landing on the results: he ended his answer on a negative rather than stating that the stakeholders were happy with the core functionality delivered on time and on budget and what the overall business benefit of this project was. He should also mention whether there is a plan in place to ultimately deliver the remaining features that were dropped in this first phase.

Ari could close out the story by summarizing that this experience demonstrates his ability to make data-driven decisions under pressure, effectively communicate complex choices, and collaborate with stakeholders to achieve the best possible outcome.

The length of this answer is about right (at approximately 90 seconds), but he would dramatically increase the impact (and he could take up to 2 minutes total) by removing the generalities while adding in more specifics, especially on how he made the decision, how it was implemented, and what the overall results were.

Describe for me your decision-making process

Interviewers want to understand your decision-making process so they can determine whether your process will fit their culture.

TRANSLATION

This job requires someone who can make difficult decisions; describe for me a decision that you faced and walk me through how you made your decision.

HOW TO ANSWER

Most people say that they have good decision-making skills, but here you'll need to demonstrate this strength by showing how you think when faced with a difficult decision (and yes, answers to both of the questions should involve difficult rather than easy-peasy decisions). Do not make the mistake many job candidates do by simply stating the needed decision, describing briefly how you made it, and then giving the result. This will not provide the window into your thought processes the interviewer is looking for.

Instead, describe the decision that needed to be made, what made it difficult or complicated, and any obstacles you faced, such as lacking time, data, or precedent. Then talk about the options, how you thought through the pros and cons of each, and why you made the decision you did. End by describing how your decision benefited the business, team, or customer.

Time and project management

Many roles require managing different projects, and interviewers will want examples of how candidates were able to get everything done in a timely manner and with high quality. They want to know if candidates will be able to handle the workload required in that role.

> ### Insider story: A project completed on time lacked a critical component
>
> An HR director friend of ours told us about a candidate she interviewed for a manager position. She asked him to describe a project he led from start to finish that he was particularly proud of. He set up the story well, describing the situation, the budget he had to work with, the time frames that were required, and the actions he took.
>
> Everything sounded great until he explained that, to get the project done on time and within budget, he had to leave out the personal protective equipment that safety regulations required. He was very proud of having completed what he considered to be a successful project, but the HR director did not agree with his assessment, and he didn't get the job. She understood the need to sometimes make compromises, but safety equipment should never be one of them!

Tell me about a time when you were juggling multiple projects with overlapping deadlines, tight time frames, and conflicting priorities

Most jobs require good time management, so be prepared to describe the tools and techniques you use to manage your time and assignments. Questions like this are frequently asked in a much longer and more complex way, such as "Tell me about a time when you were juggling multiple projects with overlapping deadlines, tight time frames, and conflicting priorities. How did you manage the projects and your time so that nothing slipped through the cracks?" If you're asked this longer question, be sure to cover all components (how you managed the projects and your time) in your answer.

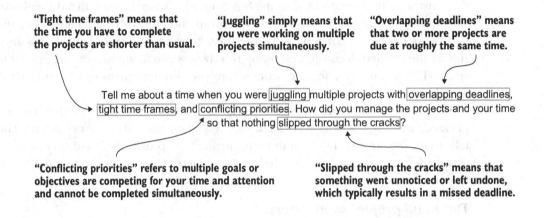

TRANSLATION

This job requires someone who is extremely organized and can successfully manage multiple things at once. Convince me you can handle that and not miss deadlines.

HOW TO ANSWER

Paint a picture of a previous work environment where you were doing just that: managing multiple projects at once with various deadlines and priorities. Then choose one particular time when things were quite busy and describe the method you used to stay organized, which could be a list, a whiteboard, a spreadsheet, or project management software. Also, state what you did when there was a conflicting priority and how you understood the difference between urgent and important (not everything that is urgent is important). Talk about your discussions with your boss if that played a part in your prioritization. Lastly, give the end result, which hopefully was that every key task was completed on time and in priority order.

Recall for me a major project you initiated and worked on through to completion. How did you proactively manage changes in project priorities, scope, and expectations?

Most projects involve changes in priorities, scope, or expectations, so you need to have an example ready.

TRANSLATION

Things here often seem to be a moving target, with constant changes in priorities and expectations. It's not uncommon to have scope creep, whereby the scope of a project

Time and project management 99

continually expands unless you can rein in expectations and priorities. To be successful in this role, you'll need to be proactive; otherwise, things can get out of hand.

HOW TO ANSWER

Describe a project you worked on that involved multiple people, teams, or departments, each with different priorities and expectations. Talk about discussions that occurred along the way when some people wanted to make changes or wanted certain things done that were outside the initial scope of the work. What did you do? How did you communicate and collaborate with the stakeholders to keep them informed and help them understand that, with added scope, either the budget or timeline would need to be increased? Discuss any approvals needed and obtained. Talk about any negotiation you did to keep stakeholders happy with the project. End with the result: what happened with the project, and what value did it bring to the company, customer, or team?

Example: Lucas, customer service

The interviewer asks, "Recall for me a major project you initiated and worked on through to completion. How did you proactively manage changes in project priorities, scope, and expectations?"

Lucas's answer

At a previous company, I ran a project that was focused on reducing our customer service response times. The initial plan was relatively straightforward around streamlining our internal processes.

However, as we started to work on this, we realized the need to address not only the response times but also how we worked with teams inside the company.

Our project team developed initial ideas and got feedback from other customer service reps to make sure that we included their suggestions and concerns. We took that information and developed a report which we reviewed with the stakeholders. We got their feedback and made changes based on what was important to them.

We then contacted other groups and asked them to create their own teams to work on this. Each group was given certain topics to address, and the entire team got together once a month.

The project took approximately six months and led to a response time reduction of 49%. In addition, we developed new procedures that sped up the handoff time between sales and customer service, leading to a Net Promoter Score [NPS] of 9 out of 10 for transfers.

The project was so successful that the CEO of the company recognized it in our annual meeting, the team was awarded an Impact of the Year award, and I received a bonus for my work. It was a big success.

What Lucas did well

Lucas selected a great project that is directly related to the position for which he's interviewing. This example also demonstrates his ability to lead teams, collaborate

(continued)

with others, solicit ideas and feedback, and gain stakeholder buy-in. He was specific in providing the six-month time frame, which shows the scope of the project, and he gave quantified results for both response time and NPS rating, which reflects customer loyalty and willingness to refer others to the company.

What would make this even better

After reading his answer multiple times, we still have no idea what the project was that Lucas worked on. What drove the need? Was it complaints, long wait times, or technical issues? He then needs to state which internal processes were evaluated and ultimately streamlined. He also needs to describe what he means by "how we worked with teams inside the company." What kinds of ideas and feedback did he solicit from the team? What suggestions and concerns were included? What kind of information was in the report that was reviewed with which stakeholders? What changes were made based on their feedback and priorities? What kinds of topics were addressed by the other groups?

In short, what actions led to the improvement in the resulting metrics that he shared? What procedures were developed (and by whom) that led to the NPS of 9, and what was their score prior to the project? Whenever a new rating (or any kind of metric) is given, he needs to include the improvement made so the interviewer will understand the movement that occurred as a result of his actions.

Lucas mentioned the word "we" around nine times in this answer, and although he did say at the beginning that he ran this project, it is unclear what specific actions he did personally as part of this project.

Lastly, it's great that the CEO recognized this project at their annual meeting and that the team received an award, but he should not mention that he received a bonus (you never want to cause the interviewer to think about your compensation).

Negotiation

For jobs that include negotiation skills, such as sales, account management, and vendor management, candidates should expect to be asked for examples. Even in jobs that do not require direct negotiation, interviewers may ask about this topic to understand how the candidate solves problems with others and develops mutually agreeable solutions in difficult situations.

Tell me about a difficult negotiation in which you were involved. What challenges arose during the negotiation, and how did you work through them?

The interviewer is not looking for a simple negotiation; the main point here is to showcase how you resolve issues that tend to arise when the people involved have different interests or priorities such as costs or time frames.

Negotiation

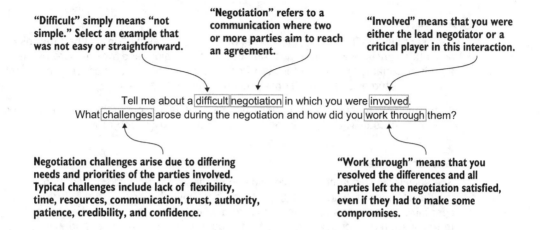

Translation

We need someone who has good negotiation skills and can get to win–win outcomes. Please tell me how you negotiated successfully through a difficult or complex scenario where, in the end, both parties walked away feeling good about the result.

How to answer

Give a scenario where you were either the lead negotiator or the only negotiator. Describe the parties involved, what was at stake, what kinds of obstacles you faced, and what you said or did to work beyond them. How did you identify the other party's true priorities so you could offer compromises they'd be amenable to? Talk through how you persuaded them to agree to those compromises and what the overall benefits to both parties were.

> ### Example: Jen, sales
>
> The interviewer asks, "Tell me about a difficult negotiation in which you were involved; what challenges arose during the negotiation, and how did you work through them?"
>
> ### Jen's answer
>
> Okay, I've got a great one for you. There was a particularly tough negotiation at my current company that I'll never forget. I was working with a potential technology client who seemed impossible to please. They had some really tight budget constraints, and our initial proposal didn't align with their price expectations.
>
> Their purchasing manager was skeptical about our pricing and the value we could provide. Even though we had been recommended to them, they were reluctant to share information about their budget. I dove deep into understanding their needs by asking a variety of questions on how our product would be used, what potential concerns they had, and what their anticipated results would be. I then customized our proposal to address each of their specific needs and concerns.

(continued)

They kept pushing for further discounts, which was a real challenge. I had to strike a delicate balance between meeting their budget constraints and making sure we made a profit. I explained the value they would get from our product and showed them real-world case studies of similar clients who had achieved outstanding results.

It took multiple rounds of negotiation and lots of patience, but in the end, we reached a very good deal. The client signed and turned out to be one of our very satisfied customers.

What Jen did well

She selected a very good example and tied her answer directly to the question, including descriptions of what challenges arose and how she worked through them successfully. Saying that she focused on the value of her product rather than the price is the right approach, and taking the time to customize her proposal to address each of the client's needs and concerns is also effective.

What would make this even better

This answer is about a minute in length, and when providing examples, answers can be that long or even up to 90 seconds for more complex stories. She should say more about the compromise reached that enabled the customer to walk away happy with the deal while ensuring her company still made a profit.

She also should define what she means by "a very good deal." What kind of revenue was this deal, and were there ongoing revenues brought in annually? She should also define what she means by their becoming a "very satisfied customer." Did they refer other customers? Did their account grow over time? Did they complete a survey that exceeded their average customer ratings?

She is missing an opportunity for impact by not mentioning specific metrics. All salespeople should include quantified results not only on their resumes but also in their interview answers.

Describe a situation that demonstrates your ability to negotiate skillfully when costs were critical

Keeping costs down is almost always a priority, so interviewers want to know how your negotiation skills can make or save them money.

TRANSLATION

In this economy, we need to keep our costs down, so we need someone who has good negotiation skills and can sell our customers on value instead of on price and/or get the best price from our suppliers. Tell me a story that shows you can excel in that type of scenario.

HOW TO ANSWER

Describe a time when you were either the lead negotiator or the only negotiator and the main sticking point was cost or price. Describe the parties involved, what the negotiation was about, and what you said or did during the negotiation. Talk through how you ultimately came to an agreement where both parties felt satisfied, even if they both had to make compromises.

Change management

Companies change, and jobs change. Interviewers want to know you're willing and able to succeed despite any adjustments you may have to make. When applying to a job in innovative or disruptive industries such as AI, cybersecurity, biotech, or financial technology, it's important to be prepared for questions about this topic. Also, if you'll be expected to implement new systems, solutions, or processes, be prepared to discuss change management. These questions are commonly asked when candidates have been at a particular job or company for a long time.

Since changes usually involve other people, interviewers want to know you can influence others and collaborate with them to ensure changes are implemented successfully and viewed positively, especially major changes that may affect many different areas of the company.

Give an example of your ability to implement change and influence people to accept that change

Interviewers want to know you can implement change and influence others to accept it.

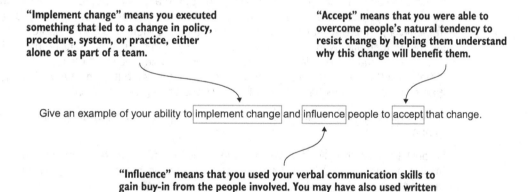

TRANSLATION

We need a change agent in this role, but there might be people here who resist change. Convince me you'll be able to get people to accept the changes you make.

HOW TO ANSWER

Describe a time when you came up with a new idea that would benefit your company, team, or customer and briefly talk through how you got the idea approved, what

104   **CHAPTER 6**   *Problem-solving, time management, negotiation, and change questions*

you did to implement it, and who resisted and why. Then describe specifically what you said or did to overcome objections. Usually this involves learning what resisters' priorities are and how they would benefit, then illustrating how their work lives will ultimately become easier rather than harder once they get past an initial learning period. Lastly, describe what the actual results were after the change was implemented, and include any anecdotes from those early resisters who were later happy about the change.

An important aspect of dealing with change is influencing people and how they deal with change. In many situations, change requires working with people and departments to make smooth transitions.

Example: Clueless Clark, marketing

The interviewer asks, "Give me an example of your ability to implement change and influence people to accept that change."

Clueless Clark's answer

People listen to me when I speak. I'm great at explaining things to people.

Let me give you just one example. A few months ago, our group needed to implement a change with our customers that affected another department. We had to change our internal response processes, so the customers we determined were the most important got priority.

It was a no-brainer change for us in the marketing team, but I wanted to make sure that the other department knew about it so they would start following the change immediately. I knew what I needed to do was to talk to them directly instead of sending them an email. I went over to their office—they're in the next building—and I said to the team lead there, "Hey, we need to talk about a new way to do things." He was initially a little reluctant because he said they were busy, but then I said, "Let's go grab some coffee and chat." He saw I was serious and agreed to coffee.

As I spoke about the changes, he nodded, and I knew my message was getting across to him.

When I finished, he didn't have any questions. I offered to talk with the rest of his team, and he said it wasn't necessary—he would make sure they all got the message.

I felt good about how I was able to tell him what to do.

The next few weeks were a little rocky, but I knew that my chat had made a difference. By the end of the month, we were all using the same new process.

What Clueless Clark got wrong

Clueless Clark started with a sentence that some may find off-putting: "People listen to me when I speak." Our response would be "How can you be so sure?" Right away, he sounds overly confident and arrogant when this question is specifically about influencing people to accept change rather than resist it.

He also lacks any specifics regarding what change he needed to implement and with which department, so it's hard to decipher what this example is about.

It's good that he knew to meet with the team lead of the other department rather than sending an email, but how he opened the meeting is also off-putting: "We need to talk about a new way to do things" is likely to put the other person on the defensive. No wonder that person was reluctant!

Going to have coffee together was a good idea, but we get the impression that Clark did most of the talking while the other person nodded. Clark said that he knew his message was getting across, but whether that was the case is doubtful, especially because that person had no questions and did not want Clark talking to their team.

The fact that Clark said he felt good that he was able to "tell him what to do" shows that he lacks understanding of the main point of this question, which is influencing people to accept change rather than telling people what to do. While the other department was using the new process by the end of the month, there is no evidence that the people there accepted this change willingly.

What Clueless Clark should have done

Clueless Clark should have clearly described what the change was, why it was needed, which other department was impacted, and how it needed to be involved. He should have asked questions to gain an understanding of how and why the other department utilized its current process and then explained why this new process was needed and would actually benefit the company, if not the department specifically.

He should have included specifics on the questions he asked, their responses, what he said about the benefits, how he gained their acceptance, how the new process was implemented, and what the overall results were.

It's quite possible that Clark feels this was a good example, but it really isn't. He should have selected a story that shows not only the specifics of the situation but also his ability to ask questions, understand why the people involved may be resistant to change, describe to them why the change was important, and articulate the benefits of the change to them. Then he should conclude the story by describing how the new process was implemented and what the overall results were.

Describe something you instituted or changed that required collaborative planning with other departments and resulted in improved customer relationships

Interviewers want to know you've made changes that required collaboration with other departments to improve relationships with customers.

TRANSLATION

We need someone who can work well with other departments to successfully implement change, even when those other departments have different priorities and agendas. Also, we find that collaborating with other departments will often improve customer relationships, so please include those results in your answer.

HOW TO ANSWER

Describe a time when you worked with other departments to plan a project involving a change that would affect many departments. Briefly talk through how you approached the people involved, what you did together, and what, if any, issues arose. Describe specifically what you said or did to negotiate and work through any differing or conflicting priorities, what the compromises were, and what you did to implement the change. Lastly, describe what the results were after the change was implemented and how customer relationships were improved.

Example: Jen, sales

The interviewer asks, "Describe something you instituted or changed that required collaborative planning with other departments and resulted in improved customer relationships."

Jen's answer

Sure, let me share a success story from my previous company. I recognized that our customer onboarding needed a major overhaul. Customers found our system very cumbersome, and many times I had to take the time to walk them through it and make sure everything was set up correctly. It was negatively affecting our customer relationships and taking me a lot of extra time. Also, I knew I wasn't the only one in our company this was affecting.

So I talked with other members of the account team and proposed to my boss that we form a task force. My boss had me give a presentation at the monthly leadership meeting outlining the problem and the benefits we'd realize when we solved this, and they approved it. I asked other departments, including customer support, product development, and IT to assign a member to work on it.

First, I initiated cross-functional meetings to get everyone on board. We discussed their perspectives on customer issues and brainstormed solutions together. Then we implemented a more streamlined onboarding process that included a modification to our CRM system and a communication plan so that our departments would stay informed.

The result was that our new onboarding was on average 55% faster for our customers, which translated to higher customer satisfaction. Our new customer satisfaction scores went from an average of 6.9 before this change to 8.5 on a scale of 1 to 10 in their first month, increasing to 8.9 six months later.

What Jen did well

Jen selected an excellent example to share, and she has a good balance of background, actions, and quantified results. She described the problem in a way that is relatable and applicable to other companies, and she was specific in describing what other departments she worked with. She also has a good balance of "I" and "we" statements. Lastly, the length of this answer is appropriate at about 90 seconds; she has some extra time to add in more specifics as described next.

What would make this even better

This is a very good answer, but it can be even more impactful (and go from a B+ to an A+) by adding in a couple more specifics:

In her description of implementing a more streamlined onboarding process that included a modification to their CRM system and a communication plan, she could provide the time frame for this implementation (was it two days, two weeks, two months?). The length of time will show the complexity of the project. Also, what was her role in the implementation? Did she continue to lead this team? If so, how did she balance that role with her sales responsibilities?

It's excellent that Jen includes quantified results, and these numbers would be even more impactful if she added the percentage improvement in customer satisfaction scores. Doing the math, they had about a 23% improvement in only one month and about a 30% improvement after six months.

It is not clear whether there was any impact on revenue as a result of this project, either for that specific account or for the product and/or company as a whole. If yes, then she should include that in her results!

Tell me about a time when you had to deal with frequent changes or unexpected events on the job

Interviewers want to know you can succeed when faced with frequent and unexpected changes.

TRANSLATION

Change is a constant around here, and things often happen that we don't anticipate. Convince me you can be successful in that kind of environment.

HOW TO ANSWER

Start by saying you are energized by change and you thrive in that kind of environment. You might even laugh a bit and say you can't remember a time when you did not work in that kind of environment! Then talk through a work situation that involved constant change and where things came up all the time that were not necessarily expected. Describe what you did to prioritize, stay organized, manage your time, and avoid getting frustrated and what the end results were. If you were in a leadership role, mention how you interacted with your team and kept them on track during these changes. Paint a picture of yourself as someone who takes things in stride and who can be agile and switch gears quickly when needed while still getting the high-priority items completed.

Think about

The following are some things to think about before moving to the next chapter:

- Which example would you select if asked to describe a complex problem you solved?
- What would you say to describe your thought process as you worked through that problem?
- What situation would you use to describe missing an obvious solution to a problem, and how would you describe what you learned as a result of this situation?

108   **CHAPTER 6** *Problem-solving, time management, negotiation, and change questions*

- Which decision would you select if asked to describe your most difficult decision?
- What would you say to describe your decision-making process?
- How do you organize and plan projects? What system or process do you use to ensure their successful and timely completion?
- Which of your previous projects changed the most throughout the time you worked on it? What caused these changes?
- What kinds of things do you do to anticipate possible changes in scope, priorities, or expectations?
- What do you do to avoid any lack of clarity in your projects' scope, deadlines, and expectations?
- What was your most challenging negotiation? How would you describe the issues that arose in a way that would show the complexity but not be overly detailed? How satisfied were you with the outcome? How satisfied do you think the other party or parties were?
- If you were not in a sales or customer-facing role, what interaction with a manager or colleague could you use as your negotiation example?
- How would you rate yourself as a negotiator? In what ways could you improve?
- Which example would you use to describe a change implementation in which you were a key player? What did you do or say to gain acceptance from the people this change impacted?
- Would you use this same example if asked for a situation that involved collaborative planning with other departments? If not, then which scenario would you describe? In what ways did the situation result in improved customer relationships?
- Which of your jobs involved frequent changes or unexpected events? How would you describe your actions and results in those situations?
- What other similar interview questions on these topics might you be asked? For additional examples, see appendix A.

Key takeaways

- Interviewers want specific examples that show how you approach solving problems and making decisions so they can understand how you think. This will help them determine if your approach matches what they need for this job.
- Answers should have enough detail that interviewers can understand your analysis process and the impact of the problem or decision described. However, your descriptions should not be so detailed that it makes your answer too long and the core message gets lost.
- Results for your customer or company should be included to show the importance of the decision or solution.

Key takeaways

- If the interviewer asks you to explain a mistake you made, the answer needs to include what was learned as a result.
- Interviewers want to find out if candidates have the skills to develop win–win solutions to problems. Candidates for jobs that require direct negotiation skills such as sales should be prepared to give specific examples that show positive results.
- Even if the job doesn't necessarily include negotiation skills, candidates may be asked about this topic to understand their persuasion and relationship-building skills.
- Interviewers often ask questions about change, especially if the job or industry involves innovation or technological advances. Some change is expected in most jobs and companies, and applicants need to show they can adapt and thrive.
- Candidates also need to show that they can influence and collaborate with others to successfully implement new changes.

Questions by job function

Now that we've covered general questions that can be asked for many different kinds of roles, we're going to look at questions for some common job functions. We'll cover senior leadership, operations, sales, marketing, finance, IT, and human resources (HR).

For each of these areas, we'll first cover what you should "be sure to sell." This is information about your skills and experience that should be included in your answers. We'll also include sample interview questions and some ideas to think about during your preparation.

Senior leadership

Applicants for senior leadership roles should expect questions that focus more on strategy, vision, and change. They should be prepared to talk about specific metrics showing how they positively affected company results. Candidates could also be asked hypothetical questions about what they would do if they were in a leadership role at the company with which they're interviewing.

These top-level roles usually involve strategic oversight across multiple divisions and functions. Interviewers may want to learn more about the applicant's interaction with their direct reports and the levels reporting to their direct reports.

Job titles in this category may include director, vice president, president, and C-suite (e.g., chief executive officer or CEO, chief operations officer or COO, chief financial officer or CFO, chief marketing officer or CMO, chief information officer or CIO, chief technology officer or CTO, and chief human resources officer or CHRO).

Be sure to sell

It's important to explain how you've improved the business both tactically and strategically, implemented mission and vision, addressed market challenges, designed performance goals and held departments and people accountable for them, interacted and influenced other department heads, implemented new ideas, and gained acceptance for those ideas. Be sure to include metrics on increased revenue, profit, market share, or customer satisfaction and decreased costs, time, and headcount.

Sample questions

- Describe for me a strategy you've implemented that addressed specific market and competitive challenges.
- Tell me about a situation in which you had to translate the mission and vision of the company into individual performance goals.
- Give an example from your leadership experience which demonstrates your ability to implement new ideas that led to company growth.
- If you were our CEO, how would you redefine our strategy to capitalize on the potential of the present market?

Think about

The following are some things to consider:

- What specific example would you use to describe a strategy you implemented to address market challenges?
- How do you go about translating a company's mission and vision into individual performance goals?
- Which new ideas of yours have led to your current or previous company's growth? How did you influence people to accept those ideas, and how would you describe the way the ideas were implemented?
- How would you describe your interactions with different levels of the organization (not just other leaders)?

Operations

People in operations positions are responsible for executing and delivering the products and services that the marketing team markets and the sales team sells. They can be involved in manufacturing, supply chain, and customer service-related processes.

Interviewers who are hiring for operations roles want to understand how the applicant has specifically improved systems and practices in the past. They want to know the specific processes and the quantified results. Interviewers are looking for specific examples to determine if the applicant will be able to be successful in this role.

Be sure to sell

Your answers should include how you improved things like efficiency, productivity, customer satisfaction, quality, vendor performance, and on-time delivery. Be sure to include metrics on percentage improvement, customer ratings, reduced costs, time, headcount, and/or errors.

Sample questions

- Describe for me a new method or process you initiated that resulted in maximizing efficiency and productivity. What performance metrics did you measure, and what were the specific improvements?
- Give an example from your leadership experience that demonstrates your ability to implement new ideas which led to reduced costs.
- Describe a situation that shows how you used technology to improve the client or customer experience.

Think about

The following are some things to consider:

- Which metrics have you achieved in your past positions that demonstrate maximizing efficiency and productivity?
- Which new ideas of yours have led to your previous company's reduced costs? How did you influence people to accept those ideas, and how would you describe the way they were implemented?
- What example would you use to describe how you used technology to improve the customer experience?

Sales

People in sales are not only selling products and services—they are also selling themselves. Therefore, interviewers will want to experience how applicants for sales roles will sell themselves. Candidates should see the interviewer as a customer and be prepared to demonstrate their sales abilities right there in the interview.

Applicants will also be expected to explain how they approach the sales process, build relationships, use best practices, and establish trust and rapport. In addition, they must show they are comfortable persuading, influencing, and dealing with uncertainty, as well as how they've handled difficult sales and customers. It is critically important for sales candidates to describe their successes using quantified results.

Be sure to sell

For a sales leadership role, show how you've built and/or led sales teams to successfully perform and achieve or exceed their sales targets. For an individual contributor role, explain how you've personally excelled and achieved or exceeded your sales targets.

Sales **113**

Also, talk about how you've identified and built relationships with customers and collaborated with other departments internally to meet or exceed customer expectations.

Sample questions

- Tell me about something you introduced that you would describe as a best practice in sales leadership.
- Describe your most complex and challenging sales success.
- Give an example of a project that required you to understand and interpret a customer's needs and requirements and relate them back to product or service requirements.
- Tell me about a project you led that provided visibility and insight to executive management based on input and feedback from prospects and customers.
- Give an example of something you instituted or changed that required collaborative planning with other departments and resulted in improved customer relationships.

Example: Jen, sales

The interviewer asks Jen, "Describe your most complex and challenging sales success."

Jen's answer

Oh, I'd love to tell you about that! Obviously, I've worked on plenty of complex deals in my career, but one really stands out because of the number of people who were involved.

It was at my previous company, which had offices all over the globe. I saw on your LinkedIn profile that you've worked for a large global company before, so you know what that's like.

Our sales team was divided by products and geography, which usually worked very well, but with some customers, there were overlaps.

One of our sales team members in Germany contacted me because he had a potential sale with a new customer who also wanted product support in the US. I was delighted to work with him, and as we met with the customer, it became clear that they also wanted product support in South America, so we brought that team in also.

In addition, the customer was looking for some unusual features, and to make that happen we had to bring in some of our team from India. All these different groups meant lots of meetings at unusual times, as you can imagine.

As the potential scope of the project grew, we involved our senior leaders, and so did the customer.

As you know, the more people who become part of the project, the more complex it becomes. In addition, the potential customer also had a subsidiary in Ireland that

114 **CHAPTER 7** *Questions by job function*

(continued)

joined the meetings several weeks into the discussions, and they had some different issues that we needed to address.

The way I managed it was to make sure we had very clear communication inside the company and with the customer.

The result was an initial order for more than $8 million, which was the biggest order we'd ever received from a new customer in the history of the company. Working with all of our teams and making sure everyone was on the same page really paid off. That sale put me and several other teammates way over our sales numbers for the quarter and earned us spots in the company's yearly reward trip to Hawaii. That was an amazing trip, and the president personally gave us each a special award for bringing in that business.

What Jen did well

She selected a good example with excellent results and definitely showed the complexity of the customer's needs. This example also shows good collaboration between Jen and colleagues in other countries and senior leaders at her company.

What would make this even better

Jen described the complexity of this situation in a bit too much detail; it was hard to follow because of the numerous people and countries involved. She should leave off the part about the customer also having a subsidiary in Ireland, because that didn't seem to be critical.

Jen spent almost her whole answer setting up the situation and gave very little information on what actions she took. All she said was, "The way I managed it was to make sure we had very clear communication inside the company and with the customer." By doing what? What kind of system or process did she set up to make sure everyone was on the same page, and what steps did she and her colleagues take to get the sale and close the deal?

Lastly, she should leave out the part about the trip to Hawaii; story results should only be about how the company, customer, team, community, or something else besides herself benefited, rather than how she personally benefited. Also, if this new company cannot afford to give that kind of reward trip to its sales staff, the interviewer might be turned off or assume she wouldn't want to work there.

Think about

The following are some things to consider:

- Which example would you use to describe your most proud sales accomplishment?
- What are some examples of dealing with difficult customers you can use to highlight your sales skills?
- What other difficulties have you faced (such as launching a new product, starting a new territory, or managing customer complaints) that highlight your skills and abilities?

- How have you worked with other salespeople and other departments to gain a new customer or close a deal?

Marketing

Marketing includes a creative side, including designing advertising, social media, and public relations campaigns; a business side, including product development and product management; and an analytical side, including researching and analyzing market and competitor data.

Applicants for marketing positions will be expected to share specific examples that include quantified results such as improved brand performance or increased revenue or market share. They should also be prepared to talk about how they worked collaboratively with other departments and with customers and external partners.

Be sure to sell

Discuss how you've developed and implemented marketing strategies that get results; conducted market analysis and research; managed projects, budgets, timelines, and business partners; and executed campaigns. Also, talk about how you've identified and built relationships with customers and business partners and collaborated with other departments including sales to meet or exceed customer expectations.

Interviewers may also be interested in your feedback about their marketing strategy, so part of your preparation should be reviewing their marketing. Consider what ideas you would have for marketing their products and how you have successfully implemented similar marketing strategies in the past.

Sample questions

- Give an example of a comprehensive and cohesive marketing strategy you developed and implemented that resulted in increased brand awareness.
- Describe a market analysis you conducted that identified challenges and opportunities for growth, including what you did after the analysis to affect change.
- Tell me about a time when you worked through the planning of a project; what issues arose, and how did you work through them?
- Describe a time when you or your team had to respond to a negative issue or a crisis very quickly.
- Tell me about a time when you successfully collaborated to diffuse a conflict between the sales and marketing teams.

Example: Clueless Clark, marketing

The interviewer asks, "Tell me about a time when you worked through the planning of a project; what issues arose, and how did you work through them?"

CHAPTER 7 *Questions by job function*

(continued)

Clueless Clark's answer

At my last company, we had a large marketing team separated into two groups that supported different kinds of customers. My part of the team focused on companies in the technical sector, and the other team focused on nontechnical companies.

We took on a big project with a new customer, and my boss decided that we needed all hands on deck for this one, so everyone worked on it. It's not the way I would have done it, but that's what my manager wanted, so I supported it.

Stacey from the other group was put in charge, and we met as a team to develop a timeline and accountabilities. The first few weeks went well, and then we hit a snag. You see, that team was not as experienced as our team, and one of the members had too many other projects he was responsible for, and he got behind on his deliverables. I recommended that someone from my team take it over because I thought that he was much better prepared, but Stacey said it was a learning experience for him. I then suggested that we could break up the deliverables and my team could take some of the smaller parts and he could still get some learning, and that's what we did.

I worked closely with my team and had brief daily meetings to make sure we met all of our deliverables, and we picked up the slack when the other team missed them.

The project was completed in the assigned eight weeks thanks to me and my team stepping up. Our boss was very happy, and the client really appreciated it.

What Clueless Clark got wrong

First, Clueless Clark should not have implied something negative about his manager ("it's not the way I would have done it") or mentioned that the other team wasn't as experienced unless he included why that was related to the snag that occurred.

It's difficult to understand this example because Clark left out specifics such as what kind of project this was, what aspect of it was Clark's team's responsibility, what department Stacey oversaw, and which deliverables did Clark's team take over. On which items did they have to "pick up the slack?" How did Clark work with his team; what did he and they do besides hold daily meetings? (What's important is not that he held meetings but rather what was accomplished in those meetings.)

Also, what were the results of this project besides being done on time? How did the project benefit the customer and Clark's company?

What Clueless Clark should have done

Clueless Clark should have clearly described what the project was, the obstacles they needed to overcome, the specific actions he and his team took, and the results/benefit/impact of the project. He should never say anything negative about anyone he works for or with, and he should give credit to everyone involved for the project being completed on time rather than patting himself on the back so blatantly ("The project was completed in the assigned eight weeks thanks to me and my team stepping up").

Think about

The following are some things to consider:

- What would you select if asked for an example of a comprehensive and cohesive marketing strategy you developed and implemented that resulted in increased brand awareness?
- What kinds of market analyses have you conducted that identified challenges and opportunities for growth? How did you use that information to affect change?
- Have you or your team ever had to respond to a sudden or unexpected negative issue or a crisis? What steps did you take, and what were the results?
- What kinds of conflicts have you experienced between the sales and marketing departments? How did you collaborate with others to resolve the issues?

Finance

Finance professionals include those in accounting, financial planning and analysis, and treasury functions. They must be able to complete complex and detailed work while also communicating and collaborating with all departments inside an organization.

Interviewers want to know applicants have the specific finance skills and experience they need and will also want examples of the ability to communicate and collaborate with other departments inside and vendors, partners, banks, and customers outside of the organization. This is especially true when the company is faced with financial challenges or other major changes.

Be sure to sell

Talk about how you've followed proper financial processes, rules, and regulations; tracked and reported on company performance; monitored company-wide budgets and forecasts; utilized financial systems; implemented improvements; conducted analysis; and made recommendations based on that analysis. Also, give examples of how you've interacted with senior leadership, investors, vendors, customers, banks, and lenders.

Sample questions

- Give me an example from your leadership experience that demonstrates your ability to implement a major change to improve a company's financial performance.
- Tell me about something you instituted that improved internal finance processes.
- Describe a situation where you worked with senior leadership to transform your company to an environment where ongoing analysis of results became part of the culture. What types of benchmarking, analysis, and reporting did you institute?
- Tell me about a difficult relationship you've had with a key financial vendor, banker, or lender; what issues arose, and how did you resolve them?

- Describe for me an early warning system you've put in place that alerted senior leadership to P&L results variations.

Think about

The following are some things to consider:

- Which example would you share that demonstrates your ability to implement a major change to improve a company's financial performance?
- What kinds of things have you instituted that improved internal finance processes?
- Have you worked for a company that had an environment where ongoing analysis of financial results was part of the culture? What was your role in contributing to or facilitating that kind of environment?
- What kinds of relationships have you had with financial vendors, bankers, or lenders? Do you have an example of a time when issues arose, and if so, how did you resolve them?

Information technology

IT professionals not only develop code and design systems; some also interact with internal and external customers to ensure the systems they develop will meet the needs of their target audience. They often manage large projects, including new technology implementations, so it will be important to demonstrate project management skills.

Applicants for these roles should be ready to explain their accomplishments to both technical and nontechnical recruiters and interviewers and articulate how the systems made a difference or delivered results for internal groups, the company, and external customers.

Be sure to sell

Be prepared to clearly describe how you've used technology to solve business problems and managed projects, budgets, timelines, scope creep, and expectations while collaborating with those outside of IT. Also, show how you've been able to communicate complex and technical information to nontechnical people and how you have saved time, money, and/or headcount and reduced errors by implementing technology solutions. For a leadership role, you'll want to highlight how you've motivated, led, and retained technical staff.

Sample questions

- Give me an example that demonstrates your ability to translate organizational needs into workable technology business solutions.
- Tell me about a time when you used technology to drive business results.

- In this role, you will need to balance your technical knowledge and your ability to communicate with a wider nontechnical audience; how have you navigated this delicate balance in the past?
- With most technical projects, it is important to balance the need for quality, deadlines, and costs. Give me an example that demonstrates your ability to balance these needs.
- Give me an example of a situation where you developed criteria for measuring the performance of the tech organization. What metrics did you measure, and what results did you report?

Think about

The following are some things to consider:

- How will you explain your technical skills to a nontechnical interviewer?
- What situation would you describe if asked for an example of using technology to drive business results?
- How would you describe how you've balanced communicating with both technical and nontechnical audiences?
- Which project would you use to describe how you've balanced the need for quality, deadlines, and costs?
- What have you done to avoid scope creep on your projects?
- If you're in a leadership role, do you use different leadership styles or approaches when leading technical staff and nontechnical staff? How would you describe those differences?

Human resources

HR professionals focus on the people side of the organization and view all employees as their internal clients. They need to be comfortable dealing with both black-and-white scenarios, where legal requirements or company policies dictate actions, and many gray areas, especially when employee performance and/or compensation is involved.

Candidates for HR roles need to show that they can work well with people in difficult situations. Interviewers want to know that you will support and help build the company culture, which can include hiring and retaining the best talent.

Be sure to sell

You will want to highlight your ability to select, hire, develop, and retain employees, as well as what you do to stay current on federal, state, and municipal employment laws, maintain confidentiality of organizational and employee information, and use both your experience and judgment when it comes to managing sensitive or delicate situations. Also, make sure to mention your ability to collaborate and influence people in management and other departments and to manage projects, budgets, and timelines.

Sample questions

- What do you think are the most important qualifications and characteristics an HR executive should possess in today's business climate?
- You've done some recruiting; if you were interviewing candidates for this position, what would you look for?
- How do you help your organization attract new talent, guard against poor hires, and retain its top talent?
- Tell me about a situation where you felt your ability to manage confidential information was being tested.
- What example can you cite of your ability to apply prudent judgment in a delicate HR-related situation?

Think about

The following are some things to consider:

- What questions would you ask if you were recruiting to fill this role?
- How would you demonstrate you can connect with people as well as enforce company rules and policies?
- How would you describe how you help your organization attract new talent, guard against poor hires, and retain its top talent?
- Can you think of a time when your ability to manage confidential information may have been tested? What did you do or say in that situation to maintain confidentiality?
- Which example would you use to demonstrate your ability to apply prudent judgment in a delicate HR-related situation?

Key takeaways

- In addition to preparing for general questions, you should also be ready for specific questions about the role you're pursuing.
- In this chapter, we've provided information on functional skills and experience that should be included in your answers if the job is in senior leadership, operations, sales, marketing, finance, IT, or HR.
- We also included sample interview questions for these job functions and things to consider as part of your preparation.

Part 3

Don't make these mistakes

In this part, we'll look at mistakes to avoid so that you'll be successful in your interviews. These include things like not doing your homework, thinking you can "wing it," not practicing your answers, and not testing out your technology in advance of video interviews.

Another mistake is not being real—that is, not being your authentic self, or trying to give a memorized answer because you think it's what the interviewer wants to hear.

We also discuss listening for the "heart" of the question and pausing if you need to think, so that you won't ramble. We provide a list of things that candidates say or do during interviews because they think they sound good, but they actually don't, and we talk about the things to find out and say to close your interview in an impactful way.

Not doing your homework, not being real, or leaving without . . .

Preparation can make the difference between an okay interview and an excellent one. You need to spend the time preparing and practicing so that the best answers come quickly and clearly. Don't make the mistake of thinking that you can wing it. Part of that preparation is getting ready to show up as you, not someone who has memorized answers to questions. Another benefit of being prepared is that you may feel more relaxed and ready to respond to unexpected questions.

Interviewers also expect candidates to follow some simple etiquette rules, which include arriving early and dressing appropriately for the role. They believe candidates display their best at interviews and will judge people negatively if they don't meet basic expectations.

At the end of the interview, you can take actions to reinforce the message that you are a good match for this role.

Not doing your homework

Interviewers expect you to be prepared to answer questions (unless the question they ask is a very unusual one that is designed to surprise you). If it appears you are not fully prepared or can't answer basic questions, that will be a red flag for interviewers. Your lack of preparation could give them the impression you're not very interested in this job or, if you're hired, you won't do the necessary work to perform well. Another way to show your interest is to prepare good questions about the job and company.

CHAPTER 8   *Not doing your homework, not being real, or leaving without...*

Assuming being an interviewer will make you a good interviewee

Those who have been in management roles have typically spent time interviewing candidates for open positions. As discussed in chapter 5's insider story, managers may have grown comfortable in that interviewer role, and consequently they assume they will do well as interviewees. But it is very different being on the other side of the desk! Interviewers know what they're looking for (which may be slightly different or more than just what is listed on the job description), know what questions they'll ask, and use their own method and biases when evaluating answers. This can make it easy for managerial candidates to think that additional preparation isn't necessary, but it is.

Not investing time in preparation or thinking that you can wing it

You probably won't make this mistake because you're reading this book! You have two roadmaps in your preparation: your resume and the job description. Be ready to discuss your experience and give examples of when you demonstrated each of the items listed. Also, think through your answers to the questions described in the previous chapters.

Example: Clueless Clark, marketing

The interviewer asks, "What are your career goals?"

Clueless Clark's answer

Career goals? Well, my immediate career goal is to get this job.

After that, I'm looking to move up in my career, which is why I'm interested in this position and company. I will be looking for an opportunity to move into management at some point because I think I would be great at managing other people. I've managed people on projects, and I think that would translate well to moving into a supervisory role.

What Clueless Clark got wrong

It's quite common for candidates to give an answer like this, saying their goal is to get this job. What they don't realize is this question refers to goals *after* getting this job. Interviewers who ask this question are looking to hire someone (a) who has career goals they can articulate and (b) whose goals will fit in with their company and culture.

This is a very common question, and Clueless Clark's short and general answer makes it sound like he didn't expect to be asked it. This could make the interviewer think Clark is not serious about the job because he didn't bother to spend time planning a good answer.

What Clueless Clark should have done

As we discussed in chapter 1, it's important to research the company and get a sense of its philosophies and practices on things like internal applications and promoting from within. Your answer should demonstrate your desire to have a long career with that company and that you don't see it as just one rung on your career ladder.

Clueless Clark should say he doesn't necessarily have specific titles and time frames in mind but he wants to continue developing his skills in project and people management (along with other relevant and needed skills in this job) so that down the road he can progress into a management role. He should talk about some of the projects where he's held a leadership role and include the relevant results he achieved on those projects. He should end by saying he'd like the opportunity to advance to other positions that might become available at this company at the appropriate time, after he's succeeded in this role and built additional experience.

Not practicing your answers to difficult or delicate questions

If anything in your background is sensitive, take the time not only to think through your answers but also to practice them so that they roll off your tongue without any hesitation or filler words such as "um" and "uh."

These can be things like your reasons for leaving your current and/or previous positions, why you have an employment gap, why you're looking to change fields or industries, why you feel you're ready for a higher-level position, or even why you have a college degree that doesn't relate to the type of job you seek.

You can practice with a friend, while stuck in traffic, or in front of a mirror. You can even record yourself using video conferencing software such as Zoom.

Not planning good questions (or enough questions) to ask the interviewer

In chapter 2, we discussed how to answer the common last question in an interview: "What questions do you have?" You must be ready for this and take the time to prepare questions to ask beyond the common "What's a typical day like?" (which is only applicable for entry-level and junior positions, because for other levels, there is no such thing as a typical day!). You have the opportunity to impress with the questions you ask, so make sure they show your experience and expertise and that you've done your homework. Also, anyone who is truly interested and excited about a job will have numerous questions.

One time, Barbara was interviewing a candidate who she thought was a great fit for the role and who had great answers throughout the interview. When the time came to ask his questions, he asked two very good ones. Then Barbara asked the candidate what other questions he had, and he said he had no other questions. At that point, Barbara concluded he must not have been as interested as he said he was, and he did not get hired.

Show your genuine enthusiasm, curiosity, and excitement by having a long list of possible questions. You can always ask how they got started at that company or in their field and what kinds of people are successful there.

Insider story: Asking good questions can get you hired

Our friend who is an HR director told us about a candidate for an inventory control specialist who had good answers to the questions he was asked in his interview but nothing had jumped out that made him especially stand out. When the time came for

126 **CHAPTER 8** *Not doing your homework, not being real, or leaving without . . .*

(continued)

him to ask questions, he asked several that demonstrated his knowledge and excitement about the work, including about the inventory systems, records management systems, product ordering systems, tracking tools, and delivery issues. After hearing the answers to his questions, he then briefly talked about his experience with those systems and issues. The HR director was so impressed by the specificity of his questions that she hired him.

Not testing out your tech in advance (for video interviews)

Video interviews are extremely common, and companies use different platforms. Make sure you have the link, the meeting ID, and any other information you'll need to join the meeting on time. Check your lighting and your web camera's angle and consider doing a test run with a friend if you've not had a video interview before.

Make sure you also check to see what will be visible to the other person on screen. What will they see that is behind you or next to you? Interviewers tell horror stories about candidates sitting in front of an unmade bed or messy room, which sends the message that the candidate isn't neat or doesn't care.

Make sure your webcam is directly facing your eyes rather than sitting low on your desk (use books if you need to elevate your monitor or laptop). Remember: if you are looking down at the interviewer, they are looking up at you, and most of us wouldn't want people talking to us while looking at our chin! Also, if you have a ceiling fan, make sure it's either turned off or not visible on screen, because it can be quite distracting.

Insider story: Tech and scheduling issues can still lead to job offers

Our friend who works in the insurance industry was recruited by a search firm for a position at a competitor of her current company. Her initial video interview was scheduled with the company's HR representative using a videoconference platform she wasn't familiar with. She downloaded the software to her PC and thought everything was working, but when the time came for the interview, she couldn't join the meeting (and she's quite tech savvy, having worked in IT). After several frustrating minutes, she ended up using her phone instead, but she was late to arrive. She was flustered and told the interviewer of her technical problems and difficulty using the platform. They said they had had similar issues with other candidates and not to worry about it. Our friend was able to make it through the interview, but she thought she did horribly (she said it was the worst job interview she's ever had).

She had written off this job, thinking she had blown it. She told herself she wasn't all that interested anyway. About a week later, she got called back for a one-on-one interview with the hiring manager, and she figured she'd do the interview as practice. It turned out the two of them hit it off well, and our friend ended up getting the job. She accepted the position because of how much she liked the person who is now her boss.

A phone interview can also have mishaps. A new college grad interviewing for his first full-time job at a small company had a phone interview scheduled with the hiring manager after submitting his resume for a position posted on their company's website. Their HR person scheduled the phone interview, and the new grad was prepared to take the call at the scheduled time. He waited and waited, but the call didn't come. Rather than giving up, he found their main phone number online and called to let them know he had an interview scheduled and with whom but they hadn't called. They found the hiring manager, who joined the call and promptly apologized, saying he was having issues with a new calendaring system. They laughed about it, had their interview, and it went well. After a couple of on-site interviews, he received and accepted the job offer.

The lesson here is problems sometimes happen; technology doesn't work properly, and calendars get mixed up, but if you can get past these issues, remain calm, be yourself, and perform in the interview despite initially feeling flustered, you can still get the job offer.

Not mapping out your directions, parking options, and commute time (for on-site interviews)

Because of mobile map applications from Apple and Google, there is no excuse for being late anymore. Check the traffic patterns during the time frame of your interview, and make sure you know how long it will take to get there (you may even want to do a practice drive, because neither the Apple nor the Google mapping system is completely accurate 100% of the time). Remember not only to find out where to park but also to allow extra time in case parking spots are limited. Lastly, make sure you have a contact phone number in case of an unexpected delay.

Not arriving early

Whether your interview is by phone, video, or in person, it's important to arrive a few minutes early. This also requires planning and preparation. You do not want the interviewer to be wondering where you are at the scheduled time. It goes without saying that being late will very likely eliminate you from consideration, and when it comes to job interviews, being on time means being a few minutes early.

Dressing inappropriately or wearing cologne or loud jewelry

For most companies and positions, there is no longer a need to wear a business suit to an interview. One step up from business casual is usually appropriate (for men, that means dress shirt and slacks but no tie; for women, that means a nice blouse and skirt or slacks), but when in doubt, ask the person who is coordinating your interview for their recommendations.

For on-site interviews, you will likely be in a small office or conference room, and what you think is an acceptable amount of cologne is likely to be different than someone else's, so it is best to wear none. Also, avoid loud jewelry, either literally (i.e., bracelets that clack with every wrist movement) or figuratively (i.e., loud colors or unusual designs). You do not want your interviewer to be distracted by your accessories!

Not being real

The focus of this book is to give you information to help you prepare for interviews, but that doesn't mean you should show up as someone you're not. Take these suggestions and put your spin on them to ensure you come across as authentic. Interviewers want to see the real you so they can be sure you will fit the job and organization. If they don't think you're being real, they will be reluctant to move you forward in the hiring process.

You may be wondering how to respond if you do not know the answer to a particular question. These questions are often technical in nature, or they have to do with a specific function in the job. If that happens, it's best to admit that you don't know the answer and then talk about something similar you are familiar with. You can even sell this as a strength: you know a lot, but you also know what you don't know. It's important to be comfortable saying, "I don't know," which will likely come across as a refreshing change from candidates who try to wing it with BS.

Insider story: Being real vs. being right

In one of my (Barbara's) past positions, we had a program whereby executive candidates could come on-site for a day of mock interviews. These included sessions on common questions, difficult questions, and questions based specifically on a job description that was representative of a job for which they expected to interview. One of my candidate clients was a CFO who had impeccable credentials and several great success stories. I had coached her prior to that day to get her resume ready and prepare her for interviews, so I had talked with her on a regular basis for weeks and felt that I knew her well professionally.

During her mock interviews, she struggled with the flow of her answers. She kept interrupting herself and asking if she could start over. Or she would remember something and include it out of order in her story. I provided her feedback on her answers, including the positive things she had said to address her self-doubt.

We went out to lunch at midday, and during our conversation about her struggling to articulate her stories, she said she was trying to give the right answers. I said, "Rather than focusing on being right, focus on being real, because there's no such thing as a perfect answer." She told me that was a light bulb moment for her, and her interviews that afternoon went much more smoothly.

Not being yourself in your answers

There is nothing more important than being real, being human, and being yourself in an interview! Even if you give perfect answers (although there is no such thing) and have excellent qualifications, if interviewers feel you are giving them canned or rehearsed answers, you're trying to tell them what they want to hear, or you're giving BS answers, you will not be hired. If you stumble, need time to think, don't understand the question and ask for clarification, or appear nervous, that is okay! People who aren't nervous don't really want the job.

Trying to pass off a memorized answer as authentic

We repeat: if interviewers feel you are giving them canned or rehearsed answers, they won't feel like they're getting to know the real you and will likely find someone else they trust more (who may be less qualified than you!). Unless you have a drama, theater, or acting background, you won't be able to make a memorized answer sound authentic, so don't even try!

Example: Clueless Clark, marketing

The interviewer asks, "Tell me about yourself."

Clueless Clark's answer

I'm glad you asked. I've been in the marketing field for more than 10 years, and I've had a lot of success in my past jobs. My managers have appreciated my good work ethic and have complimented me on that in my performance reviews.

In my current job, I ran a project that increased our number of new leads by more than 25%. This meant that the sales team had a lot more to work with. In the following quarters, our sales increased 10% in one quarter and more than 15% in the next quarter. My boss agreed that our updated focused marketing strategies had a lot to do with that increase.

At this point, the interviewer interrupts, and asks, "What do you mean by focused marketing strategies?"

Clueless Clark continues his answer

The company was looking to increase the number of customers for a new product line. Without getting into the details, we researched what kind of customers would be most interested in this new offering and created profiles of this target audience, including their media habits. We then tailored our marketing strategies to connect with those audiences.

The interviewer then says, "Okay, thank you. Tell me more about you."

Clueless Clark's answer

Oh, getting back to me: as I said, I've been in the field 10 years and have had a lot of success, and my managers have appreciated my good work ethic.

Outside of work, I'm a real baseball nut. I'm a huge fan of the Arizona Diamondbacks and have sometimes put together customer promotions around a baseball theme and had customers come to a private box area at one of the games.

I also help coach my daughter Ginny's T-ball team. She's only five but she's great.

What Clueless Clark got wrong

Clueless Clark had a pretty good opening and started to describe some of his projects, including impressive results, but when he was interrupted, he clearly lost his

(continued)

train of thought. He was likely interrupted because the interviewer wanted more specifics after his general statement about "focused marketing strategies" (this could be a key component of the marketing job for which he's interviewing).

He answered the interviewer's question and gave a brief description of what he meant, although he prefaced it with "Without getting into the details," which could be off-putting. If the new product offering is confidential, he should have said he's unable to go into details due to confidentiality.

When the interviewer then asked for more about him, Clark returned to the beginning of what he had prepared for this answer, which is a sign that he was likely giving a memorized answer. After his initial statements, he gave mostly personal information about being a baseball fan and coaching his daughter. He briefly mentions customer promotions, which could be relevant, but since he provided no specifics or results, there was very little impact.

What Clueless Clark should have done

Clueless Clark should have prepared his answer by knowing his talking points without memorizing his answer word-for-word. As discussed in chapter 2, he should start by thanking the interviewer for their time and saying something to build rapport. He should then name some of his top skills that relate to the position and describe one or two specific accomplishments with results. He should close by talking about why he's interested in this position and the company. His complete answer should be less than a minute in length.

Trying to pass off a BS answer as authentic

We'll say it again: if interviewers do not feel you are being authentic, they will find someone else who is. When Barbara first started out as an interviewer, she read many books that tell you what to say in response to interview questions. Therefore, whenever she was given one of these answers, she would respond, "Yeah, I also read the book that told you to say that, so now give me your real answer." Needless to say, she got many deer-in-the-headlights facial expressions after she said that!

Ignoring the importance of rapport-building

Employers will hire someone they like who is 75% qualified over someone who is 100% qualified who they don't like or don't feel they got to know during the interview. We cannot emphasize it enough: building a human connection with the interviewer is crucial. Therefore, showing genuine interest in them; listening; and being prepared, curious, enthusiastic, and excited will go a long way in building rapport.

Leaving without . . .

You're just about at the end of the interview and you're feeling good; however, you're not done yet. There are a few specific things you need to do before you finish.

Finding out the next steps and time frames

At the end of chapter 2, we discussed how best to answer the most common last question that is asked in interviews: "What questions do you have?"

After you ask your questions as described in that chapter, your last question should be to find out their next steps in the selection process and what their anticipated time frame is for hiring someone. If, for example, the hiring manager is about to go on vacation, or they have other fires they're putting out before they can hire someone, it will help you avoid stress when a couple of weeks go by and you haven't heard anything.

Getting the names and contact information of all interviewers

While it's no longer necessary to send a handwritten thank-you note, thank-you emails and messages are still important and will show you're not someone who just does the bare minimum. They also give you an opportunity to get your name in front of your interviewer again, reiterate why you're excited and feel you're a great fit for the role, and show your respect by being appreciative of their time.

To send a thank-you, you will need the names and contact information for all your interviewers if you don't already have them. Even for group interviews, send all interviewers their own individual thank-you message. If you're on-site, you can ask for business cards or stop at the reception desk to get this information. For virtual interviews, ask the person who scheduled you for names and contact information. Don't do what Clueless Clark did after one of his interviews: he was so confident and pleased with himself after completing what he thought was a great interview that he left without getting the names and contact information of his interviewers. He was then stuck and couldn't send a thank-you or do any kind of follow-up with his interviewers. It is not much of a surprise that he received a standard "decline" email from the company about two weeks later.

Closing the sale

An interview is just like a sales meeting, where you are the product being considered for purchase. Any good salesperson knows how important it is to close the sale before letting the prospective customer walk away. To do this, at the end of the interview, reiterate your interest and enthusiasm about the job and briefly summarize why you're such a great fit for the role and organization.

You can say something like, "I'm excited about this job and feel that I'm a great fit because of X, Y, and Z, as we've discussed. I really look forward to continuing the conversation in the next stage of your selection process. What are our next steps and time frames?" (Notice that by referring to "our" next steps, you are already acting as if you work there.) Then, with a firm handshake (if on-site), direct eye contact, and a smile, thank them for their time and say goodbye.

Think about

The following are some things to consider before moving to the next chapter:

- Think back to previous interviews; what questions were the most difficult for you? How can you be more prepared now?

- Which method of practicing your answers will be most effective for you? Would you do it in front of a mirror, with a friend, recording yourself on your computer or phone, or can you think of another way?
- Are there any answers that could sound canned? How can you adjust them so they sound real and authentic?
- What are some ways you have built rapport with people in a short period of time? Which of these can you use in your interviews?
- What are some good questions you could ask the interviewer that show your interest in the job and the company?
- What can you say to close the sale?

Key takeaways

- Interviewers expect you'll be ready for the interview, so it's important you are. You will need to prepare answers, practice, and be ready with your own questions. It's important to look and sound your best.
- Successful applicants show up authentically. They do not use canned answers. Instead, they review interview questions and suggestions and create real answers that are right for them. They also know the importance of building rapport with interviewers.
- You should do a few things at the end of every interview to wrap up the process. This includes ending the interview with a positive message that reinforces why you're a great fit for the job.

Not hearing the question, the whole question, and the heart of the question

Many candidates think they need to quickly answer all interview questions. This can add a lot of pressure and increase stress. They may start planning their answer after they hear the first part of the question, which means they might miss other important information. It's better to focus on really hearing what the interviewer is asking and then taking a moment to process it. That pause can give you time to give the best answer, which is not necessarily the fastest one.

Not letting the interviewer finish their question before planning your answer

It is important to listen intently and allow your brain to fully drink in the question before deciding how best to answer it. Sometimes the most important part of the question comes at the end. In all her years of conducting mock interviews with clients, Barbara has often received answers that didn't fully address the question. When debriefing afterward, the client focused on the first part and completely missed the heart of the question.

To make this point, Barbara sometimes asks a question such as, "Tell me about a time when you led a difficult, complex, long-term project from start to finish that required collaborating with other departments."

She has heard so many clients describe glorious examples of difficult, complex, long-term projects they led from start to finish. But they often made no mention of collaborating with other departments, which is the main point (or heart) of the

134   CHAPTER 9   *Not hearing the question, the whole question, and the heart of the question*

question! Had they forced themselves to listen to the whole question before formulating their answer, they would have talked through their story in a way that directly gave Barbara what she was looking for in their answers.

Not taking a brief pause to allow yourself to truly understand the question prior to starting your answer

As we've stated, interviewers are not fond of canned or rehearsed answers. Therefore, it's okay to stop and think for a few seconds before beginning to talk. There is a lot that your brain can do in those few seconds:

- Seek first to understand the question; then decide how best to answer it.
- Select which of your stories would most fit the question.
- Decide how to customize that story to directly relate to the organization and this open position.
- Begin your answer and enter the starting gate strong.

One of Barbara's pet peeves is when a candidate or client, when asked for an example, responds with "The first example that comes to mind is . . . ." She then thinks (but doesn't say), "No, I want your *best* example, which is often not the first one you think of!"

The best example is one that includes positive results. If you can't come up with a story that directly relates to the question, use one that is similar or adjacent to the topic being asked about. It's okay to say something like, "I haven't had that exact thing happen, but here's an example that is similar."

If you need to buy time to give yourself a chance to think of an answer, it's also okay to admit that you're not thinking of one immediately (interviewers will appreciate your not giving a canned answer). You can say "Hmmm, let me think" or "I know that's happened before; let me take a few seconds to think."

There are some questions you should be ready for without having to stop and think, such as "Tell me about yourself" and "Why are you interested in this job?" (see chapter 2), but for other questions, especially those asking for examples from your past, it is appropriate to pause a few seconds before answering.

Insider story: Unusual questions

There is a wide world of unusual, unexpected interview questions an interviewer might ask, many of which have no right answer. Some of these questions are asked as a way of getting you to describe yourself in a unique way, such as, "If you were an animal, which animal would you be and why?" My favorite of this type of question is "If you were a superhero, what would your superpower be and why?" A graphic designer was once asked, "If you were a font, which font would you be and why?"

Some firms might ask questions that require candidates to guesstimate an answer, such as "How many airplanes do you think are in the sky right now?" or "How many diapers do you think are sold each year in the US?" Marketing candidates may be asked to guesstimate the market size of a particular product or service. The interviewers in these cases are not looking for a correct answer; they want to get a sense of how the candidate approaches and analyzes problems when there is no easy answer or clear solution.

To answer these types of questions, it's important to pause, think, decide on your answer, and explain the thought process that led you to arrive at that answer.

Some interviewers like to ask brainteaser questions to see how a person thinks and how they react under pressure. These questions have a correct answer, unlike the previous ones mentioned. One of my favorite questions of this type is "You wake up one morning and the power is out. You know you have 12 black socks and 8 blue ones. How many socks do you need to pull out before you've got a match?" (Answer: you only have two colors, so to get a matching pair, pull out three socks.) Another favorite is "You're on the road to Truthtown. At a fork in the road, one road leads to Truthtown (where everyone tells the truth) and the other to Liartown (where everyone lies). At the fork is a man from one of those towns, but you don't know which town. You can ask one question to discover the way. How do you do it?" (Answer: ask the man, "Which way is your hometown?" and go the way he points. If he's from Liartown, he'll point to Truthtown. If he is from Truthtown, he'll point to the correct way.)

Once again, it's important to pause, calmly think through possible answers using logic, and, when ready, share both your answer and how you came up with it.

Interviewers looking for salespeople may ask a question that puts the candidate on the spot, such as "See this pen? Sell it to me." The correct answer is not to begin by describing the pen and its features. The correct response is to ask, "What are you looking for in a pen?" Then describe only the specific features and benefits that align with the customer's needs.

Candidates for creative roles may be asked to display their creativity in the moment, with questions such as, "How many uses for a paperclip can you think of besides holding paper together?" or "Give me 10 different things you can use a paperclip for besides holding paper." The most famous of these questions is "Why are manhole covers round?" There are a variety of possible answers for these questions; what the interviewer is looking for is your ability to remain calm, show your creativity, and brainstorm possible answers.

The bottom line is to remember what we said at the end of chapter 5's insider story, because it applies here as well: you never know what you're going to be asked in an interview, so you need to be prepared for anything.

Rambling as you try to come up with an answer

If you ramble while trying to come up with an answer, rather than thinking prior to speaking, two things will happen:

1 Your brain will work less efficiently because you're talking while thinking.
2 Your interviewer will likely start tuning you out just as you're getting to the good part of your answer.

136   CHAPTER 9 *Not hearing the question, the whole question, and the heart of the question*

It is far better to pause for a few seconds and let your brain fire on all cylinders so you can give your best answer from the start.

Example: Clueless Clark, marketing

The interviewer asks, "If you could wave a magic wand and get one special super-power, what would that be?"

Clueless Clark's answer

Oh, wow, I've never been asked that before. I've never thought about it. Let me see, let me see. That's a good question. Okay, here's what comes to mind: I think I'd like to be invisible so other people couldn't see me but I could see them. Yes, I'd like to have a Harry Potter cloak of invisibility type of thing. Wait a minute. Uh no. Actually, I don't think that's such a good idea. That sounds a little weird. Uh, what else can I come up with . . okay, actually what I'd like is the superpower of being able to read minds. That way I could read the minds of our customers and really find out what they want so we could meet those needs. Yes, that's it. I would want to be able to read minds. That's the superpower I would like to have.

What Clueless Clark got wrong

This is the kind of question that has no wrong answers, but Clueless Clark committed two of the mistakes mentioned previously: he didn't pause to give himself time to think of his best answer, and he rambled as he tried to come up with an answer. He said the first thing that came to mind (being invisible) but then didn't explain why he chose that superpower. He then called that answer weird (and the interviewer may not have thought that) and changed his answer.

What Clueless Clark should have done

Clueless Clark should have taken the time to brainstorm some possibilities and then selected one that he could explain, including why he would choose that superpower and what that says about him. The point of this question is to enable the interviewer to get to know him, so not saying more about the "why" and the "what" are missed opportunities.

Not explicitly tying your answer to the heart of the question

While giving your interview answers, there is a lot going on in your mind, so it's easy to lose track of the question you're trying to answer. It's okay to jot down a quick note if you want to remember a keyword or words from the question (this can also give you a few seconds to think).

In the question discussed previously ("Tell me about a time when you led a difficult, complex, long-term project from start to finish that required collaborating with other departments"), you could jot down the words "complex project" and "collaborate."

Then, before finishing your answer, you can glance at your notes to be sure you have covered both sets of keywords. If you've finished talking through the actions you took, or even the results you obtained, you could circle back and explain how the project involved collaboration with other departments. That will then connect the dots for the interviewer and ensure they understand how your answer ties directly to their question.

Example: Jen, sales

The interviewer asks, "Tell me about a time when you had to build credibility with different levels of the organization on a difficult project where changes had to be made? What did you do and how did you do it?"

Jen's answer

One project that I worked on that had a lot of different levels involved was choosing new sales software. We needed all of our teams to use integrated sales software. Unfortunately, some teams were using Salesforce, and other teams, including our European team, were using Microsoft Dynamics.

It was a difficult project because all the teams had their own preferences and, of course, no one wanted to change. We put together a project group to review options and interviewed people at different levels of the organization to find out what was important to them. Some of the members also surveyed some of our key customers to determine what would be most important.

Once we had that information, we compared the functions and made our recommendation. We chose to go with Salesforce based on what the senior leaders had said we needed.

It was not an easy transition for some of the teams, but in the end the feedback was very positive, and we felt good that we had been able to make a good choice.

What Jen did well

Jen selected a good example that is relevant to the sales position she is interviewing for and also conveys her experience working with teams on complex technology projects. This example also shows her ability to interact with people at different levels to identify their needs and priorities.

What would make this even better

This question has four components: building credibility, different levels, a difficult project, and making changes. Jen focused her answer on working with different levels and a difficult project but did not address credibility or change. She set up the story well, describing the situation and what made it challenging, but she did not describe the actions she took or the results obtained, other than mentioning that the feedback at the end was positive.

Jen's answer would be much better if she included her actions regarding building credibility with the different levels involved, what her specific role was on the project, who she interviewed to learn their needs, the part she played in the selection of Salesforce and its implementation, what changes needed to be made, and what the overall benefits of the integrated system were. As we described in chapter 1, Jen also needed to explain the "I" part of the "we" in the actions she described—that is, what she did individually as part of the project team.

CHAPTER 9 *Not hearing the question, the whole question, and the heart of the question*

> *(continued)*
> She also should have explained why, after interviewing a variety of people and customers to determine their priorities, the team ultimately decided to recommend Salesforce based on what the senior leaders said was needed. Many interviewers would hear that as an inconsistency and then probe her to explain it further.

Think about

The following are some things to consider before moving to the next chapter:

- Think about your past interviews; have there been situations when you found yourself rambling? Why? What could you do differently in the future?
- In the past, have you decided how you were going to answer a question or jumped in with your answer before hearing the entire question? How could you practice listening to the whole question and briefly pausing before answering?
- Have you ever forgotten an interview question in the middle of talking through your answer? What did you do? What will you do differently if that happens again?

Key takeaways

- It's important to listen to the entire question instead of just focusing on the first part of the question.
- Take a brief pause after the question to give yourself time to choose the best way to answer it. Pausing will also help you to avoid rambling as you try to develop an answer.
- It's better to take the time to give an answer that addresses the most important parts of the question than to rush and give a quick response.

Giving answers that sound good to you (but aren't)

You may think you're prepared, but there are some common mistakes that people make without realizing it. It's important to review your answers and compare them to the list of potential problems to make sure you avoid them.

It can be hard to see the flaws in our own answers, so try to look at them from a different point of view. Imagine you're looking at someone else's answers as you review the following potential mistakes.

Answers that are too long

A very common mistake is to give answers that are too long (i.e., more than 2 minutes). This can be due to many possible reasons:

- Rambling either because you're nervous (everyone is in job interviews!), you don't really understand the question, or you're trying to make something up.
- Providing too much context or background information prior to describing your actions.
- Giving too much detail about your actions before describing your results.
- Using too many filler words such as "um" or "uh."

To avoid this mistake, you must properly prepare (see chapter 1) and practice answers to anticipated questions. Do not simply talk faster so your answers will take less time!

Answers that are too short

Preparation and practice can help you be ready with answers that include the appropriate information without being too long or too short. Answers need to describe the complexity of what you do or did rather than gloss over any difficulties; otherwise, the interviewer will (wrongly) assume that what you did previously was so easy that you won't be able to deal with the challenges involved at their organization.

The challenge is to describe this complexity and any obstacles you had to overcome without going overboard and getting stuck in the weeds. The way to avoid making this mistake is to properly prepare (see chapter 1) and practice answers to anticipated questions.

Using acronyms, talking in Tech Speak or Industry Speak that may be unknown to your interviewers

Companies often have their own system of acronyms that are used so frequently you might think they are well known to the general population. Or you might use technical jargon so often that you forget that nontech folks won't know those terms. Or you might think anyone in your field or industry would know the acronyms or industry terms you use.

However, remember that, in addition to your hiring manager, you will likely be interviewed by recruiters/talent acquisition folks and people in other parts of the company who may not be as well versed in these acronyms and jargon. If the interviewer can't follow your stories or understand your answers, it will be difficult to get hired!

Focusing your answer mostly on what you did rather than how you did it and why it mattered

Simply describing what you did is less impactful than conveying how you did something. The "how" can include things like

- Who did you collaborate with?
- What tools did you use?
- What approvals did you need?
- What obstacles did you overcome?
- How did you gain acceptance or buy-in?

Also, interviewers have an implied question: "Why did it matter that you did those things?" Forgetting to include results in your answers will be a missed opportunity for impact. Even if you lack quantitative metrics, you can give a qualitative result—that is, how your actions benefited the customer, team, organization, community, or society.

Not giving answers that relate to the job, company, and industry

If your interviewer doesn't see the connection between your answer and their job, company, or industry, then they likely will conclude that you're either not qualified, overqualified, or not a fit. If you don't have any experience in their industry, you should talk about your experience in a similar job. If you don't have any experience in that kind of job, talk about your experience in a similar industry. Make sure your answer is relatable to this job or industry, even if you think you have a better answer from your experience in a different kind of job or industry. This is why it's so important to deconstruct the job description as shown in chapter 1, so that you can identify the skills needed and provide examples of demonstrating those skills.

> ### Insider story: Different industry examples may cause inaccurate impressions
>
> I (Barbara) once referred a client to an aerospace company because I used to work with someone who was now in the HR department. He had a great manufacturing background and saw they had an opening for someone with his operations expertise. His early career was spent working for an automotive manufacturer in a variety of roles prior to switching to the aerospace industry.
>
> He had a phone interview with my prior colleague, and he felt it went well because he answered all of her questions with specific examples that included quantified results, such as how he saved money, time, and headcount. A couple of weeks later, as he was still waiting to hear about their next steps, my prior colleague called me to let me know that they wouldn't be moving forward with his candidacy. She wanted to give me feedback because she knew I was coaching him.
>
> She said that while he had examples with good results, they all came from the automotive industry, and they wanted to hire someone with more aerospace experience. I knew he had the aerospace industry experience they needed, but because he didn't include enough of those stories in his answers, they formed an impression of him as lacking experience. This underscores the importance of tailoring your answers to fit the industry, even if you think you have a better example from a different industry.

The lesson here is that an example you think is better because the project was more complex, the metrics were more impactful, or there was some other important factor is not better if the interviewer feels the answer doesn't pertain to their particular organization's needs.

Leaving out the results in stories

As stated previously, when interviewers ask for examples, they have an implied question: "Why did it matter that you did those things?" Forgetting to include results in your answers means other candidates' answers will have more impact (and they just might get the job offer). Do not assume the interviewer will probe you further if you leave this out; most will simply move on and consider your answer mediocre rather than stellar.

> ### Example: Ari, engineer
> The interviewer asks, "Tell me about a time when you were most persuasive in overcoming resistance to your ideas or point of view."

(continued)

Ari's answer

Last year, I was given a project to work on that meant coming up with a different way of doing something for one of the plants.

To do this, I had to first review the current processes that were being used. I then reviewed the new specs with my manager and his manager to make sure we were all on the same page. Then I reviewed the budget and some other things that could affect the new process.

After doing a thorough review, it became clear to me that, to reach our goals, it would be necessary to purchase some new equipment. This was a potential problem since there was no money in the budget for that. I expected that would be an issue, and I was right.

To deal with this issue most effectively, I prepared by putting my analysis into spreadsheets that clearly showed how long it would take for the increased efficiency to pay back the initial cost of purchase.

I met with my manager and his manager, and even though they were initially reluctant to approve the expense, the data supported the decision to purchase.

I'm pleased to say that we did purchase the new equipment, and it was a good decision.

What Ari did well

Ari selected a relevant example and was clear in his use of "I" so it is understood that this was his project rather than his sharing the responsibility with others. He clearly articulated his actions of reviewing the current processes, the new specs, and the budget. He also stated the obstacle he needed to overcome (gaining approval for an expenditure when there was no budget for such an expense).

What would make this even better

Ari described the project in such general terms that it's difficult to understand what this was about and the impact the project had. He might have missed an opportunity to highlight who gave him the project and why he was selected, which would demonstrate that he is valued and trusted. Also, the following comments do not say much: he needed to come up with a "different way of doing something" (doing what?), he reviewed "the current processes" (which processes?), "new specs" (what kind of specs?), and "some other things that could affect the new process" (what other things?). Talking about generalities waters down the impact of his story.

He also could have given more information about the analysis he did that showed the time frame for a return on their investment. The analysis is more important than putting information into spreadsheets.

What is more critical here, though, is he failed to describe what he said to his managers to persuade them and overcome their resistance. As discussed in chapter 9, this is the heart of the question, yet all Ari said is that "the data supported the decision to purchase." What did he say to increase their understanding of why it would benefit

> everyone involved to purchase the new equipment? How did he use the "what's in it for them" approach to get their agreement?
>
> Lastly, Ari mentions they did end up purchasing the equipment and it was a good decision, but didn't include any results or benefits to the company, team, or customer. Providing performance or return on investment metrics would dramatically improve the impact of his answer.

Overusing "we" and underusing "I"

As mentioned in chapter 1, it is important to use both "I" and "we" when describing what you've done, both as a leader and individually. Many candidates overuse "we" when describing what they personally did. If every pronoun you use is "we," the interviewer will not have a clear idea of what they would be getting if they hire you. On the other hand, some people describe every action as if they did those things alone, when in reality there were others involved. If every pronoun you use is "I," the interviewer may conclude that you're not a team player who is good at collaborating with others. Also, avoid starting your sentences with "you" (as in "You need to do X"), because that can be perceived as lecturing.

Failing to balance confidence with humility

It is important to be confident in what you do and have accomplished while still being humble and knowing you're not perfect. If you go too far in either direction, you could be perceived as either arrogant or insecure, which means it will be very unlikely you'll be hired.

Bringing things up that you shouldn't: lack of experience, negatives, compensation, time off or other benefits

As discussed previously, there are questions you need to anticipate and be ready for if asked, especially if you have an obvious negative, such as lack of experience, coming from a different industry, or a gap in your employment. However, you should never bring these things up!

You also should never ask about compensation, time off, or other benefits, because if you do, you may be perceived as someone who cares more about those things than the activities and responsibilities of the job.

Not answering the "why should we hire you?" question from the employer's perspective

This question does not mean "Why do you want this job?" As we stated in chapter 2, it instead gives you the opportunity to sell why you think you're a good fit for the position. The translation of this question is "Please summarize for me the top qualifications you have for this job and what makes you unique among all the other candidates I'm interviewing?"

144   **CHAPTER 10**   *Giving answers that sound good to you (but aren't)*

Example: Clueless Clark, marketing

The interviewer asks, "We have several candidates for this position; why should we hire you?"

Clueless Clark's answer

Because I'm awesome! Okay, I'm joking a little bit, but I really am awesome. The stuff I do is really great and would make a big difference for your company.

Let me tell you about a project I worked on earlier this year. We wanted to reach new potential customers. I said we should try something totally different, and I got planes to fly banners over events, parks, and beaches with our logo and message. It made quite a splash and got a lot of press. Did you hear about it?

The interviewer says, "No, I'm not familiar with that."

Clueless Clark then says, Well, anyway, I came up with it and used the additional press to increase our brand awareness. It was fabulous, and that's the kind of thing I want to do here. I can bring game-changing ideas like that to help the business. That's my specialty.

What Clueless Clark got wrong

Even though Clueless Clark says he's joking when he says, "Because I'm awesome," he runs the risk of coming across as arrogant. He says that "the stuff" he does is "really great" and would make a "big difference" to their company but fails to describe any of his specific skills and experience, making his statements sound hollow.

He goes on to describe one specific idea, flying banners over events, parks, and beaches, but doesn't provide any metrics or results other than it "made quite a splash and got a lot of press." We're left wondering what "quite a splash" means, what press they received, and, most importantly, whether this idea achieved the intended result of reaching new potential customers.

While Clark is trying to answer this question from the employer's perspective and is trying to sell himself, his generalities make his answer weak.

Before we discuss how Clark should have answered, let's look at how Lucas answers this same question.

Example: Lucas, customer service

The interviewer asks, "We have several candidates for this position; why should we hire you?"

Lucas's answer

Based on what I've heard about the team, I think I would be a very good addition. I can bring my skills in working with global customers to support the expansion you mentioned that will be happening soon.

I'm looking to make a change, and I want an environment that I think will really support me and the great service that I like to give to customers. From what I know about this company, it really seems like customers are valued, and that aligns with what's important to me.

I'm a great team member, and I want to work with a team that values teamwork. At the end of the day, I want to know I have made a difference for customers, and I'm very interested in doing that here.

What Lucas did well

Lucas mentions several of his strengths that would be valuable to this employer: his experience in being a great team member, working with global customers, and providing great customer service and his values of both teamwork and making a difference for customers.

What would make this even better

Lucas started his answer in an impactful way, aligning his experience in working with global customers to the employer's expansion plans. But in the rest of his answer, he made a very common mistake: he answered the question "Why do you want this job?" or "Why are you interested in working here?" rather than "Why should we hire you?" While he did mention some of his strengths, he stated them as things he's looking for rather than how his specific background, skills, and experience match the employer's needs.

What both Clueless Clark and Lucas should have done

Both Clueless Clark and Lucas should have stated several of their selling points that align with the job description and company. Their answers would be much more impactful if they described specific skills and experience and any relevant performance metrics as evidence of achieving results in their previous positions.

They should summarize their answer by saying they bring a unique combination of skills and experience in three to five areas—for example: "I not only have A and B but also C and D." By ending that way, both Clueless Clark and Lucas would imply how difficult it would be to find that unique combination in another candidate and in only one person, therefore emphasizing they are perfect matches for that job.

Giving a general answer instead of a past example

As we described in chapter 1, many interviewers use behavioral interview questions (also known as competency-based questions), because they know that real-life examples are better at indicating experience than generalities or hypothetical scenarios. Therefore, if you hear a question that starts with something like "Tell me about a time when . . .," "Give an example of . . ," or "Describe for me . . ," provide a specific past example from your experience that directly pertains to the position.

Do not pretend that talking through how you typically handle that kind of situation will suffice. The interviewer might find it annoying that you are not providing an example even though they asked for one, and they may even conclude that you haven't had that specific experience previously.

Think about

The following are some things to consider before moving to the next chapter:

- Have you made any of these mistakes in past interviews? What would you do differently now?
- Which of these potential issues would be most likely to cause you problems? What can you do instead to prevent that?
- Which of the answers you've prepared match these problems? How can you adjust your answers to avoid these mistakes?

Key takeaways

- Applicants may think they have great answers, but that might not be true.
- The issue could be a simple thing that gets in the way, such as giving answers which are too short or too long, or it could be something more critical, like not including or clearly describing results.
- It's important to review the list of potential problems, compare your answers, and make adjustments if needed.

Part 4

Interview stages and interviewers

In this part, we'll look at interview stages and mindsets of the people who are commonly involved in the hiring and selection processes. We also provide translations of other things interviewers say before, during, and after interviews and talk about how to succeed if you're being interviewed by a difficult interviewer, which could be either someone who is simply bad at interviewing or very good at it.

We provide an example of a candidate who received an interview invitation and show how she prepared for the interview. She interviewed with an experienced interviewer, and we show you the transcript of that interview. We also include our notes and insights so that you can learn from her experience.

Interview stages and translations before, during, and after

Every company handles its hiring process differently, and even in the same company, some departments or managers may have different approaches. However, there tend to be some general interview stages. Understanding the stages can make it easier to know what is expected. It's also helpful to understand the reasons for meeting with certain people and what they look for in the interview process. Everyone you speak with will be able to provide input and feedback on your candidacy.

In general, employers want to know three things during their interview process:

1 Can you do the job? (Do you have the skills, knowledge abilities, and experience needed to perform well in this position?) These questions are asked very early in the interview process and typically include verifying whether your resume is accurate and asking about your technical or job function's specific skills.

2 Will you do the job? (Is this the kind of job that suits your interests, motivations, and career goals?) These questions may come in early interview stages and continue later in the interview process.

3 Will you fit? (Do you have the kind of personality and work style that will be a match for the culture of our company and team?) These questions primarily come during the middle and late interview stages.

150   CHAPTER 11   *Interview stages and translations before, during, and after*

These items are sequential, because if you don't pass the first "can you do the job" phase, you won't be invited to subsequent interviews, and if you don't satisfy the "will you do the job" component, you won't be invited to continue. If you don't succeed in the "will you fit" phase, it is highly unlikely you'll get the job offer.

Interview stages and mindsets

The hiring process typically has several stages, starting with an initial first screening to determine if the candidate meets some basic requirements. Selected candidates then move to interviews with various people who are all connected in some way to the position and hiring process. These vary depending on the company, and each hiring manager will have their own approach depending on their role and individual preferences. The following is a list of the interview stages we discuss in this chapter. You might not go through all these types of recruiters and interview stages; nonetheless, it's good to be prepared.

- First screening
- HR/talent acquisition
- External recruiters, headhunters, and staffing agencies
- Hiring manager
- Direct reports
- Peers
- Boss's boss
- Internal clients
- External clients
- Panel interviews
- Presentations

First screening

After review of your application/resume, if you are selected for an interview, you will likely begin with an initial screening interview, either with a live person (typically a relatively junior person in talent acquisition or at a recruiting firm or staffing agency) or as a one-way recorded interview, where you are given a list of video prompts and instructed to record your answers via a webcam (with no one from the company present).

These systems have become quite common, and many employers use them to save time and resources; because they no longer need a staff member to conduct these initial screenings, they can narrow their pool of candidates more efficiently. They also can send candidate recordings to the people on the hiring team for review. Some of these systems include AI to assess candidate responses. AI can analyze verbal answers for key words and phrases as well as nonverbal behavior including facial expressions and tone of voice and then offer a ranking based on a variety of criteria based on the employer's needs.

Initial interviews may be limited to basic questions like "Why are you interested in this position?", "Why did you leave your last position (or are looking to leave your current position)?", and "What is your desired salary?" One-way recorded interviews typically are like that.

However, you must be prepared for a more in-depth interview, which could happen if you are meeting live with a recruiter or HR person. You may be grilled on the knowledge and experience presented on your resume, or you may need to walk through your work history in detail and provide examples of your successes that pertain to the job. You should also be ready for any of the questions described in chapter 2—both the most commonly asked questions and the special situations questions.

Because this interviewer at this stage may be at a junior level, it may feel like they're following a script or simply reading predetermined questions. That's okay; remember that it's only the first step in the process. Do everything you can to try to build rapport and recognize that they are serving as the initial gatekeeper who will ultimately decide whether you get to interview with anyone else.

THEIR MINDSET

They will determine if you have the basic qualifications for the job and whether they think this job matches your interests and career goals. Also, they want to know whether you will make them look bad if they recommend you for the next round of interviews.

HR/Talent acquisition

After the initial screening, you may be invited to an interview with a more senior HR person. This person will typically be a more experienced interviewer and may ask any of the questions listed previously but will likely not be following a script and may also probe your answers by asking follow-up questions. Treat this the same as the initial screening; it's important to be likeable and build rapport as much as possible.

THEIR MINDSET

They will determine not only if you qualify for the job but also if you would want the job, would stay for the long term, and would be a fit for the company's culture. And again, will you make them look bad if they recommend you to the hiring manager?

External recruiters, headhunters, and staffing agencies

If the company or hiring manager needs outside assistance in finding and selecting candidates, they may engage a staffing agency or an external recruiter (commonly referred to as a search firm or headhunter). These job postings often refer to "their client" as the employer rather than naming the company so candidates don't bypass them and apply directly to the company.

Their fees depend on the level of the position. For temporary, clerical, and hourly roles, the staffing agencies typically get a markup above the worker's hourly rate. For professional and managerial roles, they typically receive a percentage of the employee's annual salary (which is usually 20% to 30%).

Search firms come in two types: contingency and retained. Contingency firms receive their fee once their candidate accepts the offer and begins work. These recruiters tend to be the most like commissioned salespeople, who also don't make any money until they close a sale.

Retained firms are paid a retainer for their services, which typically include fully defining the role; sourcing, identifying, and interviewing potential candidates; and referring only the top candidates to their client employer. Retained firms operate more like an outsourced selection committee, because they get paid regardless of where the candidate was sourced. They typically receive a portion of their fee up front, another portion upon presentation of candidates, and the final amount once the candidate is hired.

You may not know if the external recruiter is contingent or retained; you can ask, but they rarely will tell you because they feel it's not your concern. However, there are clues you may notice. If they won't tell you who the employer is until later in the selection process, you'll know they're working on contingency (and they don't want you going straight to the employer, because then they won't collect their fee). Some of these recruiters can be high pressure, just as salespeople who work solely on commission can be.

If the job description is a multipage document, with detailed information on the company, the candidate profile, the job skills, and personality traits needed, the search firm is probably on retainer.

THEIR MINDSET

External recruiters want to know if you qualify for the job and will fit with all of their client's preferences for personality, ambitions, and backgrounds. They are looking for ideal matches, because their clients are paying them to find perfect fits. They will not want to risk their relationship with their client, so they will be highly conscious of whether you will make them look bad if they recommend you.

Hiring manager

Once you make it past HR (and the recruiting firm if there was one), you will likely be interviewed by the hiring manager—that is, the person to whom this position reports. They will commonly be a functional expert and may grill you more on the details of what you did in your previous jobs, how you did it, with whom you interacted, what problems arose, and how you solved them. They will also be listening for the results you achieved and how you added value to your team, the company, and its customers.

THEIR MINDSET

The number-one question this person will want to answer (either explicitly or implicitly) is "Why should I hire you?" They will also be trying to determine whether you will ultimately make their jobs easier (not only because you'll be successful in the job but also because you'll be easy to manage) or harder (either because you will have a steep learning curve and need a lot of handholding, want a promotion right away, or just be difficult to manage).

Direct reports

For managerial positions, it has become common to include direct reports in the selection process to ascertain the extent to which you'd fit in as a leader of the current team. It will be important to ask questions during these interviews and to demonstrate your listening skills. The philosophy of servant leadership (meaning you're there to help them succeed rather than the other way around) will be important to exhibit.

THEIR MINDSET

The main question on their mind is what you'll be like to work for and whether you'll make their jobs easier (because you'll listen to their ideas and concerns and make appropriate changes to improve their jobs) or harder (because you'll be more demanding, expect them to do even more than they're already doing, or just be a difficult boss overall).

Keep in mind direct reports may be stressed and anxious about the idea of getting a new boss. In addition, one or more may have applied for this role through internal channels. You could also be asked about how you would solve a problem they're currently experiencing. Be supportive but careful not to make any promises.

Peers

It has also become quite common to include peers and teammates in the interview process to determine whether the new person will be a fit for the culture.

THEIR MINDSET

These people will generally want to know what you'll be like to work with and whether you'll make their jobs easier (because they can depend on you to get your work done and you'll be a good team-player) or harder (because you won't be reliable, you'll need them to pick up your slack, or you won't play well with others). If they are in technical roles, you may also get asked about your knowledge of technology platforms, tools, or software.

Boss's boss

For many positions, it is common to be interviewed by the person to whom your boss reports. This may just be a get-to-know-you or rubber stamp type of interview but may also be more in-depth (so you'll need to be well prepared).

THEIR MINDSET

They will be looking for your overall fit with the culture of the company and may also be thinking about your eventual promotability based on how you communicate and present yourself.

Internal clients

If the job you're interviewing for involves a good amount of interaction with other departments, the company may have you interview with staff from those departments (i.e., your internal clients).

154 **CHAPTER 11** *Interview stages and translations before, during, and after*

THEIR MINDSET

These people will want to know what you'll be like to work with and whether you'll make their jobs easier (because they can depend on you to get your work done and they can be successful in their jobs) or harder (because you won't be reliable, you'll cause them problems, or you won't be easy to interact with).

External clients

If the job you're interviewing for involves interaction with key clients, the company may have you interview with those clients to get their buy-in. This meeting could either come early in the interview process or later for final candidates.

THEIR MINDSET

Similar to internal clients, these people want to know what you'll be like to work with and whether you'll make their jobs easier (because they can depend on you to be responsive and get your work done with an eye for quality, timeliness, and cost-effectiveness so they can be successful) or harder (because you won't be reliable, you won't be easy to interact with, or you'll only care about closing a deal with them). Clients may also want to know that you will be a problem-solver and a creator of client-specific solutions.

Panel interviews

Interviews with these various stakeholders may be held as one-on-one interviews scheduled on separate days or occur all on the same day round-robin style. They also are commonly held as a group all in one room or as a virtual meeting, often referred to as panel interviews. Panel interviews may include the hiring manager, direct reports, peers, and/or internal clients.

THEIR MINDSET

The mindsets of the individuals included in the panel are the same as those previously mentioned, depending on which stakeholders are included in the panel (e.g., direct reports, peers, clients, etc.), so try to get information about the panelists in advance, including what their relationship is to the open position. During the interview, it will be important to connect with each panelist. Look directly at them if on-site. Address the person asking the question directly, while acknowledging the others in the room as well. Remember they will each be asked for their feedback and impressions following your interview.

> ### Insider story: Perfect isn't perfect
>
> I (Barbara) was once a panelist in a group interview and, based on the candidate's resume, he looked like a perfect match for the role. He answered each question, sharing relevant stories and including impactful results. We also asked him questions about his leadership style and how he solved problems and collaborated with other departments.

> As the interview progressed, I got the feeling that something was off. His answers seemed too perfect, and he came across as somewhat of a know-it-all. Although this wasn't one of the questions I had planned to ask, I couldn't help it; I wanted to see if I could crack his shell. I asked him to tell us something about himself that wasn't perfect. He stumbled, tried to make a joke (that wasn't funny), and just said something general about being very good at what he does. He did not answer the question, and he did not endear himself to any of us on the panel. Despite his being perfect on paper, he showed no likeability, and he wasn't offered the job.

Presentations

For roles requiring presentations to management, staff, customers, or business partners, it's common to expect you to give a presentation as part of the interview process. The employer may give you the topic, or they may have you select one that is relevant to the position for which you're interviewing. You may be free to structure the presentation as you wish, or they may provide you with an outline of material to include (they might even provide you with PowerPoint slides to use). They will give you the time frame in advance, so you'll know how much time you'll have to present.

THEIR MINDSET

The mindsets of the individuals included as audience members are the same as those previously mentioned, depending on which stakeholders are present (e.g., manager, boss's boss, direct reports, peers, clients, etc.), so try to get information about the attendees in advance, including what their relationship is to the open position. During the presentation, make eye contact with each audience member if you can.

At some point during your presentation, you will need to ask if there are any questions, and you can do so either throughout your presentation or at the end, depending on the time frame allocated. There may be some questions you're unable to answer, so try to anticipate what those might be and have a statement ready for those instances, such as "That's an excellent question, and I'd like to gather more information before answering that. If you provide me with your contact information after the presentation, I'd be happy to get back to you."

> ### Insider story: Hecklers at interview presentations
>
> I (Barbara) once had a client who was interviewing with a company known as one of the top think tanks in the US. After several rounds of interviews, he was asked to give a presentation to a group of their executives. They gave him a brief outline of topics to cover within a required time frame and even gave him a PowerPoint template to use for his slides. He spent a great deal of time preparing and was quite comfortable with presenting to groups because that had been a part of his previous position. When we debriefed after the presentation, he thought it went well for the most part but said

156   **CHAPTER 11**   *Interview stages and translations before, during, and after*

(continued)

there was someone in the back who kept asking questions that he felt were quite basic given the audience. This person was just shouting them out, as if he were a "heckler" at a stand-up comedy show.

My client addressed these questions as best he could. He later told me he thought this person had been planted there for a reason: the person in this job would need to handle themselves professionally and calmly even when faced with irrelevant or even silly questions, so he thought this was part of their selection process. We never found out if that was the case, but he did get the job, so he obviously passed their test.

Translating other things interviewers say before, during, and after the interview

In addition to being prepared for questions, candidates should also understand other things that interviewers may say. Each company has its own processes; however, some common things are said verbally and in written correspondence.

Before the interview

Here are some messages you may receive before you are invited to interview and their translations:

Message you receive	Translation
"We received your application and will notify you if there is interest." or "We are evaluating candidates and will notify you if there is interest."	We received hundreds of applications and have very little time and resources to go through each one in detail. We will likely use an applicant tracking system to help us search resumes for keywords and similar job titles. Do not contact us to inquire about the status of your application, because we won't be able to answer (we have multiple jobs posted and receive hundreds of responses for each one). If we are interested in learning more about you, we'll contact you.
"Thank you for your interest in X position. We are pleased to invite you for an interview."	Congratulations—you made it past our resume/application screening system and now get to interview for the position! (This initial interview may or may not be with a live person; it may be a one-way recorded video interview as described earlier in this chapter.)
"Thank you for your interest in X position. Although your background is impressive, we have other candidates whose backgrounds more closely match our needs."	Sorry, but you didn't make it past our resume/application screening system.

Translating other things interviewers say before, during, and after the interview **157**

During the interview

Here are some messages you may receive during your interview and their translations:

Message you receive	Translation
"Excellent, thank you, that was a good answer."	I'm acknowledging that you finished your answer and taking a second to gather my thoughts before asking you my next question.
"We're still interviewing other candidates and will let you know when we're ready to move to the next step." or "We will be going over the candidates with the hiring team and will then make a decision on next steps."	I do not yet know if you'll be selected for the next round in the process. It could also mean: It's doubtful that you'll make it to the next round, so I'll just give this general statement to let you down easy. You'll probably get a decline by email in the coming days or weeks.

Example: Clueless Clark, marketing

The interviewer says, "We're still interviewing other candidates, and we'll let you know when we're ready to move to the next step."

Clueless Clark's answer

Do you have any idea when that will be? I think I'm a great fit for the job, but I want to let you know that I'm talking to some other companies. They've expressed their interest, and my skills are really in demand. I think I'm going to be getting several offers to choose from so let me know as soon as possible.

What Clueless Clark got wrong

Clueless Clark should not have started his response by asking about when they'll be ready to move to the next step, as that could be perceived as putting pressure on the interviewer. He also should not have volunteered that he's in discussions with other companies and that his skills are "in demand" as that comes across as arrogant. And he shouldn't have said he thinks he'll be getting several offers to choose from.

Imagine that you are dating someone who tells you that they are dating several other people and they are "in demand" and think they'll be getting engaged soon. Would that be someone you'd want to continue to date? We don't think so!

What Clueless Clark should have done

Clueless Clark should have said something like, "Absolutely, I understand that you have a process to ensure you make the best decision for your company and team." He then should reiterate his interest and enthusiasm for the position and company and briefly summarize why his experience and skills are a great fit for the role and organization based on the job description and their discussion. He should close by saying that he looks forward to continuing the conversation when they are ready to proceed.

CHAPTER 11 Interview stages and translations before, during, and after

During the interview, continued

Message you receive	Translation
"You will be notified within the next X number of weeks if you are selected for the next round." or "We need this role to be filled by X date." or "We need this person to be on board by X date."	It is my hope that we'll know something in the next X number of weeks (or we'll be able to fill the role or have the person on board by that date), but these things always take longer than we expect, so don't hold me to that date. If you want to follow up, please wait until at least a few days after that date to email me.
"Would you provide your references?" Or "Are you actively interviewing?" Or "When are you available to start?"	(These are all "buy signs.") We're very interested in you, and . . . References: So that we can expedite the process of moving you to the next step, please give me your references. Interviewing: I'm worried that if you're interviewing with other companies, you may get hired before we're able to put a job offer together for you, so I need to know how quickly we need to move through the selection process. Start date: We'll want you to start as soon as you're available.

Example: Jen, sales

The interviewer asks, "Are you actively interviewing with other companies?"

Jen's answer

Yes, I am pursuing other opportunities. I do want to let you know that I think this job is a great match for me, and I'm most interested in joining your company. As I mentioned before, I think the values of your company are very aligned with mine, and I'm very excited about the upcoming expansion into a different market. I believe my experience in that market will be a great help for the team and I'll be able to support the growth.

What Jen did well

It's good Jen said she is pursuing other opportunities without providing any specifics (this is the one time that you should *not* give specifics!). Even if she isn't yet having any other interviews, her answer is implying that she is. While it's never okay to lie, changing the wording to be truthful is fine.

She also uses this as an opportunity to state she's a great match for the position, and her use of the words "most interested" implies that among all of the other companies she's talking with, this employer is her number-one choice. She mentions her alignment of values and her experience in the new market they are expanding into.

What would make this even better

Jen's first two sentences are perfect as is. She can improve what she said after that by summarizing why they should hire her, which we discussed in chapter 2 and in our examples in chapter 10. Even though being asked this question is a sign of interest from the interviewer, Jen should know that, until she receives the job offer, she is still selling herself.

Jen should emphasize why she is a perfect match by saying she brings a unique combination of skills and experience in three to five areas that come directly from the job description and her interview discussions—for example: "I not only have A and B but also C and D, so that's why I feel I'm a perfect match."

She then should go on to close the sale as we discussed in chapter 8. She can say something like, "I'm excited about this job and I really look forward to continuing the conversation in the next stage of your selection process. What are our next steps and time frames?"

During the interview, continued

Message you receive	Translation
"What other companies are you interviewing with?"	I'm worried that if you're interviewing with other companies, you may get hired before we're able to put a job offer together for you, and I'd like to know what companies we're up against.
	This is analogous to having someone you're dating ask you, "Who else are you dating?" (Translation: I'm worried that I don't stack up.) Do not tell them the other companies you're talking to! Unless there is a ring—or a job offer—it's none of their business!
	Simply answer by saying something general such as, "I'm talking to a variety of companies, but I don't have an official offer yet." If they press you further, just say that you're not comfortable revealing the other companies since there is nothing official.

After the interview

Here are some messages you may receive following your interview and their translations:

Message you receive	Translation
"Thank you for your interest in X position. We are still interviewing candidates and will notify you of the next steps."	We are interviewing several people for this role after having received hundreds of applications. We have not yet decided who will move on to the next step in the process and cannot tell you how long that will take, so please be patient. If you make it to the next round, we will contact you.
"Thank you for your interest in X position. We are pleased to inform you that you have been selected for the next round of interviews."	Congratulations—you made it to the next round and now get to continue to interview for the position!
"Thank you for your interest in X position and for the time you spent with us in your interview(s). Although your background is impressive, we have other candidates whose backgrounds more closely match our needs. We will keep your information in our system and will notify you if another suitable position becomes available."	Sorry, but you didn't make it past the last round in the interview process. We may or may not keep your information active in our system, so if you see another position posted, please apply.

Think about

The following are some things to consider before moving to the next chapter:

- What can you do to be prepared for the different people you'll be meeting with?
- Which interview stage causes you the most trepidation? What can you do prior to your next interview to overcome that?
- Which of the mentioned messages have you received before, during, or after your interviews?
- How can you use the information in this chapter to help you better understand the messages you receive from employers?

Key takeaways

- You'll go through typical interview stages, starting from the first screening to meeting the hiring manager and possibly meeting with their manager or others.
- During the process, interviewers will be trying to determine if hiring you would be good or bad for the business, the team, and themselves as your manager.
- There are typical messages many interviewers and companies will send out at various stages of the interview process. Understanding what the messages mean can help you choose the best response and decide what to say if a response is needed.

How to deal with bad interviewers (and really good ones)

You will undoubtedly encounter different kinds of interviewers, and you have to be prepared. We wrote this chapter to give you the opportunity to think through the different experience levels and personality types so you can prepare for each type.

When you think about interviewers, there are two big differences to consider: how talkative or quiet they are and how experienced they are as interviewers. Those who do all or most of the talking make it difficult to get a word in and share your successes. Those who are quiet and unexpressive make it difficult for you to know how you're doing in the interview or what they think of your answers.

Interviewers who are inexperienced and don't know what they're doing make it difficult for you to truly sell yourself and shine in the interview. Those who are highly experienced have heard the BS answers numerous times and don't think twice about asking one follow-up question after another, probing you for more and more information until you put your foot in your mouth by saying something you may later regret.

In this chapter, we share the best ways to succeed when being interviewed by a variety of different types of interviewers.

The poker-faced interviewer

Many people adopt this persona when interviewing others, and it is not necessarily a reflection on you. Realize you may not be able to build rapport with them even if you try and simply do your best to answer their questions. Many people have been

The lackadaisical or disinterested interviewer

You may be interviewed by someone who gives the appearance that they don't want to be there—they may remain on their computer working, check their phone, or answer phone calls while conducting the interview. This could be because they are very busy, they were asked by their boss to interview you, or they already know who they want to hire. This very likely has nothing to do with you, so don't take it personally!

The best way to handle this type of interviewer is to try to build rapport with them at the beginning and throughout the session, accept that you may not be able to, and sometimes ask temperature check questions once you finish some of your answers such as, "Does that answer your question?" or "How is that issue handled here?"

The talkative interviewer

Some interviewers like to hear themselves talk, making it difficult to share your stories. The best way to deal with this type of interviewer is to demonstrate your active listening skills, show genuine interest in what they have to say, and inject brief comments or questions that allow you to provide examples of your successes. You can say something like, "That's very interesting; I had a similar situation happen to me at my last job" or "That reminds me of the time I got great results when I faced a similar challenge." We have learned interviewers often walk away from an interview loving the candidates who don't get to say much during their interview, because they felt the candidates related well and made them feel quite comfortable.

The interviewer who asks very few questions

Some interviewers ask very few questions after their initial opening and might be talking to you just to give a rubber stamp to the hiring manager's preferred candidates. They could be your boss's boss, a peer of this position, or your boss's peer.

The best way to handle this type of interviewer is to remember your strongest examples that showcase your successes relevant to this job and to ask questions that could serve as a transition to those stories. For example, if one of your main selling points is you've solved problems pertaining to a similar role or department, you may want to ask a question such as, "What types of problems has this department experienced when doing X?" Their answer would then enable you to share examples of how you've solved similar problems.

The interviewer who tests you

In some cases, an interviewer may give what can be considered a test during the interview, which is usually given verbally, although there are written tests to assess technical, writing, mathematical, or problem-solving skills. Verbal tests may simply quiz candidates on their functional or technical knowledge or their ability to solve problems while under pressure. There are also in-box tests, which assess how candidates make decisions on how to handle tasks they would encounter on the job.

There are also interviewers who try to simulate the kind of interactions that would be critical components of a job, such as an unhappy customer, a prospective client, or an executive whose buy-in would need to be obtained for the person to be successful in the job. In those cases, the interviewer may pretend to be that customer, client, or executive, and you may or may not know they're planning to role-play a situation during your interview. It's important to recognize these situations and anticipate the possibility so you can demonstrate your ability to remain calm, ask questions, and handle the situation confidently.

Insider story: The test

One of our friends told us about an interview she had several years ago with a hiring manager. She said he was rude and challenging, questioned everything she said, interrupted her constantly, and in general made the interview extremely difficult to get through.

The interviewer offered her the job immediately. When our friend asked him why he had treated her that way, he said because the engineers she would be working with would treat her the same, so he wanted to see if she could stay calm and collected in those kinds of situations.

It's interesting the hiring manager didn't consider the fact that she'd worked successfully within engineering departments for many years as proof she could handle them, and instead he wanted to test her during the interview.

The situation left a bad impression on our friend, and since she would have reported directly to this person, she decided to decline the job.

Multiple interviewers

As discussed in chapter 11, you will likely go through several stages with different interviewers prior to receiving a job offer. Some of these people may be good at interviewing, and others may not. Don't let your experience with one bad interviewer affect your impression of the company as a whole or lead you to change your interest in their open position. Instead, think about who you'll be working directly for or with, because those are the most important people impacting your job satisfaction.

We've heard from several clients who were first interviewed by an inexperienced HR talent acquisition representative. Or they had one interviewer from another department who they didn't feel they clicked with. It's important to recognize that the person may just have been uncomfortable interviewing potential hires. Don't dismiss a job if you don't seem to get along with one of the interviewers, especially if you won't be interacting with them on a regular basis. The most important relationship is with your direct boss, so if you're able to build rapport with that person, then you're more likely to be satisfied in the job.

The inexperienced interviewer

These interviewers may follow a prescribed set of questions and/or a script. They may not give you any visual cues on whether your answers are what they're looking for and instead just move to their next question as soon as you finish an answer. The best way to handle this type of interviewer is to first try to build rapport at the beginning and throughout the session and to sometimes ask temperature-check questions once you finish some of your answers, such as, "Does that make sense?" or "How would that work here?"

The highly experienced interviewer

These are typically people who work at recruiting firms or in HR talent acquisition and interview for a living. They will have thorough and detailed questions and may continually probe you during your answers, interrupt you, and/or ask several follow-up questions. The best way to handle this type of interviewer is to pause, take a breath, and think prior to starting your answer. This will allow you to slow down the process and not feel rushed or reactive, which could lead to your providing an answer that you later regret.

Interview example

Let's look at an example of what it's like to be interviewed by a highly experienced interviewer. We'll listen in on an initial phone screening interview and see how a great interviewer builds on what the applicant says and probes to get additional information.

Maya is a marketing and communications coordinator working at CNU Management Software, which sells inventory software. She likes her job but wants more—more pay, more growth opportunities, and more learning. She started looking at online job postings and found a social media specialist position at Lextare, a larger software company. It's a brand she's familiar with, and she's excited about working for them. She applies and receives an invitation for an initial interview.

Valerie is the interviewer. She has been in HR talent acquisition for eight years and at Lextare for four. She has a list of questions she frequently asks, and she also customizes some questions about areas mentioned in the job description. She focuses on learning about the person but has heard many of what she considers to be BS answers and will quickly push back when she hears them.

She wants to bring the best people into the company, so she wants to feel the applicants would be a good fit. The managers in her company are very busy, and she doesn't want to waste their time. She only moves applicants forward in the process who she really believes would be great employees. The following is the job for which Maya is interviewing.

> **Lextare job posting**
>
> **Social Media Specialist**
>
> The social media specialist is responsible for managing the company's brand reputation through response on social media and review sites. This individual is also

responsible for managing the company's online customer support site, including writing and editing articles and videos and providing analytics to gauge site effectiveness.

What you will do to contribute to the company's success:

Monitor and manage social media channels for customer inquiries and feedback.

Respond to comments, messages, and mentions on social platforms, reviews sites, and other platforms in a timely and professional manner.

Identify and escalate urgent issues or negative sentiments to the appropriate teams.

Manage customer support site, including updating existing articles, creating new self-help articles and videos based on customer feedback, and making continuous improvements to maximize customer self-help and satisfaction.

Maintain brand voice and consistency in all interactions.

Track and analyze response metrics to improve engagement and response times.

Create monthly metrics/KPIs reporting.

Monitor social media platforms on weekends twice monthly.

Other duties as assigned.

Additional Responsibilities

Collaborate with content creators to ensure alignment in messaging.

Stay updated on industry trends, tools, and best practices in social media engagement.

Participate in the development of FAQs and response templates.

Conduct regular audits of social media interactions to identify areas for improvement.

Provide insights and feedback to marketing teams on customer sentiment and trends.

Qualifications

3+ years' experience

Experience in social media management

Strong written and verbal communication skills

Ability to handle challenging situations with empathy and professionalism

Proficiency in social media platforms and analytics tools

Excellent organizational skills and attention to detail

Preferred Skills

Knowledge of social media management tools (e.g., Sprout Social)

Familiarity with crisis management strategies in a digital context

CHAPTER 12 *How to deal with bad interviewers (and really good ones)*

(continued)

Ability to work independently and as part of a team

Core Competencies

Committed: Values each customer while working hard to keep their business and support our communities.

Helpful: Delivers support in the ways that are most useful to our customers and addresses their needs with expertise, respect, and empathy.

Proactive: Understands what our customers need and actively works to make their relationship with us seamless, easy, and rewarding.

Personable: Knows our customers well and tailors our communications and interactions to address their needs and expectations.

Our Commitment

Diversity lies in the communities we serve and among the employees who dedicate themselves to ensure our continued success. At Lextare, we believe it is our individual and unique talents, backgrounds, and perspectives that truly make us an unstoppable force.

Interview preparation

To prepare for the interview, Maya went through her resume line by line to refresh her memory about what she did in older jobs and to make sure she could substantiate anything on there the interviewer might want further details on. She also went through the job description in detail and prepared for potential questions.

Here is how Maya "deconstructed" this description to identify possible interview questions:

In the job description	Key words and phrases	Possible interview questions
The social media specialist is responsible for managing the company's brand reputation through response on social media and review sites.	Managing brand reputation through social media and review sites	What experience have you had managing brand reputation through social media and review sites?
This individual is also responsible for managing the company's online customer support site, including writing and editing articles and videos and providing analytics to gauge site effectiveness.	Managing the company's online customer support site Writing and editing articles and videos Providing analytics to gauge site effectiveness	Tell me about your experience in managing online customer support sites. Describe your experience in writing and editing articles and videos. Give an example of your providing analytics to gauge site effectiveness.

Interview example

(continued)

In the job description	Key words and phrases	Possible interview questions
Monitor and manage social media channels for customer inquiries and feedback.	Monitor social media channels for customer inquiries and feedback	Describe a situation where you found an important customer inquiry or feedback item as a result of monitoring social media channels.
Respond to comments, messages, and mentions on social platforms, reviews sites, and other platforms in a timely and professional manner.	Respond to comments, messages, and mentions Timely and professional manner	Give an example of a difficult post you drafted in response to a comment, message, or mention on a social media site. How do you organize your time so that you can respond to multiple posts in a timely and professional manner?
Identify and escalate urgent issues or negative sentiments to the appropriate teams.	Identify and escalate urgent issues or negative sentiments	Give an example of you escalating an urgent issue or negative sentiment.
Manage customer support site, including updating existing articles, creating new self-help articles and videos based on customer feedback, and making continuous improvements to maximize customer self-help and satisfaction.	Updating existing articles Creating new self-help articles and videos based on customer feedback Making continuous improvements to maximize customer satisfaction.	What experience have you had in keeping customer support site articles up to date? Describe some of the new self-help articles and videos you've created and posted as a result of customer feedback. Give an example of an improvement you made that resulted in maximizing customer satisfaction.
Maintain brand voice and consistency in all interactions.	Consistent brand voice	What kinds of things do you do to ensure your company's brand voice is consistent in all interactions?
Track and analyze response metrics to improve engagement and response times.	Track and analyze response metrics Improve engagement Improve response times	Give an example of something you instituted as a result of tracking and analyzing metrics that resulted in improved engagement and better response times.
Create monthly metrics/KPIs reporting.	Monthly metrics/KPIs reporting.	What metrics and KPIs did you initiate that became part of your regular reporting in your current or last position?
Monitor social media platforms on weekends twice monthly.	Twice monthly weekends	We need someone who can work twice monthly on weekends. What are your thoughts on that requirement?
Collaborate with content creators to ensure alignment in messaging.	Collaborate with content creators Ensure alignment in messaging	Describe your experience in collaborating with content creators. What kinds of things do you do to ensure they are in alignment with your company's messaging?
Stay updated on industry trends, tools, and best practices in social media engagement.	Stay updated on industry trends, tools, and best practices	What do you do to stay current on industry trends, tools, and best practices?

168 CHAPTER 12 *How to deal with bad interviewers (and really good ones)*

(continued)

In the job description	Key words and phrases	Possible interview questions
Participate in the development of FAQs and response templates.	Develop FAQs and response templates	What experience have you had in developing FAQs? Describe a response template you developed that was particularly challenging.
Conduct regular audits of social media interactions to identify areas for improvement.	Conduct regular audits Identify improvement areas	Give an example of an improvement area you identified because of one of your regular social media audits.
Provide insights and feedback to marketing teams on customer sentiment and trends.	Provide customer insights, trends, and feedback to marketing teams	Tell me about some of the customer insights, trends, and feedback you provided to your marketing team.
Strong written and verbal communication skills.	Strong written and verbal communication	Tell me about a time your ability to articulate a written response resulted in a positive interaction with a colleague or customer. Give an example of a delicate situation with a colleague or customer that required you to use your verbal communication skills.
Ability to handle challenging situations with empathy and professionalism.	Handle challenging situations with empathy and professionalism	Tell me about a time you used your professionalism and ability to empathize during a challenging situation.
Proficiency in social media platforms and analytics tools. Knowledge of social media management tools (e.g., Sprout Social).	Social media platforms, analytics and management tools	What social media platforms and analytics tools have you used? Which ones are your most and least favorites and why? What experience have you had with social media management tools such as Sprout Social?
Excellent organizational skills and attention to detail.	Organizational skills and attention to detail	Tell me about a time when you were juggling many projects simultaneously; what did you do to stay organized? Give an example of a situation where your attention to detail paid off.
Familiarity with crisis management strategies in a digital context.	Crisis management strategies	Describe a crisis management situation in which you were involved; what role did you play, and what were the outcomes?
Ability to work independently and as part of a team.	Work independently Work as part of a team	Tell me about a project in which you worked independently and are proud of your results. Describe a project that required you to collaborate as part of a team.

(continued)

In the job description	Key words and phrases	Possible interview questions
Committed: Values each customer while working hard to keep their business and support our communities.	Values each customer Works hard to keep their business	Give an example of you going "above and beyond" to keep a customer's business.
Helpful: Delivers support in the ways that are most useful to our customers and addresses their needs with expertise, respect, and empathy.	Addresses customer needs with expertise, respect, and empathy	Describe a situation where you addressed a customer's needs with expertise, respect, and empathy.
Proactive: Understands what our customers need and actively works to make their relationship with us seamless, easy, and rewarding.	Actively works to make customer relationship seamless, easy, and rewarding	Give an example of something you instituted that resulted in making customer relationships seamless, easy, and rewarding.
Personable: Knows our customers well and tailors our communications and interactions to address their needs and expectations.	Tailors communications to address customer needs and expectations	Describe a communication that you customized to fit a particular customer's needs and expectations.
Diversity lies in the communities we serve and among the employees who dedicate themselves to ensure our continued success. At XYZ Corp, we believe it is our individual and unique talents, backgrounds, and perspectives that truly make us an unstoppable force.	Believes in individual and unique talents, backgrounds, and perspectives	Tell me something about yourself that demonstrates your ability to value diverse backgrounds and perspectives.

When Maya finished this, she added a fourth column. In that column, she added specific stories and examples with results she could use to clearly illustrate how she handled each of the situations listed. She knew these stories and examples would be important so her answers wouldn't sound too general.

Maya then went back to chapter 2 to review common questions that she could be asked and prepared answers for those. She looked at other chapters to prepare for additional possible questions on relevant behavioral competencies. For each question, she identified stories and examples that she could share. She chose the most positive stories and examples and realized some of them could be used to address several different questions.

All this preparation took some time; however, Maya knew that she was doing this preparation not just for this interview but also to prepare for future interviews at this company. And if she didn't move forward with this job, much of this preparation could be helpful for interviews at other companies. Maya felt good about her preparation and was ready for the interview.

170   **CHAPTER 12** *How to deal with bad interviewers (and really good ones)*

Initial phone interview

Let's listen in to Maya's initial phone interview with Valerie:

> **Valerie:** Hi, Is this Maya?
>
> **Maya:** Yes, it is.
>
> **Valerie:** Hi, Maya. This is Valerie Harrison from Lextare. How are you doing today?
>
> **Maya:** I'm doing great, thank you. I'm very excited about this interview. How are you doing?
>
> **Valerie:** I'm great, thank you. Let's jump right in. Thank you for applying for the social media specialist position. Please tell me a little about yourself.
>
> **Maya:** Thank you for meeting with me. I saw on your LinkedIn profile that you're located in San Francisco, and I lived there for a while. It was so nice there. Now I'm in New York, but I remember what a wonderful place that was.
>
> **Valerie:** Yes, it's a great place. I love it here. So tell me about you.
>
> **Maya:** Thanks for asking. Some of my top skills are my strong communication skills, my focus on being proactive, and my ability to calmly manage a crisis when needed. I work hard to have a good relationship with the teams I work with, and part of that is making sure we communicate on a regular basis.
>
> One of the things I'm most proud of at my current company is I was on a team that was awarded the Presidential Impact Award two years ago for work I did when we had a crisis. An unhappy customer posted about their experience, and it blew up. I was part of the team who managed the responses and turned it into positive coverage. Each year, only three teams get this honor, and it meant a lot to me that my work was recognized by the executive team.
>
> **Valerie:** Great; why are you looking for a new job?
>
> **Maya:** I'm very proud of the work I've done at my current job and really enjoy working with my team. I've gotten some great experience, but I feel the opportunities for growth are limited. While the business is expanding with new customers, the company has less than 500 people, and there is little room to grow in the area I'm interested in.
>
> At my current job, my time is split between communications and social media management. I can do both, but it has really helped me to see that my main interest is in social media, and that's what I want to focus on. I'm looking to work for a much larger company that has a greater social media presence. That would give me the opportunity to do much more.
>
> One of the things that really interests me about this role is the increase in scope. I'm looking to broaden the reach of my messages. I also want to work with a larger team and have the opportunity to learn more and build my skills.
>
> **Valerie [interrupting]:** So why do you want to work at Lextare?

Maya: I'm impressed with how innovative your company is and the solutions you offer to your customers. The latest version of your software got very high reviews, and the stories of customer results were extremely interesting. You're at the forefront of the industry.

Your corporate values of being the best really resonate with what's important to me. I want to give customers the best possible experience.

I also appreciate the emphasis on contributing positively to society. That's something that's important to me personally and professionally. I saw on your website how your company supports the local community and offers each employee a volunteer day a year to work with a charity they choose.

This sounds like a place where I would fit in well.

Authors' insights

Maya did a good job of establishing rapport at the beginning by commenting on something they have in common. This underscores the importance of learning a bit about your interviewer in advance.

She answered the "Tell me about yourself question" pretty well by talking about her skills that are relevant to the position and sharing an accomplishment of which she's proud. What would have made that answer more impactful was to include more specifics about her communication skills (e.g., she could have described both her written and verbal skills because they are mentioned in the job description) and more specifics on how she is proactive, rather than just saying that is a focus of hers.

Maya answered the question about her looking to leave using a version of the negative sandwich approach that we described in the first chapter: she started with a positive about her current position, gave her specific reason for looking to leave (the negative), and ended on a positive by answering the implied question, "Why are you interested in this position?" She gave good reasons here, but she didn't include why Lextare in particular. Because Valerie is an experienced interviewer, she didn't hesitate to interrupt Maya to get additional information.

Valerie: Describe your experience managing brand reputation through social media and review sites.

Maya: In my current role, I developed a strategy that included monitoring social media channels and review sites for mentions of our brand.

Valerie [interrupting]: Which channels?

Maya: Facebook, Twitter, Instagram, LinkedIn, and YouTube.

Valerie: Thank you; please continue.

Maya: Anyway, I was able to provide insights for our marketing and customer service teams, allowing us to proactively address potential reputational risks. We use Hootsuite, but I'm familiar with Sprout Social, and I know that I could very quickly pick it up.

Valerie [interrupting]: Tell me about some of the insights you provided to marketing and customer service.

Maya: When we launched a new version, we got specific feedback on customer preferences and pain points. The reports showed a trend that response time to customers needed to be addressed.

One of my key responsibilities was to track customer feedback and respond promptly to both positive and negative reviews. I started a 24-hour response rule for negative comments, which helped us address concerns quickly and publicly demonstrate our commitment to customer satisfaction.

Valerie [interrupting]: How did you implement this rule, and were you the only one responding or did this rule involve others?

Maya: As I mentioned, one of the customer insights was about faster response time. Even though my team did not work directly with customers, we wanted to respond to reviews as quickly as possible. Three of us worked on responses. I suggested the 24-hour response rule, and they agreed.

Valerie [interrupting]: How did you get them to agree?

Maya: There had been an unofficial 48-hour rule in place, but waiting that long meant that by the time we addressed it, there could be a lot of negative comments that had to be dealt with. We were in a meeting discussing some of the recent posts, and it became obvious that the quicker we responded, the easier it was to handle it. So, when I said, let's try 24 hours, they quickly agreed.

Valerie: Thank you. Please continue.

Maya: We developed a schedule to make sure that even on weekends and holidays, someone would check in once a day to ensure that all negative comments were seen. If it was a holiday or weekend, we had a general message that could be used until it could be fully addressed.

I also organized a campaign that encouraged satisfied customers to leave positive reviews, which helped improve our overall rating on key platforms. This enhanced our online reputation and also fostered a sense of community among our followers.

Overall, my experience has taught me the importance of engaging authentically with our audience and using feedback to improve our brand image.

Authors' insights

Because Maya included several generalities as she was talking through her answer, Valerie interrupted to probe further. When Maya talked about monitoring social media channels, Valerie asked for more specifics. When Maya mentioned providing insights for marketing and customer service, Valerie probed for more details. When Maya said that she started a 24-hour response rule, Valerie wanted more information on how she made that happen. When Maya said that her colleagues agreed to the new rule, Valerie wanted to know how she got them to agree.

Interview example **173**

While we'll never know whether Valerie interrupted to see if it would throw off Maya's timing or concentration, it's important to note that by leaving off key specifics, one of two things could happen if you're talking with an experienced interviewer. Either you'll have to deal with the interviewer continuing to push you for the details, or worse, they won't bother to interrupt and will just continue on with their list of questions. You would then leave the interview thinking you did well, never knowing the interviewer wanted more specifics. In our view, these interruptions should be considered gifts, because they are telling you exactly what the interviewer wants more information about.

Valerie: In what ways do you collaborate with content creators in your current role?

Maya: I regularly coordinate with the communications team, which includes people who write the copy, record the videos, and design the graphics. We want to make sure that the social media content aligns with the brand image and goals.

For example, when we were putting together a recent campaign launch, I organized a brainstorming session with the group. We discussed key messaging and visuals that would resonate with our target audience. I helped by sharing insights from our social media analytics, which enabled us to focus our ideas. We came up with the slogan "Count On Us," which played on our software's inventory counting features.

Throughout the campaign, we maintained open lines of communication, using tools like Slack and Trello to keep everyone updated on deadlines and feedback. This collaboration resulted in a series of posts that significantly boosted engagement. We had more than a 30% increase in reach in comparison with previous campaigns.

Overall, I think that having a collaborative environment not only enhances creativity but also leads to more effective content that truly connects with our audience.

Valerie: Give an example of a time when a content creator you worked with was not in alignment with your company's messaging.

Maya: At my current job, I worked with a freelance content creator who was hired to develop a series of blog posts highlighting our software. I appreciated the creativity he brought to the role, but one of the blog posts he drafted focused on the complexity of our software. He saw that as a benefit, but when I read it, the message I got was that the software might be difficult to use. Obviously, this contradicted our brand messaging, which focuses on how easy it is to use the software.

I scheduled a call with him to discuss the potential issue. He was a little surprised at first but realized it would be better for him to rewrite it. The result was a much better blog post that reinforced our brand message. He appreciated my suggestion, and after that he sent me other blog post drafts to get my opinion prior to being published.

174   CHAPTER 12   *How to deal with bad interviewers (and really good ones)*

Valerie [interrupting]: What did you say to him?

Maya: I started off by letting him know how much I liked one of his previous posts, and he appreciated that. Then I mentioned that I'd seen the draft of a post that he had sent to the group, and I said I had some ideas that he might be interested in. He said yes right away, and I told him I really like the message that the software had a lot of features. I added my concern that some readers might see that as an indication that the software could be too hard to use, especially if they were not yet customers. He was surprised and said he didn't mean that, and I said of course, but he might want to look at it again from that point of view. He said he never thought of it that way and said he would review it and keep that in mind.

The next day he sent me his revision. He took out the sentence that mentioned the many features and replaced it with one that said how user-friendly it was. He thanked me for giving him a different perspective.

Authors' insights

Maya clearly is learning to provide specifics in her answers, as evidenced by fewer interruptions as the interview continues. When asked about her collaboration with content creators, she included relevant details, like which content creators, for what project, the communication tools she used, the slogan they came up with, and a quantified result.

For the next question about when a content creator was not in alignment, Maya gave a good example and included specifics on the situation and the misalignment.

Maya included the result but made it sound like she didn't have to do much to resolve it ("he realized that it would be better for him to rewrite it"). Because the heart of this question is about how she communicated the delicate message of being out of alignment, Valerie probed further to find out what she said.

Anytime someone asks for a negative example (in this case, a time when a content creator was not in alignment), there is an implied second question, which is, "How did you handle that situation and bring it to a resolution?"

Valerie: Tell me about a time when you were juggling many projects simultaneously. What did you do to ensure that nothing slipped through the cracks?

Maya: Last year, one of our team members left, and I had to cover both jobs temporarily. I had a very busy quarter where I was managing multiple campaigns, content calendars, and community engagement efforts simultaneously. I used Trello project management tools to organize tasks, set milestones, and monitor progress. I reviewed this daily and weekly to make sure I was on track and was able to address any changes. I also set up reminders for myself to make sure I didn't miss anything.

The other members of my team also use Trello, and this helps us all to support each other and keep each other accountable.

Interview example

I'm proud that I delivered all my projects on time for that quarter, and my boss told me how pleased he was I was able to get it all done.

We hired a new team member soon after that, and I was able to shift some of the work to her. I still use those time management processes now so I can continue to meet all my deadlines.

Valerie: Have you ever worked for a company that required you to deal with frequent changes or unexpected events on the job? How did you react, and what did you do to maintain a positive attitude?

Maya: Yes, my previous company was known to make frequent changes, especially during product launches. One particular time I remember was when there was a major change in the product right before a scheduled campaign launch. One of the features that had been expected was not ready, and they pulled it from the final product and said it would be made available in the next version.

This unexpected change required us to pivot and modify our messaging and content quickly.

To adapt, I first took a deep breath and focused on what we could control. The team met for a quick brainstorming session to discuss the change. We created a revised content plan that highlighted the benefits of the update without mentioning the feature coming out in the next release.

It was a stressful time that meant some really long days to get it all done. To maintain a positive attitude, I concentrated on the opportunity this presented to engage our audience with the new content. I also made it a point to celebrate small wins during this hectic time, like drafting the revised posts ahead of schedule. The entire team focused on being upbeat during that time. My boss brought dinner in for all of us during those late nights, and we took a few minutes to have a little fun. We gave ourselves the nickname "the warriors" and joked about that as we worked hard to get it all done.

The result was that the campaign had no negative responses posted by customers. The previous time something like that happened, there were more than 40 negative comments the team had to address. We were really pleased we did not have to do that this time. Yes, it was stressful, but I learned that staying positive made a difficult time easier to manage.

Valerie: Describe the last time you escalated an urgent issue or negative sentiment, including why you chose to escalate it rather than respond yourself.

Maya: Two years ago, there was a situation where a customer complained on Facebook about a software issue. One of the important features of the software is a low-stock alert. After an upgrade, this feature stopped working for some customers. They were surprised when their inventory was depleted and they had not received the reminder to order more. The customer complained about how much it had cost them in both money and problems with their customers. The comment quickly gained attention, and other people started commenting. One other company posted that they had the same problem.

I recognized the importance of the situation, and I chose to escalate the issue to our customer support team because I wanted to make sure the customer received accurate information and effective support, rather than a general response that might not address their concerns.

I also wanted to make sure that the customer support team addressed the problem as quickly as possible before other customer companies had to deal with the same problem.

Our typical way to handle this is to document the issue for our customer support reports. Instead, I called the manager right away to emphasize the importance of the issue. I mentioned the possible negative impact on our brand reputation.

They quickly reached out to the customer with a solution, and they appreciated the fast response. In addition, the engineering team developed a patch for all customers. We were able to avoid problems with other customers and showcased our commitment to customer care.

That reinforced to me the importance of collaborating with other teams and knowing when to reach out directly to get things taken care of.

Valerie: Did you ever have to work on weekends in any of your last positions? How do you feel about that being a requirement twice monthly here?

Maya: In my current role, we monitor social media on weekends and holidays on a rotating basis, so I'm already used to that.

Working weekends twice a month is fine with me. I believe it's important to be available when our audience is most active, and I see weekends as an opportunity to connect with followers.

Valerie: What do you do to stay current on industry trends, tools, and best practices?

Maya: To stay current, I regularly follow leading social media blogs, newsletters, and podcasts, such as Social Media Examiner and Hootsuite's blog. I also participate in webinars and online courses to deepen my understanding of new platforms and features.

Additionally, I engage with online communities, such as LinkedIn groups, where I can connect with other professionals to share insights and experiences. I make it a point to experiment with new tools and features firsthand to understand their potential and applicability. I also like networking with other professionals at conferences and local events. I went to the Social Media Marketing World conference, and it was fabulous. I made some great connections and got some new ideas. In just the last month, three of my posts had an increase in audience engagement rate of over 50% from the previous month because I implemented some of these new ideas from the conference.

One of the biggest challenges we face is how to consistently create engaging content. I shared information from several of the conference presentations with my team and showed them how others were managing that. It helped us adjust our approach to focus more on connecting with the audience instead of primarily focusing on the number of content pieces we post.

This is a field that is constantly changing, and it's important for me to stay up to date and bring fresh ideas and strategies to my work.

Authors' insights

Notice that Valerie no longer felt the need to interrupt Maya because she included the relevant specifics in her answers. She concisely talked through her time management process and the tools she uses (with enough but not too much detail) and included a result. Her answer about frequent changes included a good description of the situation and her actions and results. Her escalation story included sufficient detail on the software feature that stopped working, how it affected the customer, and why she chose to escalate the issue. She clearly described both her actions and results and closed her answer nicely by stating how this example reinforced the importance of collaborating with other teams (which, although this wasn't mentioned specifically in the job description, is a common element of working in a marketing position such as this one).

Because she had performed a job description deconstruction as part of her planning, she was prepared to discuss all the items in the job description, and she had good answers ready about working weekends and staying current on industry trends.

Valerie: Why do you feel that you're a great candidate for this position?

Maya: I believe I'm a strong candidate for this position because I bring a unique combination of organizational skills, communication abilities, and technical expertise.

First, my excellent organizational skills enable me to manage multiple campaigns and deadlines efficiently. As I mentioned, I use Trello with my current team to keep us all on track. Because of my strong skills in this area, I was chosen to manage our department's social media content calendars. Team members let me know each week what they are working on so I can update the group schedule. If I don't get an update on a piece of content, I check in with the other person and update it for everyone.

As part of this calendar, I keep track of how each post aligns with our overall strategy and goals to make sure we are focused on our priorities. I've been able to handle busy times when I had to manage multiple campaigns, content calendars, and community engagement activities.

Second, I have strong written and verbal communication skills, which are needed for creating engaging content that resonates with target audiences. I understand the nuances of brand voice and can adapt my messaging across different platforms to maximize impact and increase audience engagement. In addition, I can handle challenging situations professionally and am prepared to work with others in crisis situations.

Third, my proficiency in various social media platforms and analytics tools allows me not only to create compelling content but also to measure its effectiveness. I regularly analyze performance metrics to refine strategies and improve engagement, ensuring that our efforts are data-driven and aligned with business objectives. I now put together weekly and monthly metrics summaries that my boss uses in the leadership presentations he makes to our executives to keep them updated on our results.

Together, these skills would help me contribute effectively to this team and drive your social media initiatives going forward. I'm excited about the opportunity and look forward to the next steps in this process.

Authors' insights

Maya did a good job answering this question. She mentions the "unique combination of skills" she would bring, and the three things she mentions are all important to the position. She goes on to talk more specifically about each of these skill areas, selling her experience and providing evidence of these skills.

She closes her answer in a powerful way, stating her ability to contribute to the team and drive social media initiatives, and then showing excitement about both the opportunity and the next steps in the selection process.

Valerie: Those were all of my questions; what questions do you have?

Maya: Thank you. I've done my research on the company's mission and values, but I'd like to know more. How would you describe the company culture?

Authors' note

We're going to pause the interview because we don't need to show Valerie's answers. Here are the other questions that Maya asks her:

- What are some of the common characteristics of people who are successful here?
- To what extent do teams collaborate with other departments across the organization?
- What do you like most about working here?
- Is there anything else I should know about the position and company that I haven't asked about?

> These are all good questions to ask in an initial interview with HR. Maya will have more specific questions ready when she meets with the hiring manager or people in her department.

Now, let's get back to the interview after Valerie answers Maya's questions:

Maya: Thank you so much. I just want to reinforce how interested I am in this role and your company. I think my skills would be a great match, and I'm excited about the opportunity to work for such a leader in the industry. Thank you for meeting with me today.

What are our next steps and time frames?

Interview review summary

Maya did many things well in her interview, and she didn't get thrown off balance by Valerie's interruptions. Her detailed preparation paid off because she had examples and answers ready for every question. She established rapport at the beginning, she used the negative sandwich in her answer to why she's looking for a new position, and her answers were all an appropriate length, with no rambling or use of filler words.

She also demonstrated a good balance of "I" and "we" in her answers, clearly stating what she did independently and as part of a team. She had good questions ready at the end, all of which were appropriate to ask an HR person rather than a hiring manager or marketing team members. She had an impactful close to her interview, showing both her relevant experience and enthusiasm.

While her initial answers contained several generalities, she learned and adapted as Valerie probed for more specifics. As the interview continued, her answers had an excellent balance of detail and brevity. We would caution her not to give away credit by making it sound like she easily attained her results (as she did in her content creator misalignment story); instead, she should make a point to clearly state what she did to get her results.

This interview example shows how an experienced interviewer may interrupt to probe further for more information on anything a candidate may have glossed over, but it's important to realize not all interviewers will do this. Some people assume that if an interviewer wants more details, they will ask, but some may simply continue asking questions and then not invite the candidate to the next round in the selection process because they didn't get the information they wanted. One can go overboard in providing too much information, so there must be a balance. Most interview answers should be no more than 2 minutes in length, but answers without specifics will have little to no impact. Remember the motto "there is power in specifics."

Think about

The following are some things to consider before moving on to the next chapter:

- What kinds of interviewers have you talked with in the past?
- Which of the types of interviewers described do you find difficult to interact with? What could you do to make it easier for you?
- What did you think of Maya's interview with Valerie? What, if anything, would you do differently in her shoes?
- Which of our authors' insights resonated with you the most?
- How will you use this information to help you prepare for and perform in future interviews?

Key takeaways

- Each interviewer may have a very different approach; some interviewers talk a lot, and some are very quiet. Some of them may be new and seem to be reading from a script, and others are highly experienced and will probe for additional details.
- Understanding the different types of interviewers can help you to be prepared and more comfortable during your interviews.
- One way to help you prepare for an interview is to go through the job description in detail to get ideas about possible questions based on the job requirements.
- An important part of preparation is choosing positive stories and examples that can be used to make your answers specific and relatable.
- If an interviewer interrupts you, see it as a gift, because they are giving you an opportunity to provide the information they want.
- Preparation of your stories in advance can help you to be specific enough without being too long-winded.

Part 5

Wrap-up

In this part, we'll provide an update on what Clueless Clark is doing and discuss what you can learn from his experience. He uses information from each of the chapters to better understand what interviewers are really looking for, and he realizes some of the mistakes he's made in the past. He decides that he shouldn't try to wing it and learns how to build his skills and prepare for his next interview.

We'll also talk about next steps for you and how to move forward now that you've mastered the art of translating Interview Speak.

Next steps

13

Let's check in on Clueless Clark. We've seen how his answers have not matched what the interviewers were looking for. It's not surprising he has not been invited back for second interviews at any of the companies. Initially he blamed the companies and told himself that he didn't want to work there anyway. Then he started wondering what he could do about it.

He complained to his friend, Ari, who had just been offered a new job. Ari suggested Clueless Clark read this *Interview Speak* book. Clueless Clark hesitated because he wanted to be himself in interviews and didn't want to follow some lame script. Ari assured him that wasn't what this book was about. Ari said, by following the ideas in the book, he prepared differently, adjusted his messaging, and was able to focus on what the interviewer was really asking. He said understanding the translations of the questions helped him dramatically improve his answers and then get the job offer. He suggested Clueless Clark give it a try.

Clueless Clark bought this book and started reading it (we made sure he received a version of the book that did not contain stories about his own interviews). He liked the idea of getting translations and thought about how much he relied on a translation app when he was on vacation in another country and wasn't familiar with the language.

CHAPTER 13 *Next steps*

What Clueless Clark learned

Let's look at how Clark used information contained in each chapter to improve his preparation and performance in job interviews.

Chapter 1: Welcome to Interview Speak

While reading the first chapter, Clueless Clark quickly realized that he had misunderstood the basic question, "Tell me about yourself." He had been one of those people who rambled on and on about his college and hobbies and personal life.

One of the things getting in his way was that he thought he shouldn't prepare for interviews because he was afraid that would feel too forced and that he wouldn't appear as his true self. When he thought about it, however, he realized there were plenty of times at work when he thoroughly prepared, and he decided he should give that same amount of time and energy into preparing for interviews. He could be himself and still be prepared.

He was surprised to read that it's a good idea to get to know the interviewer in advance a bit to help make a connection with them. He had a lot of connections on LinkedIn, so that would be easy for him.

He found it interesting to look at the different kinds of interview questions. One type of question he had difficulty with was hypothetical questions. He found himself trying to make up answers on the spot that he realized later didn't make much sense. He learned it would be much better to either describe a real situation or talk about something similar from his background. He made a mental note to do that the next time he was asked a similar question.

He really liked the negative sandwich technique. This gave him a way to start with a positive, share the negative, and then end with another positive. In past interviews, he had said there were no problems, which probably didn't go over well. Instead, using this model would give him a way to soften the description of a failure or mistake by emphasizing the positive of both what he learned and what he was doing differently now. This seemed to be a much better approach.

Reading chapter 1 also made him realize he was way off with his answer lengths. He thought his answers should be much longer than 1 to 2 minutes. Now it made sense why some interviewers interrupted his longer answers. He decided part of his planning would be to practice answers while timing them and make them shorter when needed.

Chapter 2: Common questions and special situations

Clark was eager to get to chapter 2, and as he read, he realized he had been asked many of these commonly asked questions. He thought it was great that he now had a list of typical questions for which he could prepare. He realized his previous answers to some of these questions were far from the best.

One thing that surprised him was what questions he should ask the interviewer. He thought asking questions would make him look uninformed, so he didn't ask any.

Actually, the only thing he typically did ask was, "When do I start?" He meant it to be funny, but it didn't usually get the positive response he wanted.

He recognized one of the special situations described him—he changed employers frequently. He prepared his answers for why he left his last few jobs. He liked the suggestion of saying he's now looking for long-term employment and is excited about growing his career with the company and giving some specifics about why he'd be a good fit. He planned to add that to his answers to practice and be ready for.

Chapter 3: Interpersonal skills questions

When Clark started to read this chapter, he thought about the answers he usually gave. Many times, he was too general, especially when describing how he influenced others. When he did give specific examples, they were good, but they didn't address what the interviewer was really asking. He hadn't realized there was a question behind the question.

He remembered a question he was asked at a recent interview: "Give me an example of a time when you found yourself in the middle of a conflict; what did you do or say to get to a resolution?" He talked about how he forced the other person to change. This information made him consider how he would address it differently in the future. He would give more details on the situation, focus on what he said to defuse the emotions so that the other person felt heard, and include the results.

He started making a list of the common questions in the chapter and how he'd answer them so he could capture these ideas and work on them prior to his next interview.

Chapter 4: Perseverance skills, failures, and negative situations questions

Clark was not excited about reading this chapter; this was an area that he was uncomfortable with. He did not want to admit mistakes because he thought it would look bad, and he had a hard time with these questions.

"Tell me about one of your failures" was a question he had struggled with in the past. He liked the idea of describing a project that didn't work out the way he had wanted and what he learned from that experience and would do differently next time. It reminded him of a particular situation that he could talk about differently. He could describe why it happened, how he changed his approach, and how he handles similar things differently now.

He thought about an interviewer who asked, "What was the most useful criticism you ever received?" Even though he thought he had given a great response at the time, reading through this helped him realize it wasn't a very good answer. He had talked about a time when his boss said he was a perfectionist and instead of saying what he learned from it, he argued that it was a good thing.

He decided he was going to find a different example of a time when he was given negative feedback and had accepted it and made some specific positive changes as a result. He added that to his notes.

Chapter 5: Leadership, hiring, and motivating skills questions

Even though Clueless Clark was not a manager, he found the chapter interesting. He had led teams informally and wanted to be ready to answer these questions.

Chapter 6: Problem-solving, time management, negotiation, and change questions

Clark eagerly read this chapter because he had been asked a lot of questions about problem-solving and dealing with change.

In the past, he found it difficult to think of good examples when interviewers asked about difficult challenges. Seeing the sentence breakdown diagram helped him realize he didn't have to describe the most difficult thing he'd ever done. He just needed to choose an example that was not easy or straightforward. That helped him to think about some stories he could use for that answer. The questions in the "Think about" section helped him come up with some additional examples he could use in his answers. In fact, he really appreciated having all of the "Think about" questions from the book listed in appendix B so that he could work through them as part of his preparation for future interviews.

Chapter 7: Questions by job function

Clark appreciated the specific questions for marketing professionals. He especially liked the "Think about" section, which gave him ideas for some different examples he could use.

Another area he hadn't thought about was the employer's brands and marketing approaches and the idea to come up with new ways for marketing the company's products. He could give examples of how he had successfully done something similar in the past. That was definitely something he was going to explore.

Reading through these interview questions also helped him see that he was only answering the surface part of the questions he heard in interviews. He wasn't addressing what the interviewers really wanted to know. He took more notes on some different ways to say things and areas to be more clear about.

Chapter 8: Not doing your homework, not being real, or leaving without . . .

Reading this chapter reminded Clark how little time he spent preparing. In the future, he would make sure he sounded ready for all of these questions because he would be.

He remembered a video interview he'd had where he didn't check the link in the invitation in advance, causing him to show up 15 minutes late. The interviewer was nice about it, but Clark didn't get another interview at that company. He would make sure he was ready for future virtual interviews.

This chapter also gave him some specifics about what to do at the end of an interview. Next time, he will clearly say why he'd be a great fit so that he can close the sale. He will find out the next steps and time frames and get the names of all the interviewers and send them each a thank-you message.

Chapter 9: Not hearing the question, the whole question, and the heart of the question

This was a major problem for Clueless Clark. He would often focus on the first part of the question and answer that without hearing the rest of it. He sometimes would even jump in with his answer before the interviewer had finished talking. Now he realized interrupting the interviewer could also be interpreted as rude, which would not help his chances of getting another interview. He added a note to himself in all caps: PAUSE BEFORE ANSWERING. In the past, he thought pausing would be seen as a negative, but now he saw it as a positive. It would give him the chance to really hear the interviewer and come up with his best answer.

When he read the part about rambling, he knew he was often guilty of that. He had thought it would be better to keep talking rather than pause to come up with a clear and concise answer. In his notes, he highlighted pausing—he needed to practice that.

He was intrigued by the idea that he should find the heart of the question. He liked the idea of jotting down some key words from the question to keep him on track during his answer. Next time, he will have a pad and pen ready to remind him to do that.

Chapter 10: Giving answers that sound good to you (but aren't)

Clark cringed when he read the chapter title, and he wondered how often he had done that. He had definitely given answers that were too long, and he rambled.

This helped him see his answers tended to focus on what he did instead of why it mattered. He hadn't connected the dots in his examples so the interviewers could understand the impact of his actions. He included another note to make sure to add why something mattered and be clear about the results.

He decided he needed to develop a better answer to the question, "Why should we hire you?" He had to see it from the company's point of view and help them clearly see the value he would bring. He would choose a few important skills and experiences to highlight what would make him a great match for the job.

He also knew he had a tendency to give general answers instead of specific examples. He decided part of his preparation was going to be to go through the job description and make a list of some examples with details he could use in the future.

Chapter 11: Interview stages and translations before, during, and after

This chapter helped Clark understand what was important to different interviewers. The translations of what they said surprised him. For example, when an interviewer said, "Thank you; that was a good answer," he believed that it really was a good answer. This helped him see that maybe it was just a way for the interviewer to get ready to ask the next question.

This chapter offered him different ways to think about the lack of responses he'd been getting from companies after his interviews.

Chapter 12: How to deal with bad interviewers (and really good ones)

Clark really liked the job deconstruction example, and he decided he was going to try it. This was also a good reminder to make his answers more specific. He found the interview in this chapter pulled all the information together for him. He saw how he could shorten his answers to make them more impactful and how he could end his interviews in a strong way.

Chapter 13: Next steps

Clark had an interview scheduled the next week after he finished the book, and he blocked out time for preparation using the interview preparation checklist in appendix C. He used the job deconstruction method to find key words and phrases, and he developed possible interview questions he could be asked. He chose specific examples he could use and wrote notes for answers he could give. He reviewed the common questions and prepared answers for each of them. He read the additional questions in appendix A and realized there were several ways that one topic could be asked. This helped him recognize a topic, even if the question he was asked was slightly different than the one he had anticipated.

He then recorded himself answering the questions and reviewed his answers from an interviewer's point of view. Then he tried something that was uncomfortable: he asked a friend to do a mock interview with him. He recorded this interview and made notes on what he could improve in a real interview. He not only took notes on how to modify his answers, but he also paid attention to adjustments he could make to his nonverbal behavior, including his gestures and facial expressions.

Part of his preparation was to learn about the company and interviewer. He reviewed the company website, searched online for current articles about them, and looked at his interviewer's LinkedIn profile.

When it came time for the video interview, he was ready. He had checked everything in advance and was there a few minutes early. He had a pad and pen ready to jot down key words, and he had a sticky note on his computer that said PAUSE.

The first interview he had was with an internal recruiter. It went well, and afterwards, he completed the post-interview evaluation in appendix D. A few days later, he received an invitation to meet with the hiring manager. He was delighted, because he finally got a second interview! During his preparation, he focused on questions his manager might ask, including those focused on his execution of marketing projects. He also put together some specific questions to ask his potential manager.

After that interview, he was invited to interview with two other people who worked in the department and would be his peers. He was ready and felt very positive about those interviews.

He accomplished his goal: a job offer he accepted. Clueless Clark's work had turned him into Champion Clark.

This applicant, please

What's next for you

Now it's your turn. It's time to take the information in this book and make it work for you.

What could hold you back

When Laura coaches people, she sees many have difficulty moving from ideas into action. People often get excited about the ideas and may even make plans to improve, but they don't take actions necessary to achieve their goals.

That could mean that, even though you like the ideas in this book, you may not work on preparation. Or maybe you do start working on it, but you put off applying for jobs until you feel ready to interview. Don't wait; if you apply and get an interview, that will motivate you to work on your preparation sooner.

Clueless Clark held himself back because he was afraid that if he prepared, he wouldn't be himself in interviews. After thinking about it, he concluded he could be his best self only if he prepared. He would be able to show up to the interview with his best stories ready, so the interviewers would learn more about him. Being prepared means he wouldn't ramble while trying to think of the right answer, because he would know it. Another thing that held Clark back was he hadn't taken time to prepare. He scheduled time for other important meetings, so it made sense he should schedule time to prepare for interviews.

Now that he's worked through the material in this book, Clueless Clark is clueless no longer. He's now Champion Clark.

190   CHAPTER 13   *Next steps*

If you're still having problems getting started, ask yourself what's holding you back. What are your concerns? Are you afraid you won't be able to utilize the information in this book to improve your interview performance? The only way to know is to try and to practice so you can get better at it.

If you're getting stuck, it can help to remind yourself of the reason you're doing this. What's your big "why?" Do you want to get a better job, higher pay, a better boss, more opportunities? Understanding Interview Speak and preparing can help you have better interviews so you can get what you want.

How to move forward

It can be helpful to first ask yourself: what were your key takeaways? What information was most helpful to you? What would you like to work on first?

If you're new to interviewing and the idea of deconstructing a job description seems a little daunting, you can start by reviewing chapter 2. Just by knowing the information in that chapter, you'll be more likely to perform better in interviews.

We recommend you go back to the "Think about" section in each chapter and ask yourself those questions (they are all listed in appendix B). The information in your answers can give you some ideas about what you need to work on. Also, review the "Key takeaways" at the end of the chapters to help reinforce your learning.

Go through the chapters and appendix A to review possible questions and think through how you would answer them. You can also practice deconstructing job descriptions to help you identify additional questions you might be asked.

Then select some stories and examples that illustrate your accomplishments, including what you did, how you did it, the results, and, most importantly, why it should matter to the interviewer at the company you want to work for. Write out notes on your answers and practice them so you can comfortably and naturally share that information.

If this feels like a lot to do, start by breaking it into small, manageable steps. Then pick one small step and commit to doing it today or this week.

Another way to move forward is to ask a friend to help you stay on track. They can be your accountability partner and can check in with you to make sure you're making progress on your plans. If your friend is also looking for a job, that is even better for both of you because you can support each other as you continue to learn and take action.

> **DEFINITION** Accountability partners help each other keep on track with their goals. Usually, each partner tells the other their goals for the week; then they check in with each other at the end of that week to see how each is doing and to set new goals.

At the beginning of the book, we asked you to think about an interview you thought you nailed, but then you didn't get invited to the next step in their interview process. We told you by understanding what the interviewer is really asking and why, you could have better answers.

You now have that information, so you can be the candidate they invite back, and you can ultimately receive the job offer. Translating the questions you hear can give you an advantage over the other candidates. Every question has a question behind the question, and when you understand what interviewers are actually looking for, you can choose your best examples and stories so they can learn about you and what you bring to the role.

Thank you for going on the journey with us and letting us provide the Interview Speak translations. We were glad to share our insights from the other side of the interview table. We hope by following Ari, Davina, Lucas, Jen, Maya, and Champion Clark, you've learned new skills that will help you move forward more easily and get the job you want.

appendix A
Interview questions
by chapter

The following are the translated interview questions from chapters 2 to 7 and additional ideas of similar questions that you may be asked. While the wording is different in these additional questions compared to the questions translated in those chapters, the topics are the same, so the information and guidance provided in "translations" and "how to answer" still apply.

Use this list and think through how you would answer them to help you prepare for your upcoming interviews.

If you are in a position to hire or are asked to participate in a selection process as an interviewer, you may also find this list of questions valuable. Feel free to utilize any of the questions related to the position and skills for which you're hiring.

Chapter 2: Common Questions and Special Situations

Most common questions

TRANSLATED QUESTIONS

- Tell me about yourself.
- Why are you looking for a new job OR why did you leave your last job?
- What are you looking for next?
- What do you not want to do?
- What kind of salary are you looking for?

Chapter 2: Common Questions and Special Situations 193

- Why are you interested in this job?
- What do you know about our company?
- What are your career goals?
- What are your strengths?
- What are your weaknesses?
- What did you enjoy most about your last job?
- What did you not like about your last job?
- Why should we hire you?
- What questions do you have?

ADDITIONAL QUESTIONS

- Walk me through your background.
- Why are you in the job market?
- What interests you most about this job?
- What research have you done on our company?
- What goals do you have for yourself?
- What three things would you like to improve about yourself?
- If I were to call your previous boss or colleagues, what would they tell me are your strengths and weaknesses?
- Define three qualities of a good leader. Which of these do you need to work on and why?
- What is your compensation range? (What are you going to cost me?)
- Why do you think you should be selected for the next stage of the interview process?

Special situation questions

TRANSLATED QUESTIONS

- What have you done since you left your last company?
- Why have you changed employers so frequently over the last several years?
- Because you were with your last employer for so long, do you think you may have a hard time adjusting to a new company's way of working?
- What makes you think you know our industry and will be able to become productive right away?
- This job is at a lower level than your current (or last) job; why would you be interested in taking a step down in your career?

ADDITIONAL QUESTIONS

- How have you stayed productive since leaving your last job?
- Convince me that you're not a job hopper.

APPENDIX A *Interview questions by chapter*

- Why did you stay so long at your last employer; do you lack initiative?
- How will you get up to speed on our industry?
- How will you stay motivated doing this lower-level job?

Chapter 3: Interpersonal skills questions

Approachability, credibility, and humility

TRANSLATED QUESTIONS

- Give an example of an initiative you led that required you to interact with various levels within the company.
- Tell me about a time when humility played a role in your being successful.
- Describe a situation where you had to build credibility.

ADDITIONAL QUESTIONS

- Describe a time when you were humble.
- How do you build credibility?
- If we were to hire you, how would you go about building credibility with the team?
- Describe a project team you were on that involved multiple levels of staff.
- What kinds of things do you do so that others view you as approachable?

Influencing and gaining support

TRANSLATED QUESTIONS

- Give me an example of a time when you convinced leadership in your organization to make a significant change.
- Describe a situation when you had to delicately let a key stakeholder know that their expectations were unrealistic.
- Tell me about a situation in which you built needed support for a goal or project from people who didn't report to you and over whom you had no direct authority.

ADDITIONAL QUESTIONS

- Tell me about a time when you were most persuasive in overcoming resistance to your ideas or point of view.
- Describe a time when you came up with a new method or idea. How did you get it approved and implemented?
- Describe the occasion when you felt best about your ability to draw out and solicit information from another person.
- Tell me about an occasion when you felt it necessary to convince your department to change a policy or procedure. How did you go about it, and whose feathers got ruffled?

Chapter 3: Interpersonal skills questions 195

- Tell me about a time when you had to influence or persuade someone to do something for you that might have been an inconvenience for him/her.
- Tell me about a time when you had to convince others to support an unpopular cause. What did you do and what was the result?

Diversity, equity, and inclusion

TRANSLATED QUESTIONS

- How has your background and experience prepared you to be effective in an environment that values diversity and is committed to inclusion?
- In what ways do you think diversity is important to someone in this role?
- What kinds of experiences have you had in relation to people whose backgrounds are different from your own?
- What programs or initiatives have you been part of focused on working with diverse populations, and what was your role in those efforts?

ADDITIONAL QUESTIONS

- Describe your current understanding of diversity and why it's important.
- What are some concerns you have about working with diverse populations?
- What challenges do you think you'll face in working with a diverse team here?
- Describe an effective strategy to introduce diversity to individuals who have only experienced a limited number of cultures.
- How would you handle a situation in which someone made a sexist, racist, homophobic, or otherwise prejudiced remark?
- How would you respond to a conversation between coworkers or colleagues that could be perceived as offensive to others?
- If you were hired, how would you use this position to increase or enhance diversity at our company?
- Give an example of a time in which you demonstrated a commitment to inclusion in your work.
- Describe the most challenging situation dealing with diversity that you have faced.

Conflict management

TRANSLATED QUESTIONS

- Describe a time when you successfully defused a conflict.
- Give an example of a time when you found yourself in the middle of a conflict; what did you do or say to get to a resolution?

ADDITIONAL QUESTIONS

- Conflict can happen sometimes between individuals or departments because of their different interests or priorities. Tell me about a time when you saw conflict as an opportunity.
- Tell me about a time when you avoided a conflict because of your actions or communications.
- How do you typically react when faced with a conflict?
- How would you react if someone disagreed with your ideas or approach?
- Tell me about a time when you had a disagreement with a customer. What happened?

Chapter 4: Perseverance skills, failures, and negative situations questions

Failures and negative situations

TRANSLATED QUESTIONS

- Tell me about one of your failures.
- What was the most useful criticism you ever received?
- Describe for me a decision you regretted after having made it.
- Give an example where you failed to persuade someone to do something you felt would be good for the organization.

ADDITIONAL QUESTIONS

- Tell me about something you did in one of your jobs that didn't work out as well as you had hoped.
- Would you describe a few situations in which your work was criticized?
- Tell me about a time when you failed to reach a goal.
- In hindsight, what risk do you regret not taking? Why did you decide not to do it, and what was the outcome?

Overcoming obstacles and difficult situations

TRANSLATED QUESTIONS

- Tell me about a time when you were most persuasive in overcoming resistance to your ideas or point of view.
- Give an example of a situation when you had to think on your feet to get yourself out of a difficult situation.

ADDITIONAL QUESTIONS

- Tell me about a time when you came up with a new method or idea. What obstacles did you face, and how did you get it approved and implemented?

Chapter 5: Leadership, hiring and motivating skills questions

- Describe a time when you had to convince others to support an unpopular cause. What did you do? What was the result?
- Give an example of a situation when you had to be very careful to say the right things at the right time.
- What is the most difficult obstacle you've faced in your career?

Perseverance and drive

TRANSLATED QUESTIONS

- Tell me about a situation that shows your perseverance, persistence, and ability to remain positive when faced with adversity.
- What can you tell me about yourself that best illustrates your personal drive and motivation?
- Describe a situation that required you to make sacrifices or put in extra effort to achieve the goal. How did your drive and perseverance contribute to your success?

ADDITIONAL QUESTIONS

- Tell me about an issue or project that really challenged you. How did you meet the challenge? In what way was your approach different from others?
- What motivates you?
- What are your demotivators?
- Tell me something about yourself that shows your ability to pursue a goal despite obstacles.

Chapter 5: Leadership, hiring and motivating skills questions

Leadership and management

TRANSLATED QUESTIONS

- What is your leadership style?
- Discuss a situation where you were able to build a high level of trust, morale, and team spirit.
- Tell me about an occasion when you pulled the team together and improved morale during challenging circumstances.
- Describe a difficult experience you've had while leading a group with different opinions and personalities. What issues arose, and how did you resolve them?

ADDITIONAL QUESTIONS

- What do you expect of your direct reports? How do you communicate your expectations?
- If I were to call your direct reports, how would they describe you as a leader?

- Describe three things you've done in the past to improve employee morale. Which of these had the desired result and which did not?
- If one of your team members wanted to do something on a project in a way that could be a mistake, how would you weigh that team member's learning experience against protecting the project?
- As a leader of a team, how do you handle someone who is not pulling his/her weight? Give a specific example.
- Describe a time when you reprimanded an employee for poor performance.
- What were your objectives for the last year? To what extent were they achieved?
- Tell me about a learning experience that affected your leadership style.

Hiring and motivating staff

TRANSLATED QUESTIONS

- What kinds of things have you done to both attract new talent and guard against poor hires?
- What do you do to create an environment that inspires and motivates your team?

ADDITIONAL QUESTIONS

- How do you go about selecting and hiring the right people for your team?
- Sometimes it is important to deal with a team member's negative attitude to build team motivation. Give me an example of a time when you confronted a negative attitude successfully with the result of building teamwork and morale.
- Describe for me how you motivate people.
- In working with new people, how do you go about gaining an understanding of who they are and what motivates them?

Chapter 6: Problem-solving, time management, negotiation, and change questions

Analysis, problem-solving, and decision-making

TRANSLATED QUESTIONS

- Describe a complex problem you solved.
- Tell me about a time when you missed an obvious solution to a problem.
- What was the most difficult decision you ever had to make on the job?
- Describe for me your decision-making process.

ADDITIONAL QUESTIONS

- Tell me about a problem you solved in your last job.
- Tell me about a problem you were unable to solve.

Chapter 6: Problem-solving, time management, negotiation, and change questions   **199**

- What was the last decision you had to make in your last job?
- How do you go about making decisions?

Time and project management

TRANSLATED QUESTIONS

- Tell me about a time when you were juggling multiple projects with overlapping deadlines, tight time frames, and conflicting priorities.
- Recall for me a major project you initiated and worked through to completion. How did you proactively manage changes in project priorities, scope, and expectations?

ADDITIONAL QUESTIONS

- How do you keep track of all the projects assigned to you?
- Tell me about a time when you missed a deadline. What did you learn and how do you avoid missing deadlines going forward?
- With most projects, it is important to balance the need for quality, deadlines, and costs. Give me an example that demonstrates your ability to balance these needs.
- Describe a project that required you to either increase the budget or extend the timeline. Which did you choose to change and why?

Negotiation

TRANSLATED QUESTIONS

- Tell me about a difficult negotiation in which you were involved; what challenges arose during the negotiation, and how did you work through them?
- Describe a situation that demonstrates your ability to negotiate skillfully when costs were critical.

ADDITIONAL QUESTIONS

- What are your strengths and weaknesses as a negotiator?
- Tell me about a time when you had to make a major compromise during a negotiation.
- What have you learned about yourself as a result of your negotiation experiences?
- Describe a situation when your ability to gain important information led to a successful negotiation.
- Give an example that demonstrates your ability to evaluate alternatives which resulted in gaining support of another person despite their different point of view.

Change management

TRANSLATED QUESTIONS

- Give an example of your ability to implement change and influence people to accept that change.
- Describe something you instituted or changed that required collaborative planning with other departments and resulted in improved customer relationships.
- Tell me about a time when you had to deal with frequent changes or unexpected events on the job.

ADDITIONAL QUESTIONS

- Tell me about a project you participated in that involved change management.
- Describe a difficult change you made. What made it so difficult, and how did you manage it?
- Give an example of a time when you had to gain buy-in from people for a change that you or your team wanted to implement.
- In what ways did your last job involve working with other departments to implement change?
- What kinds of things do you say to get buy-in from others for your ideas?
- Around here, change is the norm; how do you think you'd adapt to that kind of environment?
- Tell me about something that happened in your last job that was unexpected; how did you react?

Chapter 7: Questions by job function

Senior leadership

- Describe for me a strategy you've implemented that addressed specific market and competitive challenges.
- Tell me about a situation in which you had to translate the mission and vision of the company into individual performance goals.
- Give an example from your leadership experience which demonstrates your ability to implement new ideas that led to company growth.
- If you were our CEO, how would you redefine our strategy to capitalize on the potential of the present market?

Operations

- Describe for me a new method or process you initiated that resulted in maximizing efficiency and productivity. What performance metrics did you measure, and what were the specific improvements?

Chapter 7: Questions by job function **201**

- Give an example from your leadership experience which demonstrates your ability to implement new ideas that led to reduced costs.
- Describe a situation that demonstrates how you used technology to improve the client or customer experience.

Sales

- Tell me about something you introduced that you would describe as a best practice in sales leadership.
- Describe your most complex and challenging sales success.
- Give an example of a project that required you to understand and interpret a customer's needs and requirements and relate them back to product or service requirements.
- Tell me about a project you led that provided visibility and insight to executive management based on input and feedback from prospects and customers.
- Give an example of something you instituted or changed that required collaborative planning with other departments and resulted in improved customer relationships.

Marketing

- Give an example of a comprehensive and cohesive marketing strategy you developed and implemented that resulted in increased brand awareness.
- Describe a market analysis you conducted that identified challenges and opportunities for growth, including what you did after the analysis to affect change.
- Tell me about a time when you worked through the planning of a project; what issues arose, and how did you work through them?
- Describe a time when you or your team had to respond to a negative issue or a crisis very quickly.
- Tell me about a time when you successfully collaborated to difuse a conflict between the sales and marketing teams.

Finance

- Give me an example from your leadership experience that demonstrates your ability to implement a major change to improve a company's financial performance.
- Tell me about something you instituted that improved internal finance processes.
- Describe a situation where you worked with senior leadership to transform your company to an environment where ongoing analysis of results became part of the culture. What types of benchmarking, analysis, and reporting did you institute?
- Tell me about a difficult relationship you've had with a key financial vendor, banker, or lender; what issues arose, and how did you resolve them?

APPENDIX A *Interview questions by chapter*

- Describe for me an "early warning system" you've put in place that alerted senior leadership to P&L results variations.

Information technology

- Give me an example that demonstrates your ability to translate organizational needs into workable technology business solutions.
- Tell me about a time when you used technology to drive business results.
- In this role, you will need to balance your technical knowledge and your ability to communicate with a wider nontechnical audience; how have you navigated this delicate balance in the past?
- With most technical projects, it is important to balance the need for quality, deadlines, and costs. Give me an example that demonstrates your ability to balance these needs.
- Give me an example of a situation where you developed criteria for measuring the performance of the tech organization. What metrics did you measure, and what results did you report?

Human resources

- What do you think are the most important qualifications and characteristics an HR executive should possess in today's business climate?
- You've done some recruiting; if you were interviewing candidates for this position, what would you look for?
- How do you help your organization attract new talent, guard against poor hires, and retain its top talent?
- Tell me about a situation where you felt your ability to manage confidential information was being tested.
- What example can you cite of your ability to apply prudent judgment in a delicate HR-related situation?

appendix B
Questions to think about

The following are all the questions included in the "Think about" sections throughout the book. We encourage you to work through these as part of your interview preparation to become a more effective candidate and get the job you want.

Chapter 1: Welcome to Interview Speak

- How have you prepared for interviews in the past? What will you do differently now?
- Which of the types of interview questions described have you been asked in previous interviews?
- Which of the traps mentioned have you fallen into? What will you do differently in your next interview?

Chapter 2: Common questions and special situations

- How would you answer the question "Tell me about yourself"?
- How would you describe the reason you exited (or are looking to exit) your last (or current) job?
- What three things would you list as your weaknesses, and how would you use the "negative sandwich" to describe each of them?
- How would you answer the "Why should we hire you?" question?

204   **APPENDIX B**   *Questions to think about*

- If any of the special situations apply to you, such as being unemployed, having multiple short-term jobs, being with one employer for a long time, or wanting to change industries, how would you address them?

Chapter 3: Interpersonal skills questions

- Which scenario would you select to describe when humility contributed to your being successful? In what way was it important to be humble in that situation?
- When you've had to build credibility, what kinds of things did you do or say that allowed others to have confidence in your abilities?
- Which project would you describe if asked about interacting with different levels of staff within your organization?
- Which projects or ideas required you to gain higher-level approval? What did you say or do to get that approval?
- Have you ever had to tell someone that their expectations of you or your team were unrealistic? If so, what did you say to help them understand?
- Which example would you select to describe a situation where you had to gain support from people who didn't report to you? What did you do or say to gain their support?
- What are your personal beliefs on diversity, and why do you think this topic is widely discussed these days? How do you think this topic relates to the kind of role you are targeting?
- Which of your experiences interacting and collaborating with people whose backgrounds differ from yours would you talk about in interviews if asked?
- How comfortable are you in sharing aspects of your personal background that may have shaped your views on diversity?
- Which example would you select to describe a conflict in resolution of which you played a key part? What did you do or say to reduce the tension between the parties?
- There is a difference between being a mediator between people who have a conflict and being in the middle yourself as someone who has a conflict with another person. Which examples do you have of having a conflict with others on a project, deadline, or priority?
- What kinds of tools or methods do you typically use to calm people down during heated discussions?

Chapter 4: Perseverance skills, failures, and negative situations questions

- Which example would you select if asked to demonstrate perseverance and persistence?

Chapter 5: Leadership, hiring, and motivating skills questions   205

- When was the last time you had to persuade someone to accept your idea or point of view? What factors contributed to their resistance? What did you say or do to gain their acceptance?
- What example would you give if asked about a time you had to think on your feet?
- What were the obstacles you needed to overcome to be successful in your last job?
- What kinds of things do you typically do to remain calm during stressful situations?
- What situation would you describe if asked about one of your failures? What did you learn after this experience, and what do you do differently now?
- What constructive criticism have you received that you would describe if asked about this in an interview? In what ways did you take it to heart and change your behavior as a result?
- Can you think of a decision you made that, if given the chance, you would change? What did you learn from that experience, and what do you do differently now?
- Which example would you share about failing to persuade? What did you say at that time, and how would you word it differently if given a similar situation now?

Chapter 5: Leadership, hiring, and motivating skills questions

- How would you describe your leadership style?
- How do you think others would describe you as a leader? Have you ever asked them?
- Do you gravitate toward one style of leadership, or do you adapt your style to the situation and people involved?
- What kinds of things do you do to build trust in you as a leader?
- Have you ever been in a situation where staff had low morale? How did you react?
- What example would you use to describe a time when you built team spirit?
- Which scenario would you describe if asked about leading a team with different personalities and opinions? What did you do as a leader to resolve the issues that arose?
- How would you describe your selection and hiring process? What works well and what can be improved?
- How would you describe your interview style? Do you follow a process or do you "wing it"? What kinds of questions do you ask?
- How do you think others would describe what you're like to work for?
- What do you do to identify what motivates the members of your team? Once you have that information, what do you do as a leader to ensure that your team stays motivated to perform at their highest levels?

Chapter 6: Problem-solving, time management, negotiation, and change questions

- Which example would you select if asked to describe a complex problem you solved?
- What would you say to describe your thought process as you worked through that problem?
- What situation would you use to describe missing an obvious solution to a problem, and how would you describe what you learned as a result of this situation?
- Which decision would you select if asked to describe your most difficult decision?
- What would you say to describe your decision-making process?
- How do you organize and plan projects? What system or process do you use to ensure their successful and timely completion?
- Which of your previous projects changed the most throughout the time you worked on it? What caused these changes?
- What kinds of things do you do to anticipate possible changes in scope, priorities, or expectations?
- What do you do to avoid any lack of clarity in your projects' scope, deadlines, and expectations?
- What was your most challenging negotiation? How would you describe the issues that arose in a way that would show the complexity but not be overly detailed? How satisfied were you with the outcome? How satisfied do you think the other party or parties were?
- If you were not in a sales or customer-facing role, what interaction with a manager or colleague could you use as your negotiation example?
- How would you rate yourself as a negotiator? In what ways could you improve?
- Which example would you use to describe a change implementation in which you were a key player? What did you do or say to gain acceptance from the people this change impacted?
- Would you use this same example if asked for a situation that involved collaborative planning with other departments? If not, which scenario would you describe? In what ways did the situation result in improved customer relationships?
- Which of your jobs involved frequent changes or unexpected events? How would you describe your actions and results in those situations?

Chapter 7: Questions by job function

SENIOR LEADERSHIP

- What specific example would you use to describe a strategy you implemented to address market challenges?

Chapter 7: Questions by job function

- How do you go about translating a company's mission and vision into individual performance goals?
- Which new ideas of yours have led to your previous company's growth? How did you influence people to accept those ideas, and how would you describe the way the ideas were implemented?
- How will you describe your interactions with different levels of the organization (not just other leaders)?

OPERATIONS

- Which metrics have you achieved in your past positions that demonstrate maximizing efficiency and productivity?
- Which new ideas of yours have led to your previous company's reduced costs? How did you influence people to accept those ideas, and how would you describe the way they were implemented?
- What example would you use to describe how you used technology to improve the customer experience?

SALES

- Which example would you use to describe the sales accomplishment you are most proud of?
- What are some examples of dealing with difficult customers that you can use to highlight your sales skills?
- What other difficulties have you faced (such as launching a new product, starting a new territory, or managing customer complaints) that can highlight your skills and abilities?
- How have you worked with other salespeople and other departments to gain a new customer or close a deal?

MARKETING

- What would you select if asked for an example of a comprehensive and cohesive marketing strategy you developed and implemented that resulted in increased brand awareness?
- What kinds of market analyses have you conducted that identified challenges and opportunities for growth? How did you use that information to affect change?
- Have you or your team ever had to respond to a sudden or unexpected negative issue or a crisis? What steps did you take, and what were the results?
- What kinds of conflicts have you experienced between the sales and marketing departments? How did you collaborate with others to resolve the issues?

FINANCE

- Which example would you share that demonstrates your ability to implement a major change to improve a company's financial performance?

208 **APPENDIX B** *Questions to think about*

- What kinds of things have you instituted that improved internal finance processes?
- Have you worked for a company that had an environment where ongoing analysis of financial results was part of the culture? What was your role in contributing to facilitating that kind of environment?
- What kinds of relationships have you had with financial vendors, bankers, or lenders? Do you have an example of a time when issues arose, and if so, how did you resolve them?

INFORMATION TECHNOLOGY

- How will you explain your technical skills to a nontechnical interviewer?
- Which example would you use if asked for an example of using technology to drive business results?
- How would you describe how you've balanced communicating with both technical and nontechnical audiences?
- Which project would you use to describe how you've balanced the need for quality, deadlines, and costs?
- What have you done to avoid "scope creep" on your projects?
- If you're in a leadership role, do you use different leadership styles or approaches when leading technical staff and nontechnical staff? How would you describe those differences?

HUMAN RESOURCES

- What questions would you ask if you were recruiting to fill this role?
- How would you demonstrate that you can connect with people as well as enforce company rules and policies?
- How would you describe how you help your organization attract new talent, guard against poor hires, and retain its top talent?
- Can you think of a time when your ability to manage confidential information may have been tested? What did you do or say in that situation to maintain confidentiality?
- Which example would you use to demonstrate your ability to apply prudent judgment in a delicate HR-related situation?

Chapter 8: Not doing your homework, not being real, or leaving without . . .

- Think back to previous interviews; what questions were the most difficult for you? How can you be more prepared now?
- Which method of practicing your answers will be most effective for you? Would you do it in front of a mirror, with a friend, recording yourself on your computer or phone, or can you think of another way?

- Are there any answers that could sound canned? How can you adjust them so they sound real and authentic?
- What are some ways that you have built rapport with people in a short period of time? Which of these can you use in your interviews?
- What are some good questions you could ask the interviewer that show your interest in the job and the company?
- What can you say to "close the sale"?

Chapter 9: Not hearing the question, the whole question, and the heart of the question

- Think about your past interviews; have there been situations when you found yourself rambling? Why was that? What could you do differently in the future?
- In the past, have you decided how you were going to answer a question or jumped in with your answer before hearing the entire question? How could you practice listening to the whole question and briefly pausing before answering?
- Have you ever forgotten an interview question in the middle of talking through your answer? What did you do? What will you do differently if that happens again?

Chapter 10: Giving answers that sound good to you (but aren't)

- Have you made any of these mistakes in past interviews? What would you do differently now?
- Which of these potential issues would be most likely to cause you problems? What can you do instead to prevent that?
- Which of the answers that you've prepared match these problems? How can you adjust your answers to avoid these mistakes?

Chapter 11: Interview stages and translations before, during, and after

- What can you do to be prepared for the different people and positions you'll be meeting with?
- Which interview stage causes you the most trepidation? What can you do prior to your next interview to overcome that?
- Which of the mentioned messages have you received before, during, or after your interviews?
- How can you use the information in this chapter to help you better understand the messages you get from employers?

Chapter 12: How to deal with bad interviewers (and really good ones)

- What kinds of interviewers have you talked with in the past?
- Which of the types of interviewers described do you find difficult to interact with? What could you do to make it easier for you?
- What did you think of Maya's interview with Valerie? What, if anything, would you do differently in her shoes?
- Which of our authors' insights resonated with you the most?
- How will you use this information to help you prepare for and perform in future interviews?

appendix C
Interview preparation
checklist

The following is a checklist to help you prepare for your job interviews. We encourage you to work through these items prior to each interview to become a more successful candidate and get the job you want.

Know the company

- Review the company's LinkedIn page and website, paying particular attention to the way they describe the company and its mission, values, culture, and people.
- Search for any recent press releases about the company.

Know the job

- Go through the job description in detail and think through each bullet point. Be ready to describe your experience in each item listed and to give examples.
- Consider doing a "job deconstruction" such as the ones we provide in chapters 1 and 12.

Learn about the interviewer

- Review the LinkedIn profiles of all interviewers to learn about their backgrounds and how they describe themselves.

- Identify anything you have in common that you can use to build rapport during the interview.

Know yourself

- Go through each line on your resume and be able to describe your projects, duties, and results, including how each example pertains to this organization and the position for which you're interviewing.
- Identify your most relevant and compelling stories to share in the interview based on the areas of experience and/or competencies listed in the job description. You may wish to put together a prep chart such as the following one.

Interview prep chart

Competency	Story including actions and results

- Practice using one of the answer frameworks described in chapter 1 to structure your stories (PAR, STAR, SOAR).
- Customize and practice your answer to the "Tell me about yourself" and exit questions (why you're looking for a new position).
- Identify your top three to five selling points for why you are a great fit for the position, including your unique combination of skills, knowledge, and experience.
- Identify any potential objections they may have (e.g., experience in a different industry, different company, or team size) and how you will overcome them; include examples.
- Develop and practice your answer to the question "Why should we hire you?" (i.e., what makes you uniquely qualified and the best fit for the position and company?). It is your job to convey this information regardless of whether it is asked explicitly.
- Develop your list of questions to ask the interviewer(s).

appendix D
Post-interview evaluation

The following are questions to ask yourself after each interview. The purpose is to reinforce what you did well so you can continue to do those things and to look for areas where you can improve going forward. Even if an interview did not go well, you have an opportunity to see it as a learning experience and use the information to better prepare for future interviews.

How did I show that I did my homework regarding the company and position?

- What information was I able to convey?
- What do I want to emphasize in the future?

Was I able to build rapport with the interviewer?

- How did the interviewer respond?
- What do I want to work on?

Which questions were the most difficult for me to answer?

- Why were these difficult?
- How will I answer them if they come up in future interviews?

What did I do well?

- How can I build on those things and use my strengths in future interviews?
- Was I able to be myself and feel authentic in my interaction with the interviewer?

Were there any interview questions that surprised me?

- Why did they surprise me?
- How can I prepare for these kinds of questions in the future?

Did the interviewer interrupt me or ask for more information after my answers?

- How did I react?
- Are there answers that I need to shorten?
- In what answers could I have provided more specifics?

What could I do differently next time?

- Is there anything else I should do to prepare for my next interview?
- Should I use the same stories, or are there better examples I can come up with if I take more time to think about them?
- Did I remember to include results in my examples?
- Did I listen to the "heart" of the question so that I can directly relate my answers to those topics?
- Did I balance my use of "I" and "we" in my answers?
- Do I recall using any weakening words or filler words in my answers?
- What else do I think I should do differently in my next interview?

How did I close the sale?

- Did I have the opportunity to reiterate my interest and review why I'm a great fit for the position and company?
- Did I ask for their next steps and time frames?

Any other ideas?

- Is there anything else I want to work on before my next interview?

index

A

accountability partners   190
acronyms   140
analysis, problem-solving and decision-making   198
answers
   avoiding mistakes   209
   common mistakes   139
   frameworks   16
   leaving out results in stories   141–143
   length   19
   providing more specifics   214
   relating to job, company, and industry   141
   shortening   214
   too long   139
   tying to heart of question   136–138
   why it mattered   140
approachability, credibility, and humility   48–52
   credibility   51–52
   humility   49

B

bad interviewers, disinterested interviewers   162
behavioral or competency-based questions   16
breadth vs. depth questions   15

C

change management   103–107, 200
   frequent changes or unexpected events   105–107
   collaborative planning with other departments   105–107
   influence people to accept   103–105
change questions   206. *See also* questions
checklist, interview preparation, company   211
companies, researching   7
confidence, balancing with humility   143
conflict management   60–62, 195
   answering questions about   61
   resolving conflict   60–62
credibility   51–52

D

DEI (diversity, equity, and inclusion)   55–59
   people whose backgrounds are different   56–59
   working with diverse teams   195
difficult questions   213

F

failures and negative situations   64–69
   criticism question   66
   failure question   65
   interview questions   196

INDEX

persuading someone question   69
regretted decisions question   68
filler words   17
finance   207
   considerations   117
   sample questions   117–118, 201
   selling yourself   117

G

general questions   16
generic answers   18

H

hiring and motivating staff   198
homework, avoiding mistakes   123–128
   assuming being an interviewer will make you a good interviewee   124
   dressing inappropriately or wearing cologne or loud jewelry   127
   not arriving early   127
   not investing time in preparation or thinking that you can wing it   124
   not mapping out directions, parking options, and commute time (for on-site interviews)   127
   not planning good questions (or enough questions) to ask the interviewer   125
   not practicing answers to difficult or delicate questions   125
   not testing out tech in advance (for video interviews)   126–127
HR (Human Resources)   4, 119, 202, 208
   considerations   120
   sample questions   120, 202
   selling yourself   119
humility   143, 204
hypothetical questions   16

I

Industry Speak   140
influencing and gaining support   194
information technology   208
initial screening questions   26
interpersonal skills questions   48. *See also* questions
   approachability, credibility, and humility   48–52
   conflict management   60–62
   diversity, equity, and inclusion (DEI)   55–59
   humility   204

influencing and gaining support   52–55
interviewers
   building rapport with   213
   getting to know   12
   highly experienced   164
   inexperienced   164
   interrupting   214
   letting them finish before planning answer   133
   poker-faced   162
   researching   211
   talkative   162
   testing   163
   those who ask few questions   162
   types of   180, 210
interviews   149, 150
   authenticity   128–130
   bad interviewers   162, 180
   barriers to success   189
   boss's boss   153
   closing   130–131
   common questions   25–29, 46, 192. *See also* questions
      what are you interested in this job   32
      what are you looking for next   30
      what are your career goals   33
      what are your weaknesses   34–37
      what are your strengths   34
      what did you enjoy most about last job   38
      what did you not like about last job   38
      what do you know about our company   33
      what do you not want to do   31
      what kind of salary are you looking for   31
      what questions do you have   40
      why are you looking for new job   29
      why should we hire you   39
   direct reports   153
   discussing negatives in   143
   example of   164–179
   external clients   154
   external recruiters, headhunters, and staffing agencies   151
   hiring manager   152
   HR/talent acquisition   151
   initial screening   150
   internal clients   153
   interviewers   161

INDEX 217

mistakes to avoid   121
multiple interviewers   163
negotiation questions   199
next steps after reading book   190
overview   3
panel interviews   154
peers   153
preparation checklist   211–212
preparation for   7, 20, 123–128, 131, 184–188, 203
preparation stage, potential objections   14
presentations   155
questions   4–5
questions about perseverance and obstacles   204
questions to think about   208
rambling   138
researching interviewers   211
stages and interviewers   147
stages of   209
translating messages from interviewers   156–159
trap   17–19
understanding interview questions   20
Interview Speak
overview of   7
using book   6
I pronoun, overusing and underusing   143
IT (information technology)   118, 192, 203, 211, 213
considerations   119
sample questions   118–119, 202
selling yourself   118

J

job descriptions, analyzing   9
job functions   110–111
questions by   110–120
job interview preparation checklist, knowing the job   211

L

leadership, hiring and motivating staff   83–88
leadership and management questions   77, 197
creating high level of trust, morale, and team spirit   80–82
leadership style   77–79, 88, 205
leading group with different opinions and personalities   83

pulling team together and improving morale during challenging circumstances   82

M

marketing   115–117, 207
considerations   117
sample questions   115–116, 201
selling yourself   115

N

negatives, discussing in interviews   143
negative sandwich   18, 203
negotiation questions   103, 199, 206
describing difficult negotiations   100
describing situations that demonstrate ability to negotiate skillfully when costs were critical   102
next steps   183

O

obstacles, difficult situations, interview questions about   196–197
operations   111, 207
considerations   112
sample questions   112, 200
selling yourself   112
"or" questions   19

P

pausing before answering questions   134–135
perseverance and drive   73–75, 197
personal drive and motivation   74–75
sacrifices or extra effort   75
perseverance skills
failures and negative situations   64–69
overcoming obstacles and difficult situations   69–73
questions about   204
post-interview evaluation   213–214
preparation   1, 123
know the company   7–9
know the interviewer   12–13
know the job   9–12
know yourself   13–14
problem-solving questions   90, 206
complex problems   91–93

218   INDEX

decision-making process 96, 198
difficult decisions 93–96
missing obvious solutions 93

Q

qualifications, why employer should hire you 143–145
questions. *See also* interviews
by job function 206–208
common 203–204
initial screening questions 26
interviewers, letting them finish before planning answer 133
tell me about yourself 26–29
tying answers to heart of 136–138
types of 15–17

R

rambling 135
resistance to ideas 69–71
rising inflection/uptalking 19

S

sales 112–114, 207
considerations 113, 201
sample questions 113, 201
selling yourself 112
senior leadership 110, 206
considerations 111
sample questions 111, 200
selling yourself 111
short answers 140
special situations 42–45
translated questions 193

staff, hiring and motivating 83–88, 198
attracting new talent and guarding against poor hires 84–86
creating environment that inspires and motivates team 86–88
stories, leaving out results in 141–143
surprising interview questions 214

T

talkative interviewers 162
team motivation 88
Tech Speak 140
tell me about yourself question 26–29
time management and project management questions 97–98, 199, 206
timing of answers 19
translating, messages from interviewers 156–159
after interview 159
before interview 156
during interview 157–159
traps, interview 17–19
answer length and timing 19
filler words 17
generic answers 18
negative sandwich 18
or questions 19
rising inflection/uptalking 19
using 'I' vs. 'we' 18
weakening words and phrases 17

W

weakening words and phrases 17
weaknesses 203
we pronoun 143
wrap-up 181